MW01154934

CITY SCIENCE
PERFORMANCE FOLLOWS FORM

Ramon Gras
Jeremy Burke

ARETIAN
Urban Analytics
and Design

Index

CITY SCIENCE

Foreword by Fawwaz Habbal, Ph.D.

Senior Lecturer at Harvard University Former Executive Dean for Education and Research at Harvard School of Engineering and Applied Sciences

Cities are born from intricate social and economic dynamics, political struggles, and the influence of geographical, cultural, and historical constraints. Throughout history, cities have been pivotal centers of civilization and have significantly shaped human life. As urban populations swell, so do the challenges of urban development. Therefore, comprehending the elements fostering sustainable city development becomes paramount.

This book delves deep into modern theories about cities, economic growth, and human activities that drive knowledge and innovation. The book assesses urban performance based on criteria like quality of life, equal opportunity, knowledge access, economic vitality, health standards, and patterns of social interaction. Moreover, it scrutinizes the amenities and services essential for cities, presents quantifications for key indicators, and discusses strategies to address intricate urban challenges. Readers will discover guidelines for fostering and preserving successful knowledge economy ecosystems.

City science theory is not new. Historically, cities underwent continuous transformation, with designs and concepts emerging from every corner of the world. China's ancient Feng Shui principles, dating back 6,000 years, endeavored to harmonize individuals with their surroundings. In the West, various urbanistic movements from Sanitary and Garden Cities to decentralized car-focused plans have shaped urban landscapes. Numerous architectural and engineering masterplans and blueprints were published in books and articles. Today, public participatory planning and system design are highlights in the discourse.

In contemporary times, city science systems theory offers techniques to evaluate the macro-level impacts of city typologies and designs on urban dynamics and performance. Systems theory encompasses elements like social interaction, agglomeration economics, innovation, wealth generation, talent attraction, accessibility and mobility, energy and water efficiency, and access to urban services and amenities, among others.

Using complexity science and network theory, this book provides insights into many global cities, establishing urban benchmarks for the modern age. The authors deconstruct cities, understand their inherent elements and urban dynamics, and offer a granular approach to gauge and comprehend urban innovation systems. Their goal is to raise the quality of life of people and create more prosperous cities and communities around the world.

By measuring and analyzing city design typologies and their impact on urban performance patterns, such as quality of work and life, and viewing urban spaces as complex systems, the authors identified overarching urban development trends. The book elaborates on how city designs, characterized by complexity features, influence human performance, urbanization efficiency, and the knowledge economy.

Leveraging parameters intrinsic to complexity, such as urban morphology, entropy, and scale, the authors correlate multiple pivotal urban components, creating compelling conclusions stemming from their meticulous study of 100 cities, each a conglomerate of thousands of sub-municipal administrative units. The ensuing insights suggest that cities exhibiting equilibrium across numerous scales – pertaining to both spatial distribution and the magnitude of connections – tend to optimize spatial and material utilization while enhancing the surpluses yielded by social interaction patterns.

Moreover, efficiency key performance indicators (KPIs) for a selected cohort of cities revealed that neighborhoods characterized by more structured city typologies – such as grids/reticular or fractal types – exhibit a heightened degree of fractality index and harness superior urbanization efficiency.

The fractality of urban form has emerged as a critical component in evaluating the interdependencies between urban form and urban performance. The Fractal city form typology manifests supreme efficiency, both in the realms of material urban infrastructure and superlinear social interaction patterns, thus fortifying access to services and amenities and fostering the knowledge economy. These fractal growth patterns orchestrate a more egalitarian dispersion of amenities compared to other network types. Furthermore, the urban form entropy index is found to be symbiotically correlated with urban development efficiency metrics. It is observed that intermediary levels of city form entropy attain the peak of urbanization efficiency.

Exploratory studies on the nexus between the urban fractality index and residents' quality of life unveiled patterns indicating enhanced urban efficiency. City designs with a pronounced fractality index were observed to consistently overshadow their counterparts in harnessing infrastructure optimally.

In summary, by intertwining city science systems techniques with network theory, this book bridges urban design best practices with the essence and dynamics of thriving cities. It furnishes guidelines and metrics for urban development efficiency, weaving in architectural and economic development best practices.

This book is a valuable read for 21st-century policy makers, urban planners, and designers. It serves citizens well as they attempt to understand how to champion sustainable development goals.

An Introduction to City Science

A Paramount Urban Development Challenge

A paramount urban development challenge for the coming decades will be to identify city design and economic development strategies able to envision, incept and shape sustainable development solutions to successfully address the needs of citizens and communities worldwide. Today, the majority of the world's population lives in cities, and it is expected that urban population will continue to grow in the coming decades. The rapid and chaotic increase in city dwellers will negatively impact urban performance measured in terms of quality of life, equal access to opportunities, knowledge, education, economic growth, healthy living conditions and social interaction patterns, as well as amenities and services if cities cannot respond to the pressures that arise from increased urbanization, technology disruption, and mass automation processes.

While urban science-derived city design and management principles can help solve these problems, up to this point the state-of-the-art concepts, methods, and heuristics in the realm of city form and urban systems analysis have often lacked the degree of advancement, solvency, and maturity required to allow for a quantification of critical key indicators, comparative benchmarking for best practices, and rigorous implementation strategies to successfully tackle the complex urban development problems facing society.

A Novel City Science Theory and Methodology

Recent advances achieved by our team at Aretian out of the Harvard Innovation Lab in the sphere of city science research and economic complexity modeling illuminate how urban development typologies and economic development strategies impact growth patterns and citizens' quality of life. Emerging research fields such as complex systems and network theory have served as the theoretical and methodological foundation for shaping evidence-based, data-driven economic development strategies. Academic studies have shown the structural impact of both quantitative growth, by means of network scaling studies, and qualitative growth, by evaluating the economic complexity, city form structures, and multiplying effects of innovation network design. But how can we deliberately shape urban design and economic development strategies tailored to each context and environment in order to incept sustainable development and inclusive economic growth?

Given the complexity of how people interact with a city, the critical question arises: How do a city's shape and social networks influence its urban performance in terms of citizens' quality of life?

In this book, we present a novel city science methodology aiming to address this fundamental question. We have evaluated dozens of metropolitan regions and hundreds of municipalities around the world and compared them with one another to identify city form patterns and their impact on urban performance with respect to their ability to satisfy a series of quality standards, focusing on urbanization and architectural quality and efficiency, mobility and logistics, accessibility to urban services and amenities, economic development and smart specialization, and innovative knowledge economy ecosystems and their ability to generate prosperity. Through the comparison and clustering of the design features of both the theoretical and empirical examples, we identify the subtle ties between city type characteristics related to urban topology, morphology, entropy, fractality, and scale, and the impact of such aesthetic and functional types on the quality of life of citizens, measured and evaluated by means of a series of urban performance metrics.

The purpose of this book is to establish the foundation for a city science theory and methodology, aiming to provide a rigorous, scientific, evidence-based global analytical process by which urban designers and leaders can provide urban diagnostics and global benchmarks, identify strengths, weaknesses, risks and opportunities, define urban development goals, and inform city design and economic development decision-making processes, thus contributing to raising the level of understanding of urban phenomena, as well as the quality of the architectural fabrics that make up the built environment.

A key insight from our city science studies shows that there is a perfect analogy between the different types of city form patterns and archetypal network typologies in terms of both their aesthetic properties and their functional characteristics. By comprehending cities and urban spaces as dynamic, ever-evolving complex systems, we can describe their most salient features and urban form elements, understand their psychological and cultural impact on individuals and communities, and identify the non-trivial causal mechanisms between design decisions and the subjective experiences of their residents. Every display of human creativity, whether individual or collective, represents a sensual manifestation of the underlying worldview or *Weltanschauung*. When we admire the beauty and harmony of an architectural design or the aesthetic configuration of an urban space, we intimately perceive the essence of a city expressed by means of the metaphors and qualities embedded within the conception of the space.

Unfortunately, some spurious intellectual trends have questioned the relationship between aesthetics and function. Aesthetic schools such as Mondrian's Neoplasticism, or Malevich's Materialism aimed to break the intimate relationship between art, craft, design, aesthetics, and function. Such trends inspired a catalogue composed of a myriad of ugly urban design interventions and architectural spaces that unleash an instantaneous, instinctive, intuitive rejection in most citizens. The reason why such buildings and neighborhoods are perceived as unappealing and poorly functional is very clear: they were based upon false premises, which led to the wrong conclusions, unattractive designs, and nonfunctional venue configurations, hence contributing to social alienation and dehumanization.

The data-driven insights presented in this book prove that in urban design and architecture, as in art, form and function are intimately related. Aesthetics follow a unique sensibility, a set of priorities, and a specific understanding of the world and the local context, hence inducing certain types of behavior, socialization, and ultimately impacting our perception and experience. Those features can now be modeled and better understood, and the advances derived therefrom enable us to anticipate how to best address the urban problems of our time. How did we achieve this? We modelled urban environments aesthetically and quantitatively by breaking them down into their critical underlying systems: the networks of (1) urban infrastructure and architecture, (2) economics and companies, and (3) talent and innovation.

Inspired by the network graph logic drawn by Euler, the ontological group classifications from Évariste Galois, the complexity science and information principles developed by Geoffrey West and his team, and stemming from the intuitions and scientific approaches stimulated by the founding fathers Louis Durand and Ildefons Cerdà, we developed a three-step method that let us draw and evaluate the complex and delicate, non-trivial, structural, systematic, and causal relationship between city form and urban performance.

The thorough analysis of the nature of the three urban networks of metropolitan areas around the globe reveals that most urban environments follow variations of 10 archetypal patterns: the Small World City, the Radial City, and the Reticular, Linear, Organic, Random, Atomized, Monumental, Garden or Fractal City. Each city form pattern is characterized not only by a set of similar morphological features but also by common network science characteristics, emergent properties, and inner dynamics. We applied this methodology to data gathered on 100 metropolitan areas worldwide and their internal subdivisions. By grouping the subdivisions into sub-municipal agglomerations based on common urban form features, it is possible to identify and characterize their internal tapestry of city form typologies and evaluate their respective urban performance metrics and indicators.

We show that each city typology has a distinct effect on urban performance, we quantify this impact, and we provide comparisons between the different typologies. Finally, we apply this methodology to evaluate the ability of each city typology to achieve not only urban development efficiency metrics and knowledge economy indicators, but also the standards set forth by the 15-Minute City, a sustainable development proposition by urban scientist Carlos Moreno, among others, for a decentralized city composed of walkable neighborhoods that provide equal access to housing, education, and amenities.

First, we propose a framework to model urban environments and the social interaction dynamics operating within them in a three-dimensional manner, in order to identify, measure, describe, and evaluate a series of urban form typologies, aesthetics, and functional properties that describe a city's shape and size generally. This offers a unifying concept to define the properties and characteristics inherent in the underlying urban design patterns. Second, we propose that the urban form typologies can be quantified through the framework to establish a disciplined methodology to compare the shape and scale of one city to another. The methodology combines topological (street network) and morphological (building form) features of urban form as well as other metrics related to geographic scale, fractality, entropy, and density. Third, we provide a unified method to evaluate urban performance in terms of urbanization efficiency, innovation metrics, and the distribution of amenities. Fourth, we apply this framework to study the structural, causal relationship between morphological design typologies and urban performance in order to determine which city design strategies are best suited to meet the demands and needs of citizens globally.

The evidence-based city science methodology reveals that the most virtuous urban systems are those composed of scale-free networks with a highly fractal urban network topology, morphology, and social network inner structure. Those systems structurally benefit from two major advantages: they harmonically integrate a distributed set of accessible services and resources (egalitarian networks protecting the most vulnerable citizens) while enabling the multiplying effect of innovation, hence unleashing merit-based prosperity based on liberty and fruitful collaboration, and liberating the latent talents of citizens in general – particularly the most brilliant ones. Naturally, each urban space, context, community, city or municipality, metropolitan area or region, and country will present a number of cultural, social, axial, spiritual, aesthetic, physical, and natural constraints and circumstances, hence the urban design solutions and economic development strategies need to be tailored for every case. But being equipped with advanced city science analysis and insights will enable us to tackle those complex problems and eventually contribute to creating a freer, more prosperous, and humane society. What are the foremost urban development challenges facing the cities of our time?

Paris / London

Urban Development Challenges Facing the Cities of Our Time

The Need for a New Science of Cities

The urban planners and designers of the 21st century face a formidable task: advancing the science of cities in order to offer viable, solvent solutions to the challenges posed by the increasing population growth in metropolitan areas, derived from an unprecedented worldwide demographic explosion, and by technological progress. In 1960, one out of three people lived in cities. Today, 57% of the world's population lives in cities, and these trends are expected to continue in the coming decades (World Bank, 2020). Population migration will continue to exacerbate existing urban issues such as housing shortages, overcrowding, traffic, pollution, and resource constraints. In addition, these trends can potentially hinder progress in terms of economic development, knowledge creation and diffusion, and equality of access to services and amenities.

Nevertheless, city leaders from all countries – particularly developing ones that are capitalizing the greatest urban growth – have entered the 21st century armed with antiquated urban analytics and design tools. Prevailing urban growth patterns in cities like São Paulo, Bogotá, Lagos, Delhi, Cairo, Mexico City, and Karachi, among others, are largely inherited from the worst urban planning practices of the 20th century: organic or random urban typology models that use resources inefficiently, thus undermining social interactivity; the abusive centrality of cars in transport systems; dispersed business activities, making it hard to develop individual and collective know-how and create opportunities; excessive suburbanization, which leads to social fragmentation; the unequal distribution of city services in different districts; architectural barriers, which exacerbate social fracture and detract from public safety; and the lack of green spaces and places for social interaction. In short, deficient urban development patterns have been applied without critical consideration, further complicating our efforts to approach the standards of quality established in the sustainable development goals.

Standing on the Shoulders of Giants

Understanding urban planning as both an art and a science allows us to build on the visions of the founders of modern urbanism – chief among them Ildefons Cerdà and Louis Durand – and modernize a method of analysis and design that has made great strides in recent decades. The renowned architect, civil engineer, and urbanist Louis Durand combined his professional practice as a designer with his academic studies, which included his foundational works *Recueil et parallèle des édifices en tout genre, anciens et modernes* (1801) and *Précis des leçons d'architecture données à l'école polytechnique* (1805), where he systematically studies the different architectural design typologies and the morphological features that characterize them.

The brilliant urbanist, civil engineer, and architect Ildefons Cerdà established the conceptual foundations of modern urbanism in his *General Theory of Urbanization (1867)*. Cerdà's revolutionary vision led him to pursue highly idealistic goals by deploying extremely pragmatic and grounded design methodologies. His creative endeavor focused on responding to the urgent need, spurred by the emergence of the Industrial Revolution, for a systematic understanding of what modern cities were, and could eventually become, by transforming a once unstructured and outdated set of minor disciplines into a cohesive, rigorous profession. He started by coining a set of concepts that would allow him to codify the fundamental elements and dynamic systems that constitute modern cities. Way before the words urbanism, *Städtebau* or city planning started being used in city-related studies, he coined the word *urbanization*. Cerdà was the very first city designer to overcome the traditional planning routines inherited from pre-Industrial times by proposing a set of rigorous methodologies to integrate all the techniques and design considerations that needed to be harmonized in order to successfully address the problems that modern cities necessarily face.

Systems Engineering: Urban Design as a Science

Cerdà understood that modern cities require the juxtaposition of complex systems to effectively deploy the multiple services enhanced by the technological advances of the Industrial Revolution. His innovative vision allowed him to systematically address qualitative challenges by developing quantitative models. His ultimate goals addressed considerations such as eradicating early child and mother mortality, increasing the standard of living of working class families, merging social classes within the same neighborhoods and buildings to reduce social stratification, drawing specific street patterns to induce egalitarian power relationships, balancing the human need for isolation and privacy with the ability for people to socialize, prioritizing pedestrian mobility and sociability over alternative means, and establishing efficient mobility and energy systems able to adapt to further foreseen technological changes. To address such challenges, he designed a series of probabilistic, non-deterministic heuristic models based on extensive avant la lettre big data analysis. Cerdà iteratively refined and sophisticated such methods, allowing him to come up with ranges for optimal building height, footprint, and density, and for street and sidewalk width, integrating all urban services in the very same way we still do to this day. His envisioning of a of a modern, distributed grid system with a self-similar morphological pattern became a reference for all grid models that came after his Barcelona Expansion Plan, including Manhattan in NYC.

Human-Centered Design: Urban Design as a Service

Ildefons Cerdà developed his main book while designing the Barcelona Expansion Plan, completed in 1859. Not only did his plan accomplish all the fundamental goals it pursued in a masterful way, but it also represented a benchmark for high-quality urban design practice. Today we can empirically contrast not only the lasting achievements that his plan brought for the city of Barcelona, but also the benefits of well-thought design methodologies. By way of example, recent studies comparing the cities of Atlanta and Barcelona show how metropolitan areas with a comparable population can embody massive differences in terms of environmental footprint or transportation efficiency. For all these reasons, Cerdà is a source of inspiration for new generations of city designers who want to contribute to addressing the enormous technical and social challenges that the discipline of Urban Design must respond to in this age of rapid and often abrupt technological changes, while using a human-centered and rigorous approach.

Sustainable and Resilient Urban Design and Economic Development

Since the late 20th century, the increasingly chaotic acceleration of the urbanization process around the world has exacerbated urban problems such as overcrowding in substandard housing, a sharp increase in peak hour traffic and average commuting time, limited opportunities for stable, decent, well remunerated employment, a widening income gap, the gradual disappearance of local businesses and everyday social interactions, the appearance of 'food deserts' in large urban areas, energy and water inefficiency, and social isolation and loneliness due to urban atomization. After the initial surge provided by the founders of modern urban planning in the 19th century, the science of cities languished for more than 100 years until the dawn of the 21st century.

Despite the emergence of various aesthetic trends in urbanism and architecture, such as the movement associated with the International Congresses of Modern Architecture (1928–1959), these contributions did not always constitute actual progress in the science of cities nor did they further our understanding of the urban phenomenon and how it affects people's quality of life. That hiatus progressively hampered the ability of urban planners to adequately rise to the challenges of their time.

Urban Development Challenges Facing the Cities of Our Time

In the 1950s, the urban activist Jane Jacobs began to denounce the fact that post-war urbanism had given cars priority over pedestrians in public spaces and vitality was being lost in historic city centers, which deteriorated significantly in the second half of the century. Harvard professor Robert Putnam and celebrated sociologist Saskia Sassen described the collapse of association and community life as a result of the detrimental effects of over-suburbanization and the social atomization it caused. The Brazilian architect and urban planner Jaime Lerner denounced the abusive nature of overambitious urban renewal projects, arguing that strategic urban transformation initiatives on a smaller scale could bring about significant systemic changes in the medium and long term.

City Design and Urban Performance: How Can We Inform Sustainable Urban Development Design?

For his part, mobility expert Robert Cervero pointed out the negative consequences of low-density suburban growth and proposed several initiatives to align compact urban development with mobility systems that prioritized public transportation, reducing commuting time and transportation costs and promoting greater social interaction. The architect and urban planner Jan Gehl underscored the decline of public spaces and the marginalization of pedestrians, which led to a lack of public safety, higher crime rates, the loss of a flourishing local business community, and the dehumanization of public space. In a similar vein, urban designer Jeff Speck defined the negative consequences of the excessive geographical dispersal of urban activities and proposed recovering dense urban centers to revitalize the social life of cities around the world.

Although several authors throughout the 20th century made valuable qualitative contributions that facilitated the definition of good criteria for citizen-friendly urban development, it was not until the beginning of the present century that a fresh batch of urban designers and researchers shed new light on the challenges that cities face in the age of globalization, automation, robotics, and artificial intelligence.

Resilient Cities: How Can We Inform Urban Economic Development Strategies to Incept Distributed Prosperity?

Urban development thought leaders, consultants, and economic development decision-makers need to shape urban and economic development as well as smart specialization strategies to strengthen their cities's industry-specific value chains and raise their global competitiveness. Urban designers, economic development consultants and civic leaders tend to be ill-equipped when facing urban development strategies: What should be the main drivers for morphological city design? Are there desirable ranges of values for urban density? What are the driving factors behind them? Can we accurately measure them? How can we properly allocate the different zoning strategies, and shape a successful placemaking strategy? How can we attain universal access to fundamental urban services and amenities? Groundbreaking research led by Bettencourt, Lobo, and West (2009) have studied the universal relationship between scale and urban phenomena, and particularly the remarkable similarity between cities and living creatures. One of the most striking and profound revelations stemming from their academic research is the nontrivial analogy between cities and animals as complex systems. The careful evaluation of animal size growth patterns reveal either superlinear or sublinear relationships between their average body weight and intrinsic, systems-level properties and characteristics. Similar phenomena can be observed when it comes to evaluating growth patterns in human settlements. Urban infrastructure networks tend to manifest an exponent that is below one with respect to the exponential relationship per capita between population growth and material infrastructure efficiency, suggesting economies of scale in the use of construction materials, transportation and communication networks. Social interactions, which culminate in innovation and wealth creation, show a power law coefficient above one, therefore implying increasing returns to scale in human interaction. By deepening our knowledge of such relationships, we can answer some fundamental urban development questions.

Innovative Cities: How Can We Shape a Successful Knowledge Economy Able to Create Distributed Prosperity and Inclusive Growth?

Urban economy thought leaders and decision-makers face the urgent need to shape their innovation strategies by emphasizing their unique areas of global comparative advantage. Over the next three decades, the middle classes in countries such as China and India are expected to triple in size. This will represent a dramatic shift in power and trade relations on the geopolitical plane. Similarly, emerging technologies based on artificial intelligence, robotics, and process automation are threatening to destroy at least one-third of jobs in the Western world as we understand them today. The West in general, and Europe in particular, is showing clear signs of exhaustion and of having lost both its flair for innovation and its leadership in developing new solutions that generate virtuous economic circles to benefit the majority of its citizens.

Recent research in the study of economic development and urban phenomena has applied insights regarding economic complexity to provide a reliable methodology to describe industry comparative advantage at the national level. This strand of research applies network theory to study the linkages between knowledge-producing agents in an economy (Hidalgo & Hausmann, 2009). The methodology enables a systematic understanding of collective know-how advancement and knowledge diffusion at the national scale, as well as the identification of smart specialization and diversification strategies.

Up until recently, the literature presented two major limitations: on the one hand, it primarily focused on international trade of physical goods, thus lacking the analysis of high-value-added intangible services; and on the other hand, the national level of aggregation did not permit a deeper understanding of geospatial dynamics, hence precluding a detailed understanding of territorial dynamics and the nonlinear benefits of the geographic aggregation of knowledge-intensive activities. As a result, the economic complexity models fell short in terms of identifying sub-national and city-level collective know-how dynamics and illustrating urban development recommendations at the regional, urban, and local levels (Hausmann et al., 2014).

City science research conducted by our team out of the Harvard Innovation Lab started to systematically breach that gap in the urban innovation literature to understand the links between best practices in urban design and the main factors, features, and underlying dynamics of successful cities. By combining city science techniques with insights from economic complexity, we are able to provide a higher resolution methodology to measure, evaluate, and better understand innovation systems at the urban scale. The geospatial analysis of innovation and knowledge-intensive activities within urban environments holds the promise of being able (1) enable a deeper understanding of the dynamics of the nonlinear benefits of a strategic geographic aggregation of knowledge-intensive activities in order to (2) identify the key ingredients and dynamics facilitating economic growth and stable employment creation; thus (3) propelling regional growth and distributed prosperity by means of providing urban development decision-making recommendations to increase urban economic performance.

How can we provide continuity to the precious legacy envisioned by authors such as Louis Durand and Ildefons Cerdà in order to create urban analytics and design techniques capable of addressing the urban challenges of our time?

City Form features derived from urban design tend to have a structural effect on the quality of life of citizens (Barcelona)

Straightness

Fractal Dimension

Streets per Node

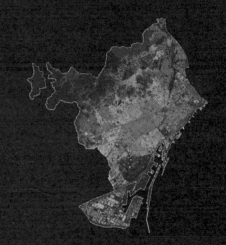

Morphological Orientation

1st percentile   100th percentile

Urban Scaling: Superlinear and Sublinear Implications

A Surprising Mathematical Analogy between Animal Species and Urban Systems

Ever since the team at the Santa Fe Institute (New Mexico) led by Professors Geoffrey West and Luis Bettencourt breathed new life into the science of cities, the discipline of urban planning has recovered and increased its vigor. Today, new methods of modeling the urban phenomenon are facilitating the diagnosis of the challenges of sustainable urban development and providing rigorous data to support urban leaders and experts in their decision-making processes. The reconciliation of the legacy built by urban planners, architects, civil engineers and other professionals over the last century with new methods for analyzing the urban phenomenon as a complex system – in other words, relying on complexity science – as well as automated learning, network theory, and artificial intelligence allow us to identify structural patterns and best practices in the field of urban design in order to come up with viable solutions to the pressing urban challenges we now face.

Superlinear Effects of Urban Scaling in Economic Development

In an influential body of research, Geoffrey West and collaborators have studied the remarkable similarity between cities and living creatures based on the scale of their body and total residents (Bettencourt, Lobo, Helbing, Kühnert and West, 2006). There are simple and universally applicable laws that link the size of mammals to their fundamental biological functions such as metabolism and energy consumption. If we display all mammals on a log-log graph and we evaluate the relationship between their body mass in kilograms and their metabolic rate, we observe a perfectly aligned regression line. Every time we compare animals doubling their weight, we observe sublinear diminishing of heartbeat speed, energy consumption, and metabolic effort. Simultaneously, we detect superlinear scaling in terms of higher life expectancy, enhanced physical capabilities, and stronger resilience overall when addressing potential threats or environmental risks. This implies that, regardless of size, all mammals are a scaled manifestation of a single, idealized mammal. Could this also be true for human cities and agglomerations?

West and his collaborators showed that this is, in fact, the case by analyzing a myriad of urban phenomena such as infrastructure, crime, pollution, wealth creation, and innovation. The research finds that there are universally applicable power laws across different geographies and economic dimensions that translate the size of a city as measured by population and other measures to the urban phenomena listed above. These laws can be classified as linear, superlinear, or sublinear determined by the exponent of the power law and have interesting implications (Bettencourt et al., 2006).

Other papers by the same group of researchers focus on related topics involving the network structure of urban infrastructure. In particular, Kühnert et al. (2016) study the supply patterns for energy, fuel, medical and food supply. Bettencourt et al. (2010) study the superlinearity of urban growth, and Bettencourt et al. (2007) study the increasing returns to patenting as a scaling function of metropolitan size. In follow-up work, Bettencourt et al. (2008 and 2009) focus on the self-similarity implications of these networks, in addition to proposing a production function for cities that illustrate these superlinear patterns (2013). Finally, Bettencourt et al. (2011) study the implications for innovation and crime patterns within these networks. Lane et al. (2009) study the patterns of self-organization of urban agglomerations that motivate the modern analysis of urban networks.

Urban Development: Scaling Trends

The revolutionary findings extracted from the research led by Professor Geoffrey West illuminate the emerging systems' advantages and disadvantages associated with population growth at a global scale. Among other finds, West's team show that the scale of human settlements structurally affects the nature of human interaction. As a human settlement grows over time, we observe three types of alterations in per citizen or per capita indicators:

1. **Sublinear growth (<1):** advantages associated with cost reduction and economies of scale, which promote more efficient infrastructure investments and improve the per capita social impact of new builds.
2. **Linear growth (=1):** proportional growth on the log-log plot, so that the ratio of population to number of houses remains essentially constant.
3. **Superlinear growth (>1):** growth in the form of multiplying benefits derived from greater social interaction and more complex human and technological networks that give a tremendous boost to the knowledge economy.

Every time a city doubles its population, the scale factor induces structural changes as a result of the multiplying, super-linear benefits of strategic aggregation. Thus, the structural effects of doubling the population of an urban settlement tend to produce a per capita increase of:

+15% in average wealth per capita indicators
+15% in average per capita knowledge economy indicators
+10–20% in patents per capita
+12–18% in average per capita social interaction indicators
+12–20% in the speed of human interactions
+12–20% in supply chain efficiency
+12–20% in average business diversity and jobs per capita indicators
+12–20% in productivity per capita

Urban and Economic Development: Agglomeration Trends

Similarly, quantitative population growth also affects economies of scale, which allow cities to benefit from positive sublinear growth. The larger and denser the city, the greater the per capita efficiency of investments in urban, transport, energy, and water infrastructures tends to be:

15% reduction in capital expenditures (capex) and operating expenses (opex) per capita (Bettencourt et al., 2010).

Analogously, their studies pointed out certain observed disadvantages associated with population growth, most notably the superlinear growth of income and wealth inequality, crime, and pollution per capita.

Why do industries agglomerate? How much of this agglomeration is explained by local advantages and how much is a result of endogenous intra-industry spillovers? Ellison and Glaeser (2009) try to tackle this fundamental question by disaggregating the effect of economic agglomeration between natural advantages and intra-industry spillovers in a sample of four-digit manufacturing industries in the United States. They study the determinants of agglomeration based on cost of inputs (electricity, gas, coal, agricultural products), cost of labor inputs (relative wage differences), relative price of skill, transportation costs, and unobserved spillovers. They find that natural advantages have a limited explanatory power, being able to explain only 20% of observed agglomeration. The implication is that agglomeration effects are an important force driving the geographic distribution of economic activity. As noted by the authors, this effect is particularly extreme in manufacturing industries, in particular, the automobile manufacturing sector.

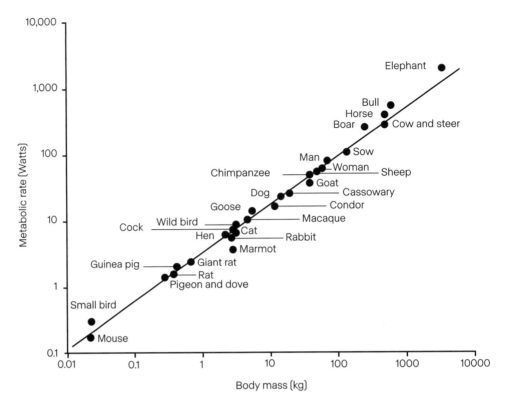

Metabolic rate of animals
Results from Bettencourt, West et al.

Previous research by Bettencourt et al. (2010) as well as Barabási (2017) shows that the scale of cities has a super linear or sublinear impact on social measures such as patents, crime, and sustainability. The measurement of the superlinear effects of the geographic aggregation of knowledge-intensive activities within urban innovation ecosystems and provide quantitative measures of the multiplying effects and the derived economic surplus in terms of knowledge advancement, wealth, and employment creation for the surrounding communities. The novel framework presented in this book will allow readers to understand these relationships by modeling knowledge-intensive activities from a network theory perspective.

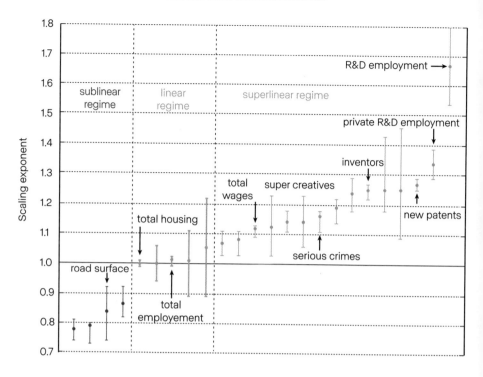

Multiplying effects of urban scaling
Results from Bettencourt et al.

The city science advances achieved by the research team at the Santa Fe Institute provide a solid foundation to better understand the impact of quantitative growth of cities on the quality of life of citizens at a very aggregate scale. However, there is a wide range of observation variance within a given population bracket, depending on the quality of the urban design, space programming, and economic development systems. How can we assess those qualities of urban environments in a scientific manner?

A New Challenge: Evaluating the Quality of Urban Design

Establishing an Analogy between Network Types and City Design Styles

The core contribution of our novel methodology is to territorialize the city science logic by means of modeling the inner ingredients and dynamics of urban systems through the lens of network theory and complexity science. When facing the challenge of how to undertake this arduous task, we opted for establishing an analogy between nodes and architectural spaces and features, and edges and streets, roads, walkways, and connectors at different scales. Such an approach allowed us to establish direct analogies between perceived design styles and well-known network typologies, hence opening the path to measure and define complex systems properties, dynamics, and patterns, and ultimately predict the functional behavior of a given system in a probabilistic manner.

Urban Development Trends

City form typologies can be described based on their three-dimensional form characteristics as a unifying framework to understand the long-term impact of city design criteria on urban performance. At a fundamental and abstracted level, cities are combinations of street networks, blocks of buildings, and the humans that populate and use these two groups of urban spaces. While all developed cities can be defined in such a way as to be considered similar or topologically invariant, it is clear that the urban form of cities in terms of the nuances of their street networks, buildings, and infrastructure varies greatly. These variations, produced through differing historical approaches to urban design, master planning, development, and redevelopment enable the categorization of developed cities into a set of explicit city typologies: small world, radial, linear, reticular/grid, organic, atomized, garden city, fractal, etc. When considering the connection between urban form and the performance of cities, city typologies and their respective urban characteristics provide a theoretical framework by which associated and potentially induced human behaviors and performance outcomes might be scrutinized. More significantly, introducing categorical divisions by which to understand cities produces a set of theoretical guidelines that are amenable to the application of network theory analysis. Accomplished city science researchers such as Michael Batty and Nikos Salingaros hinted in the direction of the attractive properties of self-similar or fractal urban growth patterns. However, the relationship between such fractal features and the quality of life of citizens remained largely unexplored. In this book we analyze at length by means of evidence-based methods the inherent relationship between self-similarity and Scale-Free properties and high performing city development patterns.

Economic Development Trends

The network science-fueled research of economic complexity and collective know-how tries to model the relation between the stock of knowledge in a region and economic outcomes (Hidalgo & Hausmann, 2009). Our work incorporates these intuitions but places the scope of analysis at the city and district levels and incorporates higher quality data such as firm-level data. Furthermore, the urban economic development analysis presented in this book accounts for power laws in urban scenarios as proposed by Bettencourt et al. (2010), which focus on the universal relation between scale and urban phenomena by using graphical descriptions of sublinear or superlinear effects with larger and larger scales of aggregation. We contribute to this literature by focusing the analysis on innovation districts and knowledge economy ecosystems in urban settings. Moreover, our work considers the study of agglomeration economies by Ellison and Glaeser (2009). This strand of the literature tries to disentangle the effect of local comparative advantage and endogenous spillovers to explain the geographic distribution of economic activity. The literature finds that intra-industry externalities play an important role, and local natural advantages have a limited explanatory power. We build upon these findings to concentrate on the powerful externalities driven by innovative activities in urban settings.

The city-level evidence-based approach to increase urban performance, developed by Kent Larson and Andres Sevtsuk, serves as a source of inspiration to bridge the gap between economic geography, economic complexity studies, and urban design (Ekmekci et al., 2016). Economic complexity is taken as a measure of collective know-how. The study of how people collaborate to add value to the economy dates back to the writings of Adam Smith (1776), who studied the division of labor. People and firms specialize in different activities, increasing economic efficiency and the impact of the interactions between them. Hidalgo and Hausmann (2009) applied this insight at a national scale to study the relationship between the human and physical capital resources in a given country and the type of goods that they export. Basing their work on the study of Scale-Free networks by Barabási (2016), they modeled the structure of an economy as a bipartite network in which countries are connected to the products they export and showed that it is possible to quantify the complexity of a country's economy by characterizing the structure of this network. Furthermore, this measure of complexity is correlated with a country's level of income, and deviations from this relationship are predictive of true growth (Barabási, 2017). This suggests that countries tend to converge to the level of income dictated by the complexity of their productive structures. The level of complexity is modeled as the combination of capabilities available in a given country or, more broadly, as a measure of collective know-how.

This body of work spurred further research including Hartmann et al. (2017), which expands the scope of analysis of economic complexity to study the implications for institutional design and income distribution. Youn et al. (2016) use similar motivation to investigate how the diversity of economic activities depends on city size. The limitation of this approach as usually applied is that it lacks the level of detail to be implemented at an urban scale. In addition, it is mainly tailored to the analysis of export data, which tend to lack measures of service industries. Our goal is to contribute to these two dimensions by focusing the analysis of collective know-how on the urban scale and, in addition, making use of firm-level data to also incorporate the production of services. In addition, we believe that a less indirect and more precise approach to measuring collective know-how is through the output of the innovation process as measured by patents and innovation-related metrics.

Knowledge Economy Trends: Innovation Districts as Catalysts for Activating the Local Talent

One novel urban and economic strategy to propel the knowledge economy and create vibrant and innovative cities involves shaping, for each metropolitan area, a network of innovation districts, strategically located to liberate the potential *collective know-how*. Professor Miquel Barceló, a renowned engineer, urban economist and researcher, conceived the *innovation district* concept as a geographic knowledge economy *hub* aiming to galvanize the intellectual potential of a given community. An innovation district is a specific urban environment based on combining urban renewal with the geographic concentration of innovation activities, where individual talent and organizations work in knowledge-intensive industries to solve complex problems. Innovation districts activate the dormant capabilities of a community and generate exponential benefits for surrounding neighborhoods and regions. When analyzing this phenomenon, we can build upon these insights to carry over the question of the agglomeration of manufacturing industries to a more general understanding of innovation activities. How much of the agglomeration in innovation activities can be explained by local comparative advantages, and how much is an endogenous spillover effect that can be replicated in different regions? This is a fundamental question since, as we will show, the spillover effects of innovative activities appear to be large.

As we will see in subsequent chapters, an evidence-based comparison between the societal effort carried out by knowledge-intensive employment to promote innovation, the tangible results attained by those professionals and teams, and the societal impact experienced therefrom reveal strikingly nonlinear amplifying effects and causal relationships and illuminate the ingredients and dynamics inherent to any successful innovation district. These results reveal that innovation districts systematically benefit from structural nonlinear innovation patterns as a result of the geographic aggregation of knowledge-intensive activities within urban environments. Representative examples of successful innovation districts include Kendall Square in Cambridge, MA, Jurong Innovation District (Singapore), MIND Milano Innovation District (Italy),

Silicon Alley in New York City (NY, US) 22@ in Barcelona (Catalonia, Spain), the Grand Canal Innovation District in Dublin (Ireland), and the Pittsburgh Innovation District (PA, USA).

Benefits from Leveraging City Science Insights and Learnings

Urban design criteria can improve upon these outcomes to promote sustainable urban environments. However, the current implementation of urban design concepts is often too abstract and lacks a unified framework to quantify and compare different cities and the best strategies to address specific problems. To create a successful design response to a given problem, an urban planner needs to understand a city's typology, morphology, and scale as well as scientific reasoning to evaluate urban performance in terms of economic development, innovation, and the distribution of amenities.

City science research efforts intend to address this complexity so that planners can better answer this fundamental question: How does a city's shape and size influence its future performance?

City Science Informing Urban Design and Management

First, we propose the concept of a city typology, based on its three-dimensional form characteristics, as a unifying framework for understanding the long-term impact of city design criteria on urban performance. Ontological, qualitative classifications of urban design typologies can be extremely insightful and revealing when their inner properties and idiosyncrasy help explain their cause-and-effect dynamics as well as the impact on the quality of life of citizens. Cities can be decomposed into a series of nodes (architectural spaces) and edges (roads, streets and other transport walkways and relationships). The nature of the underlying topological structure defines the mobility and logistics efficiency of an urban area, whereas the particularities of the morphological structure of buildings and activity programming of architectural spaces severely impacts the social relationships that can emerge and evolve within a particular urban setting. More holistic measures such as fractality, density and entropy tend to conform to archetypal growth patterns that share similar aesthetics and functional properties. The city typology as defined in this methodology serves as a useful means of characterizing cities across the world and captures cardinal facets involving urban topology, morphology, and scale.

Second, we propose that city typologies can be quantified and compared to one another and provide a disciplined methodology to quantify a city's shape and size. There are many ways to measure a city's shape and size in terms of street and building layout, street length, building shape, distribution of amenities, density, resource use, etc. Our classification of city typology is a useful metric that summarizes these characteristics and allows for comparisons across space and time. The methodology combines topological and morphological features of urban form as well as other metrics related to geographic scale. We apply this methodology to gather data for 100 cities worldwide and identify their internal tapestry of urban form typologies.

Third, we provide a method to quantify and evaluate urban performance measured by urban design and environmental efficiency, innovation metrics, creation of knowledge, and distribution of amenities. Current urban design efforts intend to maximize access to high-quality urban services and promote local networks of talent in order to ensure egalitarian access to resources and amenities, and to support upward economic mobility. Our methodology enables the collection and quantification of data for many cities worldwide in a unified manner to drive comparisons of urban performance across time and space.

Finally, we apply this framework to study the relationship between city typology and urban performance. We show that city typologies have a distinct effect on urban performance, we quantify this impact, and we provide comparisons between the different typologies. This methodology is applied to evaluate not only the urbanization and architectural efficiency, but also the quality of the local knowledge economy ecosystem, as well as the concept of the 15-Minute City, a proposition of a decentralized city which provides equality of access to housing, education, and amenities. Research into urban design models such as the 15-Minute City had yet to systematically address explicit city typologies and their links with concrete urban performance metrics; the framework proposed in this work can be used as a guiding principle upon which to develop urban design proposals embracing proximity urbanism.

Economic Development and Smart Specialization Strategy

The intensity of social interactions is a key metric in the evolution of innovation districts. The scaling exponent of urban infrastructure networks with population by means of log-log scale analyses is usually estimated below one, therefore suggesting economies of scale in the use of buildings, transportation, and communication networks. On the other hand, social interactions, which culminate in innovation and wealth creation, present a scaling exponent above one, therefore implying increasing returns to aggregation in human interaction. The latter effect can be so powerful that it creates jumps in innovation with cycles shorter than a typical human lifespan, in contrast with biological phenomena where large innovation jumps occur sporadically and in a timeline longer than many lifespans of a living creature.

The network model proposed is not tested on empirical data but could serve as a solid ground for future tests with urban innovation empirical patterns. Schläpfer et al. (2014) study the superlinearity of communication networks in urban environments by analyzing mobile phone interactions within European cities.

Our contribution to this body of literature is to territorialize the notion of economic complexity at the submunicipal scale in order to further understand how to concretize smart specialization strategies for a given city, neighbourhood, industrial cluster, or innovation district. This is an area of analysis that deserves a set of data sources and a methodological approach of its own. Within the economic geography literature, there has been a large body of work focusing on agglomeration economics. Successful examples of nurturing a successful smart specialization strategy include Tallinn (Estonia), Dublin (Ireland), Bangkok (Thailand), Seoul (South Korea), Pittsburgh (PA, USA) and Cambridge (MA, USA).

Knowledge Economy Strategy: Networks of Innovation Districts

In recent years, a rising number of innovative firms and talented workers are choosing to congregate and co-locate incompact, amenity-rich urban settlements in the cores of central cities, known as innovation districts. These patterns were proposed by Miquel Barceló and described by Katz and Wagner (2014) as well as Burke, Gras Alomà, Yu and Kruguer (2019, 2021, 2022). These districts are geographic areas where leading-edge anchor institutions and companies cluster and connect with research centers, universities, start-ups, business incubators, and accelerators. Innovation districts tend to be physically compact, transit-accessible, technically wired, and offer mixed-use housing, office spaces, and retail.

A winning strategy to propel the knowledge economy is to envision, plan, design, shape, build, and operate a network of innovation districts that are strategically located, liberating the latent economic forces of the community and unleashing global competitiveness, thus contributing to improving the quality of life of citizens. The work of Bettencourt et al. (2008) addresses power law trends at the scale of the entire city. Furthermore, the findings of this body of work reveal much greater variability in the ranges of empirical power law exponents with respect to the various urban metrics evaluated. This increased variability suggests that as cities grow and scale the performance outcomes observed are affected by variations at smaller scales. These variations are no doubt a consequence of the heterogeneity of social and infrastructural networks and structure in different global cities. Narrowing the focus of the study of innovation from the city to the district level allows us to study in particular the superlinear effects of agglomerations of knowledge intensive activities around innovation districts. We can incorporate these measures of scale into our work to analyze the implications of population density and city size in the context of different urban layouts (Bettencourt and Lobo, 2006; Bettencourt, Lobo, and Strumsky, 2007; Arbesman et al., 2009; and Ellison and Glaeser, 2009).

City Science-led Policy Strategies: Informing Urban and Economic Development Strategies

Cities can strategically benefit from recent advances in the city science research area. By combining City Science techniques with traditional Urban Design methodologies, city leaders can harmonize art and science in urban development, informing their urban design and economic development strategy in an evidence-based manner to shape innovative and resilient cities. How can we better inform urban and economic development at the metropolitan scale to shape innovative and resilient cities? By harmonizing three main strategies:

Urban Design Vision: Fractal Metropolis Strategy to improve citizens' quality of life and achieve universal access to services, while capitalizing on the exponential benefits of the geographic concentration of knowledge-intensive activities.

Economic Development Vision: Evidence-based Smart Specialization to activate the dormant capabilities of collective know-how, by strengthening industry-specific value chains and informing product diversification and sophistication strategies.

Innovation Strategy: Network of Innovation Districts to liberate the potential of local talent by clustering knowledge-intensive activities geographically and linking research with knowledge transfer and production at scale.

Urbanism as an Art and a Science

City Form Features and Network Properties

The main research thesis of this book is to measure how different city design typologies impact urban performance patterns with respect to quality of work and life, and to prove the intimate relationship between city form and urban performance. We also seek to understand how the performance patterns for each city typology compare to the desired characteristics of sustainable development, including the ability to attain the standards of the 15-Minute City. A combination of network theory and complexity science provide a theoretical foundation for our work, enabling us to systematically analyze the relationship between urban form types and their associated urban dynamics and performance.

City form types are a useful theoretical framework, given that, historically, urban development patterns can and have been depicted by typological categories, each of which can be visually described and modeled mathematically. We have distilled these commonly understood typologies into a comprehensive set including the following categories: Small World, Monumental, Radial, Garden, Linear, Atomized, Random, Organic, Grid, and Fractal. While cities are composed of the same elements (roads, buildings, open spaces, urban furniture, supporting infrastructure and technology systems, etc.), each urban design type is differentiated and characterized by the specific layout of these elements. As we demonstrate in subsequent chapters, these layouts can be characterized systematically and quantified by specific urban form metrics. Our principal hypothesis is that these characteristics structurally impact urban dynamics, thus inducing specific patterns for urban performance in accordance with the different typological urban systems. The overarching assumption, more generally, is that cities have developed common patterns that can be categorized into specific archetypes. The type of urban form present in each city then influences the urban dynamics: social, economic, mobility, and otherwise. The dynamics created by form are inherently unequal, and therefore it is worth studying the performance of each type to determine how to continue to evolve our existing cities and design new ones.

We can sculpt a framework for understanding and evaluating the shape and size of cities by associating them with ontological groups or city typologies, subsequently measuring urban performance in a comparable manner across different geographies and time. This framework allows us to examine the concept of the 15-Minute City and to define and study which city types and urban characteristics enable achieving its quality standards.

Urban Design Typologies:
100 Representative
Global Cities

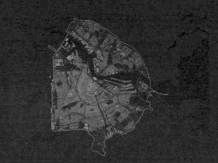

Amsterdam

Boston

Frankfurt

Hong Kong

Istanbul

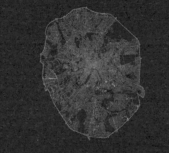

Las Vegas

Moscow

New York City

Osaka

Shanghai

Seoul

Analogy Between City Design and Network Typologies

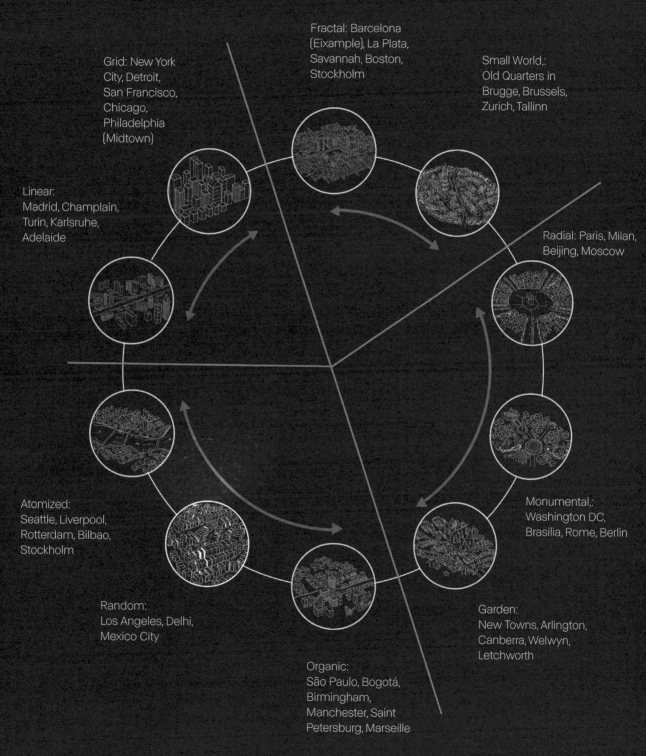

Fractal: Barcelona (Eixample), La Plata, Savannah, Boston, Stockholm

Small World,: Old Quarters in Brugge, Brussels, Zurich, Tallinn

Grid: New York City, Detroit, San Francisco, Chicago, Philadelphia (Midtown)

Linear: Madrid, Champlain, Turin, Karlsruhe, Adelaide

Radial: Paris, Milan, Beijing, Moscow

Atomized: Seattle, Liverpool, Rotterdam, Bilbao, Stockholm

Monumental,: Washington DC, Brasilia, Rome, Berlin

Random: Los Angeles, Delhi, Mexico City

Garden: New Towns, Arlington, Canberra, Welwyn, Letchworth

Organic: São Paulo, Bogotá, Birmingham, Manchester, Saint Petersburg, Marseille

CITY TYPE	NETWORK THEORY ANALOGY	REPRESENTATIVE CITIES
Small World	Small World Network	Old Quarters in Brugge, Brussels, Zurich, Tallinn
Radial	Radial Network	Paris, Milan, Beijing, Moscow
Garden	Tree Network	New Towns, Arlington, Canberra, Welwyn, Letchworth
Linear	Linear Network	Madrid, Champlain, Turin, Karlsruhe, Adelaide
Atomized	Modular Network	Seattle, Liverpool, Rotterdam, Bilbao, Stockholm
Random	Random Network	Los Angeles, Delhi, Mexico City
Organic	Poisson/ Lognormal Network	São Paulo, Bogotá, Birmingham, Manchester, Saint Petersburg, Marseille
Monumental	Hierarchical Networks	Washington DC, Brasilia, Rome, Berlin
Grid	Reticular Network	New York City, Detroit, San Francisco, Chicago, Philadelphia (Midtown)
Fractal	Scale Free Network	Barcelona (Eixample), La Plata, Stockholm, Boston

City form typologies and their representative features (urban topology, morphology, entropy, and scale) have an effect on urban performance with respect to urbanization efficiency, access to urban amenities, and the knowledge economy. We identified 10 core city form typology trends. By way of example, urban density superlinearly correlates with urban infrastructure efficiency and access to services. Every time we double population density, we observe on average a 19% sublinear increase in economies of scale in terms of access to amenities, all else being equal.

Urban form fractality is a key urban form component when evaluating the relationship between urban form and urban performance. When we double the city form fractality (2x growth), we observe on average a 31% superlinear increase in efficiency in terms of access to amenities and social interaction surplus, all else being equal.
The Fractal city form typology is the most efficient in terms of both material urban infrastructure efficiency and superlinear social interaction patterns, boosting the access to services and amenities as well as the knowledge economy. Fractal growth patterns achieve a more egalitarian distribution of amenities than other network types.
The urban form entropy index is correlated with urban development efficiency metrics, and intermediate levels of city form entropy achieve the maximum/optimal degrees of urbanization efficiency.
The geographic aggregation of knowledge-intensive activities within physical proximity with an innovation network hierarchical logic tends to facilitate fruitful interaction, hence producing multiplying effects benefitting the overall urban economy, by increasing wages, diminishing unemployment, and producing new inventions, products and services that raise the quality of life of citizens.

City Form Metrics

CITY FORM CHARACTERISTICS	URBAN FORM VARIABLES
Urban Form Fractality & Entropy City Design Harmony and Order	Urban Form Fractality Index Area Compactness Street Orientation Order (Shannon Entropy)
Urban Topology Street Layouts	Avg. Length of Street Segments Density of Intersections Density of Street Segments Avg. Circuity of Street Network Avg. Intersection Connectivity Avg. Betweenness Centrality Avg. Closeness Centrality (local) Avg. Closeness Centrality (global) Avg. Straightness Centrality
Urban Morphology Building Form	Avg. Area of Building Footprints Avg. Area of Tessellations Avg. Building Orientation Avg. Tessellation Orientation Avg. Street Alignment Avg. Building Compactness

Urban Performance Indicators

URBAN PERFORMANCE	KEY PERFORMANCE METRICS
Network of Talent Knowledge Economy	**Superlinearity:** **Multiplying Effects of the Knowledge Economy** Innovation Intensity Innovation Performance Innovation Impact
Network of Industries Access to Urban Amenities	**Superlinearity:** **Access to Urban Amenities per building node** Education Amenities per Km2 Mobility and Public Transit per Km2 Healthcare Amenities per Km2 Sustenance Amenities per Km2 Entertainment Amenities per Km2
Network of Urban Design Urban Development Efficiency	**Superlinear Efficiency (Economies of Scale):** Total Urbanization Efficiency Total Built Area Efficiency: Architectural Efficiency Total Street Length Efficiency Street Flow Centrality Urban Network Centrality and Opportunity KPI Urban Mobility Efficiency

We focus on the application of this framework to the study of possibilities for maximizing economic opportunities as well as the qualities of urban services in order to ensure egalitarian access to resources and amenities. It is demonstrably clear that it is possible to evaluate urban performance metrics using data from open street maps and business databases to describe the ways in which urban form contributes to helping or hindering innovation performance, access to amenities, and infrastructure management.

During our research, we identified 10 core urban form design typologies based on similar city form features, which helped to establish urban performance KPIs that were used to define the 15-Minute City urban performance KPIs. We validated five city science hypotheses. Our results show that when creating urban performance indicators to measure the quality of urban life, it is important to understand the degree to which different urban development patterns satisfy such standards. Super linear and sublinear components will need to be understood in relationship to one another, not just for the entirety of the city. This will change the urban planning, design, construction, and maintenance of such systems. By completing the existing empirical analysis, the methodology takes a fresh look at how current systems are organized and their benefits, drawbacks, and tradeoffs.

City form fractality exists on a spectrum and superlinearly correlates with urban performance. It may be possible to achieve the 15-Minute City by reinforcing the degree of fractality in the layout of urban spaces, in combination with increased density. Our results show that by reinforcing specific network features such as fractality, it is possible to increase urban performance in multiple ways. Further studies could help discern what pragmatic actions may help reinforce fractality in terms of the redevelopment of existing urban spaces. Without easy access to jobs of various types, it is not possible for individuals to capture that income for their own livelihood or advance their professional development. Without a diverse set of industries, the economy is fragile and the city will not be able to capture the taxable income from a diversified portfolio of industries. Without fruitful human interaction, cities become isolated and quality of life diminishes. Without access to public transport, cities become congested, air pollution rises, and health decreases. In our research, we have developed systematic and quantitative methods and applied them to real empirical cases to understand the connections between metrics describing urban form and the impact they have.

Deepening the understanding of the relationship between city form and innovation performance dynamics enables to determine desirable ranges for urban density, street orientation patterns, architectural space morphological features, building height, space programming, placemaking strategies, amenity distribution, and knowledge economy ecosystem building, among others. When evaluating the Boston, MA underlying city form patterns we observe a gradient in urban performance for knowledge economy KPIs (innovation intensity, innovation performance) positively correlated with the degree of city form fractality present in each neighborhood, whether it is shaped following an organic, reticular, linear, garden or fractal layout. This is to be expected but also shows the uneven distribution of economic opportunities within the city. The neighborhoods are separated by program and there is very little overlap between urban features, causing certain areas of the city to outperform others socially and economically, which limits the opportunity for citizens to capture the value created. Of course, the success of innovation ecosystems is not determined exclusively by urban form; yet, as is consistent with our results for urbanized efficiency and access to amenities, the urban form qualities that result in higher degrees of fractality – enabling easier reciprocity, connectivity, and more efficient positioning and allocation of amenities – serve as fruitful space design frameworks supporting high quality social interaction patterns, helping to propel corporations, businesses, research teams and startups that require talented employees and strong connections to neighboring industry verticals, residences, and other services.

Urban environments are host to a myriad of issues that can be solved with rigorous analysis and coordinated action. We intend for the analysis, methodologies, and results set forth in the proposed city science methodology to help catalyze further transition towards quantitative methods of understanding cities that work cohesively with design and policy to create more prosperous urban environments that are better equipped and more adaptable to future challenges and change.

Aretian's novel research and city science methodology make distinct contributions to three strands of the academic literature linking city design with economic development and social outcomes:
(1) urban scaling analysis at the municipality level
(2) urban network studies
(3) economic complexity and geography studies

By modeling urban space as a three-dimensional complex system characterized by morphological design features, a specific space programming configuration, an underlying urban fabric infrastructure, and dynamic human networks, we can identify global types of families of urban development patterns and their impact on the quality of life of their citizens. But how did we break through the methodological stagnation affecting the discipline of urbanism?

A New City Science Methodology: Deductive, Inductive, Abductive Reasoning

Cities as Complex Systems: Overcoming Methodological Stagnation

The noble endeavor aiming to shape a solid, actionable and solvent city science theory and heuristic practice has often encountered periods of methodological stagnation. The main reason is the inherent difficulty in devising a viable heuristic methodology that both captures a great deal of the complexity that we observe in urban phenomena and is able to model the urban infrastructure and systems manifested worldwide in a universal and benchmarkable manner, while providing valuable pattern recognition methods, rigorous predictive modeling to reduce uncertainty, and evidence-based insights related to design and management.

The good news is that by harmonically integrating complex systems modeling and network theory principles, paired with a set of demonstrable hypotheses and assumptions, we have been able to break through some of the legacy limitations in the realm of urban science that have accumulated in recent years. A key difficulty most urban scientists face when shaping a city science model is the need for combining a generalizable, universal model with the myriad of specificities observed in city design and urban systems around the globe. In a way, every architectural space, urban setting, neighborhood, district, city or municipality, and region is unique. Simultaneously, we perceive common patterns, fundamental structures, and social network properties that can be described, defined, modeled and understood. Furthermore, network science provides a series of system typologies, each of which is characterized by common properties, features, and dynamic cause-and-effect relationships.

For instance, the research efforts conducted by West and his team out of the Santa Fe Institute offered a number of insights and fundamental lessons that help us understand the scaling or purely quantitative factor when it comes to observing the urban phenomena and the emergence of complex systems in city development. However, their advances are subject to a fundamental limitation: they presented aggregate results at the municipal scale but failed to describe the inner dynamics experienced within a city at the pedestrian level. Such an approach would require a combination of urban design, architecture, and civil engineering knowledge with network science principles and modeling.

How Did We Break Through a Core Methodological Stagnation Affecting City Science Modeling?

By establishing a structural and rigorous analogy between well-known network typologies and specific urban design patterns and architectural styles, we are able to: (1) ontologically classify city design types into fundamental typologies of network science; (2) understand the properties, characteristics, and inherent dynamics associated with each network type and its archetypal features; and (3) measure, evaluate, and predict the impact of each type on individual and collective psychology and functional qualities, therefore allowing for tailoring design strategies and placemaking decision-making to satisfy the needs and unleash the potential of every site and community.

A Source of Inspiration: Eratosthenes, Columbus

Ever since the brilliant mathematician Eratosthenes devised a clever strategy to indirectly estimate the radius and diameter of the Earth, many scientists have attempted to validate and take advantage of such a non-trivial and powerful concept. The wise man from Alexandria estimated the radius of our planet with over 99% accuracy by means of a creative geometry exercise consisting of taking partial measurements of the sphericity of the Earth by calculating the sun's projections over vertical structures during different times of the day. His outstanding intuition led him to validate and refine what were, by then, well-known assumptions about the globe's physical properties among educated citizens. However, while Eratosthenes' and Ptolemy's treaties and studies were preserved and transcribed throughout the middle ages in Europe, there had been no empirical validation of their estimations and hypotheses.

It took cosmographer Christopher Columbus to pose a bold validation strategy: aiming to reach Asia and the potential unknown territories by traveling west from Europe via the Atlantic Ocean. The strategy proved correct, and the rest is history. Columbus convinced the Catholic Monarchs to allow him and his crew to navigate to the west well beyond the Açores islands, aiming to reach East Asia and the newfoundlands in between. The epic led by Columbus opened a new era, characterized by the consolidation of the scientific method as an empirical construct aiming to discern the validity of measurable and demonstrable hypotheses and assumptions. The knowledge acquired by mankind and the vast opportunities open for peoples around the world enabled the birth of an era of great discoveries and advances for humanity. In his audacious effort, Columbus combined the top-down hypothesis that the world we inhabit is fundamentally spherical, the bottom-up learnings derived from partial observations of the sphericity of the earth revealed by ships as they disappear on the horizon, and the abductive conclusion that if the sphericity can be estimated, we can properly size the naval infrastructure and operational resources required in order to reach a specific destination across the ocean. Such fantastic progress can serve as a powerful metaphor and help us draw direct inspiration in order to chisel out a set of urban science assumptions, construct a robust methodology to validate them, and project the learnings in order to make better decisions when tackling complex urban problems.

A Fundamental Intuition: Euler and Galois

Given the need to better understand why certain cities and urban areas attain remarkably better results than others in constituting attractive, desirable, and highly functional urban environments, our first task is to capture the essence of a given urban setting. By understanding cities as three-dimensional networks composed of specific, yet dynamic city form features, we can build off prior knowledge in the domain of complex systems. Euler defined the foundations of graph theory and network science when he drew the very first known graph depicting the bridge system of the Prussian city of Königsberg by means of a mathematical and aesthetic abstraction. The immense progress achieved in the sphere of network science since Euler drew his sketch has resulted in a wealth of knowledge that presents revolutionary applications for a vast array of fields, ranging from intermodal mobility to medical research, all the way through electromagnetism and beyond. A key takeaway from Euler that we can apply when modeling cities as complex systems is the ability to decompose a given urban territory into its fundamental topological and morphological features, a strategy that allows us to define the unique bi-dimensional patterns of street layouts and morphological features of architectural space, hence providing both an analytical and representation system to evaluate and conform urban environments.

A genius mathematician in his own right, Évariste Galois developed his entire career between the ages of 16 and 20. His tragic and epic death, which occurred at the height of the Romantic era, amplified the legend built up around him and inspired the admiration, sympathy, and compassion of gentle souls worldwide. His theories and ideas established the foundation for today's satellite systems and geopositioning techniques, contributing immensely to enabling the birth and eventual expansion of the internet. A paramount contribution achieved by Galois was the ability to define ontological, categorical, qualitative groups characterized by common features, properties, and nontrivial cause-and-effect relationships. His influence can be seen in the establishment of the analogy between network typologies and city form patterns and archetypal structures. By being able to group urban development growth patterns based on common design features such as street orientation patterns, underlying street hierarchies, morphological characteristics of architectural space, and activity programming distributions, we can better understand how people interact with one another and the impact of different aesthetic and functional designs on the subjective urban experience of citizens.

Aretian Methodology: Deductive, Inductive, and Abductive Reasoning

We envisioned a three-step methodology in order to build a systematic analogy between network science typologies and city design patterns. Deductive reasoning allows us to establish top-down, conceptual hypotheses defining the correlation between fundamental archetypal urban growth patterns and their network science counterparts. Inductive reasoning permits empirically validating the causal relationships by measuring a series of key performance metrics over time. Abductive reasoning equips us to successfully transition from a leap-of-faith intuition into a well-known analytical territory by establishing a traceable set of relationships that can explore the landscape of urban phenomena and confirm specific hypotheses in the absence of complete information. Abductive reasoning launches the arrow of the hypotheses that we can formulate via deductive reasoning and validate and refine by means of inductive reasoning based on systematic empirical observations and measurable dynamics.

The core underlying hypothesis is that the morphological design and activity programming set up of cities tends to have lasting effects on the human subjective and collective perception, behaviour, relationships and dynamics. Simultaneously, it is in our hands the ability to deliberately embed within our designs and compositions a more humane worldview, one that stimulates the most noble impulses of people, rather than hindering them. As Winston Churchill put it, "we shape our buildings, thereafter they shape us".

The combination of abductive, speculative definition of hypotheses based upon the analogy between network dynamics and human interaction dynamics within the urban space; deductive, ontological conceptualization of network typologies with city design archetypal patterns, with inductive, empirically driven statistical validation of hypothesis reveals highly insightful relationships, thus allowing for more precise development diagnostics and higher quality design methodologies.

A fundamental observation is that the highest quality environments are manifested whenever we observe the juxtaposition of Scale-Free networks with fractal topological and morphological compositions with respect to the three fundamental urban systems: the networks of talent, industries, and urban design. Just like in the classic Parable of the Talents, where the individuals that make the most of their abilities and gifts are the ones producing yields exponentially related with their merit, hence benefitting the broader community; a society will be much better off as long as it raises the potential prospects of each of the citizens in a moral manner, rather than curtailing it.

Self-similar organizational structures, such as the ones observed historically in medieval guilds that worked in their *ateliers*, tend to reward personal merit, teamwork collaboration, and effort, whilst stimulating a communitarian and egalitarian foundational relationship.

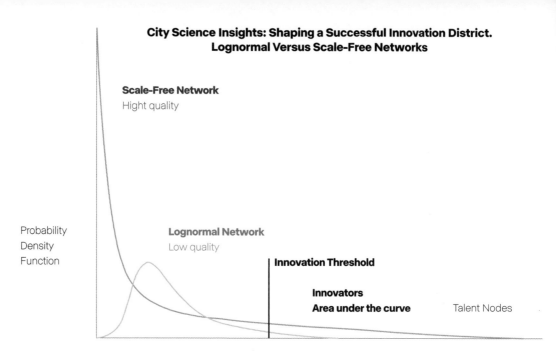

**City Science Insights: Shaping a Successful Innovation District.
Lognormal Versus Scale-Free Networks**

Scale-Free Network
Hight quality

Probability
Density
Function

Lognormal Network
Low quality

Innovation Threshold

Innovators
Area under the curve   Talent Nodes

When such a healthy, generous worldview crystallizes in broader organizational networks and industries, the overall community raises the bar in terms of their personal and collective outcome, morale, and sense of belonging. In order to achieve those gold standards, the physical environment needs to provide the proper habitat and ambiance. A highly fractal urban design with a highly fractal network of industries in which a highly fractal network of talent operates is the secret recipe for envisioning attractive and functional urban development strategies that make the most out of the human experience.

Unfortunately, the most prevalent network structures in urban design and organizational life are not the highly self-similar, Scale-Free, fractal ones characterized by their harmonic polycentrism, but rather the mediocre, lower quality, Poisson-based Lognormal networks. Mediocre or poorly articulated collaboration organizational schemes functioning on top of stagnant, marginally innovative industries, operating in an environment often characterized by unfortunate degrees of density, banal architectural spaces and urban environments are more often than not the business-as-usual constraints of everyday life for many citizens worldwide. Being able to determine the ingredients and dynamics that can help us ascertain how to conform to higher quality urban environments whilst advancing an urban economy based upon egalitarian and merit-based systems is a paramount goal of this book. A virtuous society will flourish more naturally within a virtuous urban environment characterized by those free, egalitarian, and merit-based relationships. Drawing inspiration from observations of fractality and high quality Scale-Free networks in nature, science, art and architecture can be one of the keys for success.

Measuring City Form and Urban Performance

Strategic urban and economic development currently lacks evidence-based, data-driven, rigorous territorial analysis. As such, decision makers, planners, and city officials do not currently have the right tools and organized information to reduce the risk of decision making in regional planning. Information is often disaggregated and separated across multiple data sets and subject matter expert teams. It is difficult to merge the information together so that different cities can be compared to one another in order to create a coherent narrative that can support decision making and long-term urban and economic planning.

Here we introduce the two primary methodologies employed in the analysis to achieve the goal of determining the linkages between city types and their performance. First, we developed a geospatial analysis framework to collect urban morphometrics (the metrics that describe complex features of urban form) and use them to classify geographic areas within cities into our set of typological categories. We use these classifications and the calculated metrics to provide quantitative descriptions of these theoretical design typologies. Second, we developed a set of key performance indicators (KPIs) to quantify the performance of urban spaces in three categories: infrastructure efficiency, accessibility, and work-related activity.

By systematically collecting variables related to scalable infrastructure efficiency, the accessibility of amenities, and the quality of economic opportunities related to innovative work we are able to provide empirical evidence for the influence of urban layouts on quality of work and life. With the two primary methodologies combined, we evaluate how the characteristics of the typological groups can contribute to or hinder the performance goals of the 15-Minute City. To understand, guide, and evaluate our analysis of representative empirical examples we developed five main hypotheses.

Greater Boston Area
Innovation Employment

Innovation Employment

- 0
- 5.000
- 10.000
- 14.089

Innovation District

- Boston Harvard Allston
- Boston Longwood Medical
- Boston Seaport
- Cambridge Harvard Square
- Cambridge Kendall MIT
- Other

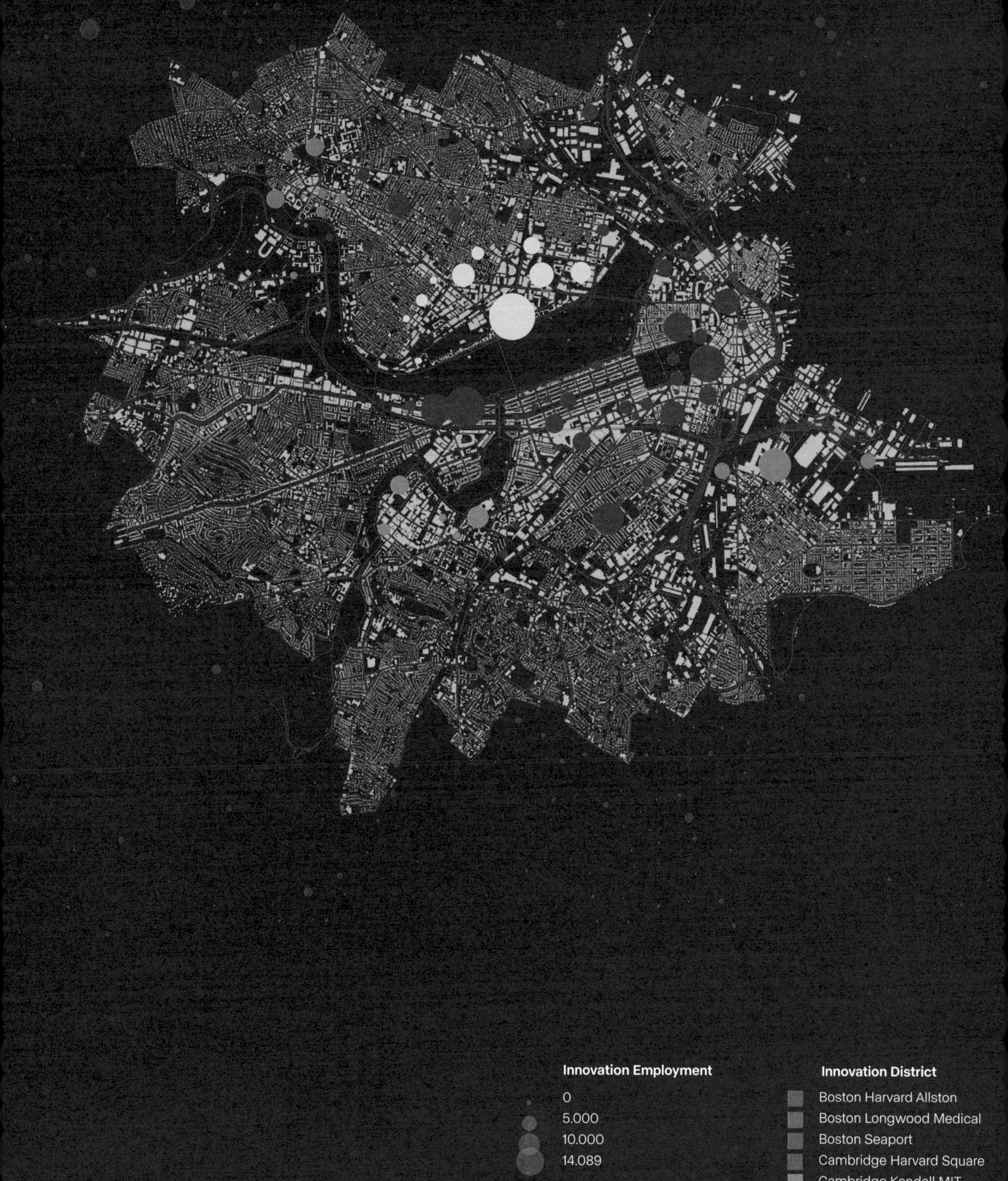

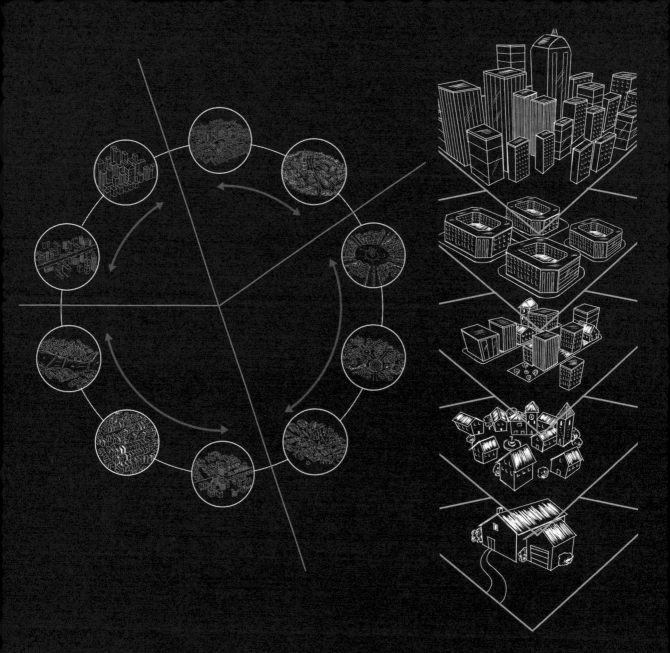

Research Hypotheses

Insight 1
City form typologies and their representative features (urban topology, morphology, entropy, fractality, and scale) have an effect on urban performance with respect to urbanization efficiency, access to amenities, and the knowledge economy.

Insight 2
The urban form fractality index is positively correlated with urban infrastructure efficiency, and the fractal city typology is the most efficient out of the 10 types in terms of urban infrastructure economies of scale and superlinear social interaction patterns.

Insight 3

The urban form fractality index is positively correlated with the access to urban services and amenities, and fractal grids achieve a more egalitarian distribution of services than other network types.

Insight 4

The urban form entropy index is correlated with urban development efficiency metrics, and intermediate levels of city form entropy achieve the maximum/optimal degrees of urbanization efficiency.

Insight 5

The geographic aggregation of knowledge-intensive activities in physical proximity with an innovation network logic tends to facilitate fruitful interaction, hence producing multiplying effects benefitting the overall urban economy.

City Form Key Performance Metrics (KPIs)

To quantify the economic performance of each typology and the influence of specific urban features on performance outcomes, we have established three categories of key performance indicators (KPIs) that quantitatively describe the **Network of Talent** (local professional skills), **Network of Industries** (access to high-quality employment and amenities), and **Network of Urban Design** (layout and size of cities that contributes to or hinders access to amenities). The KPIs can easily be deployed to describe the potential for a successful economy with a focus on innovation in cities around the world. Network of Talent KPIs describe the innovation and knowledge economy over specific geographic areas of cities as designated by the local authorities. They are useful for comparing innovation across multiple different landscapes. Network of Industry KPIs track important amenity categories and their location in space. For this category of KPIs we look at amenities that are accessible roughly within a 15-minute walking shed or a distance of 1,000 meters. Therefore, we are able to determine which urban spaces have easier access to essential services for daily life and work. Lastly, for the Network of Urban Design KPIs, we collect several infrastructural efficiency indicators. These indicators serve to explain how efficiently a particular typology might scale in terms of the resources and space required to accommodate particular structural patterns versus others.

We can understand all three performance indicator categories (talent, industry, and urban design) through the concept of sublinearity and superlinearity, which describe a system's ability to deliver resources, access amenities, and provide infrastructure to a given community. Based on the city typology, each system (talent, industry, and urban design) will either be more or less efficient depending on the scale and size of the city.

We define superlinearity as the enhanced performance of merit-based economic and innovation-related activity based on the city type and scale. For sublinearity, we define the term as the efficiency associated with the distribution of infrastructure required to meet the needs of the community to support transportation and water distribution, for example. In addition, cities can be super- and sublinear in relation to the distribution of amenities, healthcare, education, access by transit, and income levels across residents and employees.

If a particular set of urban layout principles are followed it may enable easier access to innovation-related job opportunities, which may have multiplying effects in value creation; thus, a superlinear scaling ensues. Similarly, if a particular urban layout allows for a more efficient placement or distribution of services, amenities, and infrastructure or a reduction in a social effect such as crime, then the city type is said to be sublinear for such categories. This can manifest in a reduction in commute time, materials used to construct core infrastructure such as streets and buildings, and the number of gas stations needed to service automobiles.

The larger a city becomes, the lower the ratio is for the amount of materials needed to accommodate an increase in the number of people. However, not all city form typologies grow in the same way. Therefore, certain patterns of urban form enable greater or lesser degrees of efficiency as a city grows and expands in size and population.

Geographies and Database Building

Included in this study are 100 global cities containing tens of thousands of sub-municipal geographic divisions. The selection of this subset of cities and the sub-municipal geographic divisions was based on three main selection criteria: relative geographic diversity, clear correlation with a theoretical typology (based on urban planning history and theory), and data availability. Geographic data serves as the backbone of this analysis. In order to ensure consistency and accuracy, shapefiles outlining municipal boundaries and sub-municipal administrative divisions making up the geographic units used throughout our geospatial analyses were sourced directly from city level, region level, and in some cases federal level geospatial portals.

A critical component of the methodology described in the previous section is consistency in terms of the relative scale of geographic aggregation.

In many countries, the most systematic sub-municipal divisions are census geographies produced by a country's or a region's census bureau. Naturally, these geographies are not consistent across countries and in some cases even across cities in the same country. As such, we have collected sub-municipal geographies specific to each city that are comparable to the U.S. Census units in terms of their positioning in the hierarchy of geographic administrative divisions in each respective case.

City Form Features

Another core aspect of our methodology is the collection of urban morphometric data belonging to three subcategories: topology, morphology, and scale. As outlined in the methodology section, we collect a number of specific metrics within each of these categories in order to comprehensively catalog complexity measurements that describe many features of urban form. These metrics are extracted from street network data and building footprint data downloaded from Open Street Maps (OSM) and Open Street Maps Buildings (OSM Buildings). The primary methods for extraction and analysis were developed in Python, making use of several key packages and libraries including GeoPandas, OSMnx, and Momepy, among others. Select data manipulation and analysis was also performed using GeoDa.

City Science Methodology
Osaka, Japan and Frankfurt, Germany

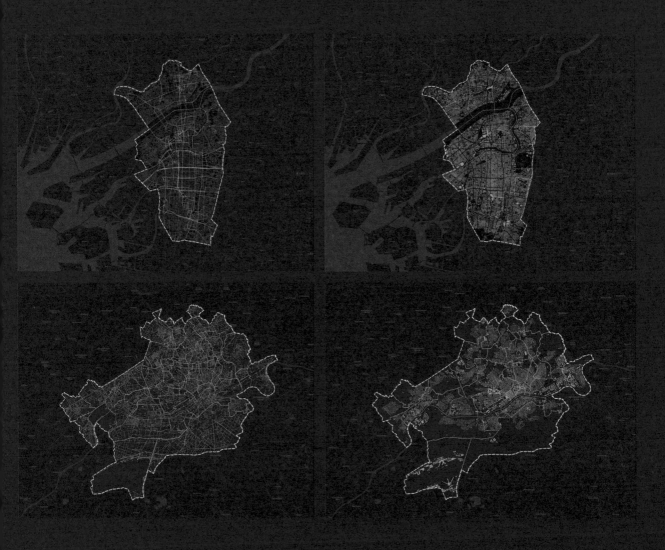

Urban Topology (2D)
Establishes the street layout pattern and dictates movement throughout the city.

Urban Morphology (3D)
Establishes the building layout, density, and programmatic neighborhoods: housing, business, entertainment, etc.

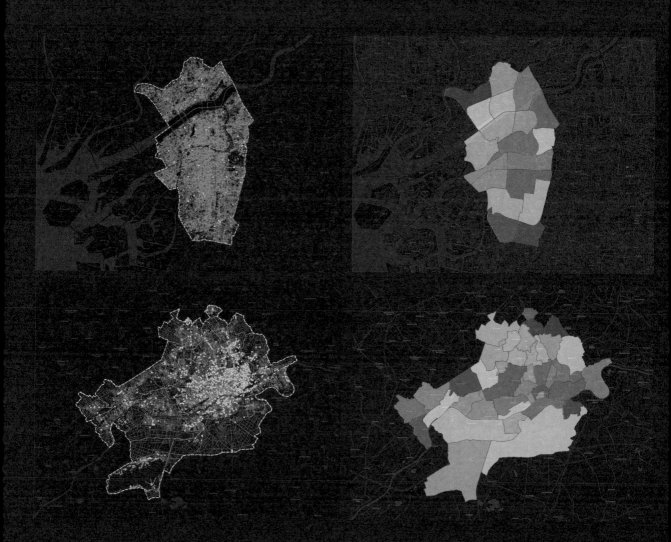

Amenity Distribution
The actual distribution of amenities as a result of morphology features, clustering dynamics, and programming.

15-minute city (KPI)
Accessibility to urban amenities determines the ability to reach critical services within walkable distance.

Urban Performance KPIs

In order to evaluate the performance of each city typology and the associated specific features of urban form, we collected two main categories of variables to serve as performance indicators. For the analysis of economic opportunities and innovation we downloaded, cleaned, and aggregated business data from several business data portals such as InfoGroup, Orbis, and Amadeus. These were combined with our own innovation datasets, in which we have tagged and mapped innovative industries (Burke, Gras, Kruguer, and Yu, 2021). Finally, in order to investigate access to amenities, we collected point of interest data from Open Street Maps for amenities related to six categories: sustenance (food and drink), education, healthcare, entertainment, transportation, and greenspace.

The data collected for spatial boundaries, street networks, buildings, amenities, and innovation are subject to standard data limitations. Specifically, spatial boundaries are cataloged and maintained by individual governing entities and hosted in geoportals or other data storage systems at the local, regional, and in some cases federal level. Data quality standards and documentation vary greatly between all cases. Great efforts have been made in this research to standardize data and ensure data quality, including temporal consistency (data from the most recent year available) and at similar levels of aggregation. Street network, building footprints, and amenities data all come from Open Street Maps, which is an open source platform. While most open source platforms are error prone, the Open Street Maps community follows very clear guidelines and as a result the data available from Open Street Maps' services has quickly outmatched all other public and private geospatial data sources for infrastructure- and urban-related data. Most recently, as of 2021, the OSM open source community includes more than 7 million contributors who collectively have produced over 6.6 billion nodes, 730 million streets/ways (e.g. streets and boundary lines), and various kinds of attribute data (OSM Wiki, 2021).

Therefore, this data represents the most up-to-date and consistent representation of the global cities we have included and is equally amenable to comparative studies given that all data is sourced from the same place. Lastly, as with demographic and census-related data, business surveys are not always entirely comprehensive. However, the business data we have collected in order to study economic opportunities and innovation has been rigorously cleaned and standardized to produce insightful metrics on innovation that are able to be compared across all contexts and cases.

We applied the geospatial analysis methodology to evaluate the relationship between city form and urban performance across a set of 100 cities from around the world, composed of thousands of sub-municipal administrative units. After completing a standardized database describing urban form features and quantifying aspects of topology, morphology, and urban scale and entropy at the level of geographic units specific to each case, we proceeded to group the geographic units into larger urban agglomerations presenting common city form characteristics.

These agglomerations were tagged by means of supervised analysis based on professional experience in urban design to identify the closest city form typology: small world, radial, garden, monumental, atomized, organic, random, linear, grid and fractal. After evaluating the relationship between the different city typologies and their urban performance KPIs, the results of the research validate the core set of hypotheses and assumptions able to help inform design and management decision-making processes.

HYPOTHESIS 1

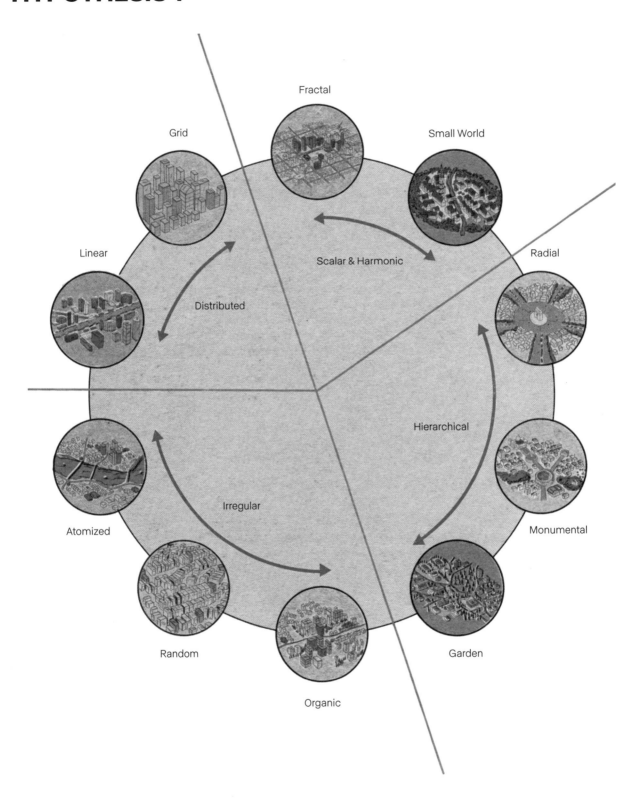

Fractal

Grid

Small World

Linear

Scalar & Harmonic

Radial

Distributed

Hierarchical

Atomized

Monumental

Irregular

Random

Garden

Organic

The Ten Archetypal Urban Design Patterns

City Typologies Have a Structural Effect on Urban Performance

City form typologies and their representative features (urban topology, morphology, entropy, fractality and scale) have a structural and universal effect on urban performance, with respect to urbanization efficiency, access to urban amenities, and the knowledge economy. The results of the city science evaluation of urban performance for each of the 10 urban design typologies shown on the circular diagram suggest that city typologies have a systematic and demonstrable effect on urban performance. We find that different typologies present distinctly different results in terms of urbanized efficiency (e.g., land use, built area, and network length).

Specifically, the relationship between the Urban Fractality Index and the Urbanized Efficiency KPI is positive and non-linear, indicating a superlinear pattern. This relationship is expressed differently for each typology, resulting in a gradient that indicates that city typologies with a higher fractality index outperform the others in terms of efficient use of infrastructure. In other words, there is a gradient of efficiency and a decreasing level of superlinearity across the typologies as fractality decreases. As a result, efficiency decreases across the typologies according to the following order: fractal cities, reticular grids, monumental, linear, organic, atomized, small world, random, garden, and finally radial models. The relationship between the Urban Fractality Index and the Network Closeness, Circuity and Betweenness Centrality, presents a clearly positive, nonlinear relationship between both variables, again indicating a superlinear pattern. This result suggests that cities that are well balanced across many scales in terms of the spatial distribution and quantity of connections (from individual streets and thoroughfares to larger highways) tend to take up less space and use less material, whilst maximizing the surplus obtained by social interaction patterns.

HYPOTHESIS 2

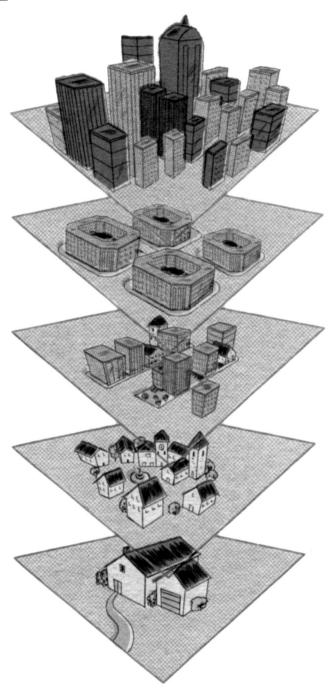

Impact of quantitative and qualitative improvements in urban design on the quality of life of citizens. Every time we double urban fractality (design quality), we observe a multiplying factor of 31% due to better social interaction and access to nearby services.

Every time we double the density without exceeding the limit of each city size, we observe 19% economies of scale: lower consumption of construction materials, energy, water, transportation, and greater access to urban services.

City Form Fractality Correlates with High Quality Urban Design and Performance

The urban form fractality index is positively correlated with urban infrastructure efficiency, and the fractal city typology is the most efficient out of the 10 types in terms of urban infrastructure economies of scale and superlinear social interaction patterns.

City Form Fractality is the most salient and analytically informative urban design feature when it comes to predicting urbanization efficiency.
The fractal layout, is the most sublinear of all typologies in terms of material infrastructure. This implies that it is the most efficient in terms of use of space and materials for construction (total length or volume of material). On the other side of the spectrum of typologies, the random and organic typologies are the least efficient in terms of material infrastructure.

By way of example, when we visualize the Urban Fractality Index, encoded via color gradient, and the Urbanization Efficiency KPI for a set of representative cities, we observe that neighborhoods that present more self-similar city typologies, such as grids/reticular or fractal types, tend to both present a higher degree of fractality index and capture a superlinearly higher degree of urbanization efficiency overall.

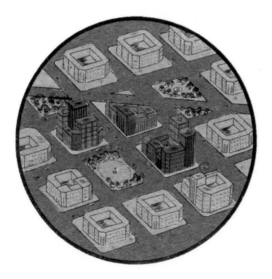

HYPOTHESIS 3

HYPOTHESIS 3

Fractal Grids Achieve a More Egalitarian Distribution of Amenities Than Other Network Types

It has been shown through the analysis, that highly fractal urban design patterns provide residents with greater access to amenities due to the fact that in polycentric, self-similar city types each amenity tends to be located closer to residents than in other layout forms in terms of Access to Education Amenities per Km2, Mobility and Public Transit per Km2, Healthcare Amenities per Km2, Sustenance Amenities per Km2, and Entertainment Amenities per Km2. In fractal cities, programs are overlaid on top of one another, therefore allowing people to reach each amenity with greater ease. The nesting factor of fractal cities also allows for programs to be distributed in an egalitarian way.

By way of example, Barcelona's Eixample and Sant Martí districts represent a preeminent example of a Fractal City Typology. The geospatially even distribution of amenities depicts how the even distribution of amenities is made possible by the neighborhoods that were designed in this style. Certain neighborhoods, such as the Eixample district and Sant Martí, present a remarkably fractal nature. Comparatively, Ciutat Vella follows a Small World City structure, Nou Barris presents a radial-organic pattern; Sants a Linear City Pattern; Gràcia a Grid-Organic pattern, and Les Corts a Monumental pattern.

When evaluating the 15 minute city quality standards for cities across the globe, we appreciate striking differences. For example, Barcelona's districts of Eixample and Sant Martí show a much higher number of illuminated amenities, and their spatial breakdown presents a highly egalitarian nature in terms of widespread distribution and accessibility to critical services. Other districts, such as Sant Gervasi or Ciutat Vella denote a more uneven distribution of amenities. In comparison with Barcelona, the city of São Paulo presents a much more organic city form layout. The careful evaluation of São Paulo's pedestrian accessibility to critical services and amenities presents a dramatically uneven distribution of services throughout the city. A steep decay in terms of accessibility throughout most of the Brazilian megalopolis underscores the unevenness of amenity distribution across the city.

Previous illustration: Concept of the 15-Minute City: accessibility to services: sustenance (restaurants and cafeterias), education (kindergarten, primary school, high school, university, research centers), healthcare (primary care, clinic, hospital) culture, leisure, retail and commerce, mobility nodes.

HYPOTHESIS 4

Intermediate Levels of Urban Form Entropy Present the Optimal Urban Development Efficience Performance Overall

The overall degree of city form regularity or specificity can be estimated by means of the urban form entropy metric. Highly rigid three dimensional urban design patterns characterized by simple replicable patterns present low levels of entropy, whereas highly idiosyncratic, unique and unpredictable city design morphologies present high entropy levels.

The results show that urban development typologies presenting an intermediate degree of urban form entropy outperform both extremely high or low city form regularity values with respect to urbanization efficiency patterns. Intermediate levels of Urban Form Entropy (Shannon Entropy Order) present the optimal levels of Urbanization Efficiency, Global Closeness Centrality, Betweenness Centrality, and Urban Form Fractality. However, the level of Urban Form Entropy is inversely correlated with Network Circuity, implying that a more rigid or highly ordered street layout pattern may contribute to increase the overall mobility efficiency. In other words, a balanced combination of a certain underlying distributed network regularity with a polycentric node and edge distribution presents the optimal features to maximize the quality of life of citizens.

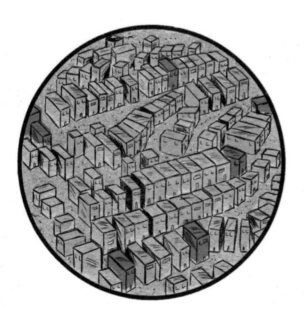

HYPOTHESIS 5

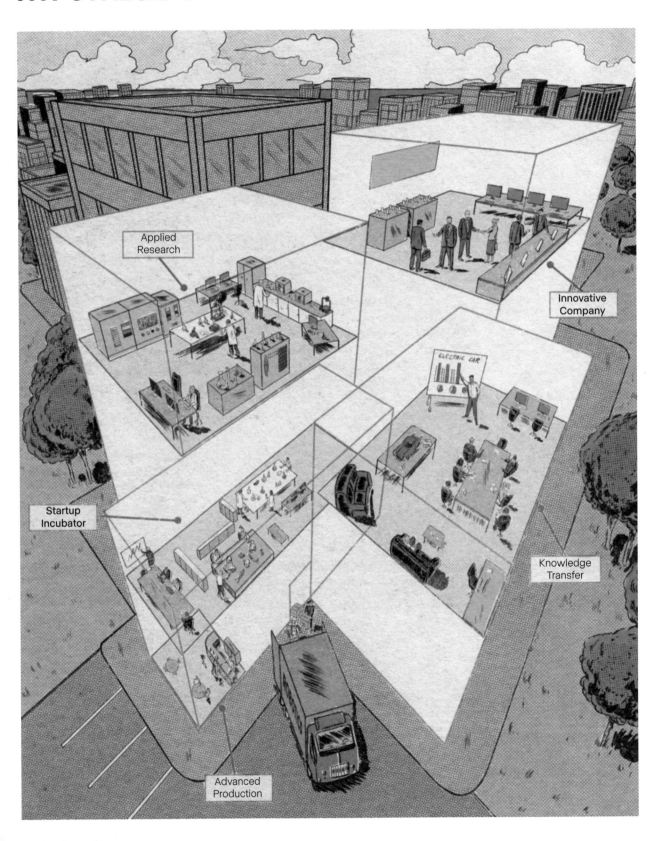

Applied Research

Innovative Company

Startup Incubator

Knowledge Transfer

ELECTRIC CAR

Advanced Production

Hierarchical Innovation Clustering Liberates Human Talent

The geographic aggregation of knowledge-intensive activities in physical proximity and structured with a hierarchical innovation network logic tends to facilitate fruitful interaction, hence producing multiplying effects benefitting the overall urban economy.

In order for people to successfully collaborate by means of generating products and services to solve complex problems facing society, a number of prerequisites need to be in place. Whilst intensive exploitation of agricultural fields led to the creation of stable, increasingly prosperous and resourceful permanent human settlements, and division of labor and a scientific approach to knowledge creation and diffusion the professional world allowed for extraordinary discoveries and magnificent human creations, we must recognize that often societies struggle to stay self-reliable and prosperous. Collaboration requires frequent communication, whether in-person, or by means of remote information transmission technologies. The geographic concentration of innovation-related activities within physical proximity in relatively dense environments, characterized by a hierarchical network structure of complementary agencies is the key for success: from research centers, technology and knowledge transfer, via startup incubators and accelerators, coworking spaces, all the way through corporations and complete innovation ecosystems. The evidence-based results of evaluating the innovation performance of hundreds of thousands of municipal units reveal the superlinear, exponential nature of the gains obtained by shaping those prosperous communities. A key success factor in shaping a vibrant innovation ecosystem is to conform a constellation of knowledge-intensive workplaces operating within physical proximity, conceived to facilitate the completion of the innovation journey, from idea inception to prototyping, Minimum Viable Product creation (MVP) down to product launch, market consolidation, and service scalability.

1) Applied Research
2) Knowledge Transfer
3) Innovative Company
4) Startup Incubator
5) Advanced Production

City Form and Urban Performance: Three Urban Systems

The overarching city science modeling framework, provided by the three networks of analysis, offers a conceptual understanding of how the data can be organized and described in detail to align with policy, resource deployment, and development decisions:

Network of Talent: Composed of individuals with valuable skills and abilities working in concert to solve complex problems. The analysis of the network of talent (innovation intensity, performance, and impact) enables describing the knowledge creation and knowhow diffusion of the city and surrounding neighborhoods based upon its demographic base, labor force, education, knowledge economy, and the Seven Phases of the Innovation Pipeline, along with networks linking industry and university applied research, technology transfer centers, and innovative companies and startups.

Network of Industries: Composed of businesses, agencies and institutions, which serve as the foundation for collaboration, and enable merit-based promotion of the best ideas. The collective knowledge, societal knowhow and sector-specific strengths and weaknesses of the business community in terms of levels of critical mass, vertical integration, product/service sophistication, and competitiveness. Identification of key industries and businesses presenting a global comparative advantage, their quantitative presence, and level of sophistication.

Network of Urban Infrastructure: The urban form, street layouts and road network hierarchies, building location, architectural space morphology, and programming needs and opportunities to make new developments accessible and attractive with the necessary programming and access to urban amenities, services, and transportation. Street network analysis for street layout design, mobility, and accessibility studies.

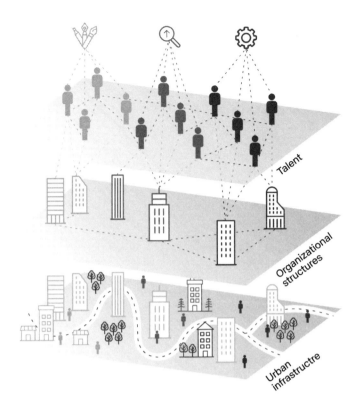

The geospatial analysis database, model, and methods used in this chapter lay out the foundation for further studies on how urban form impacts human experience, resource management, transportation and mobility, and economic opportunities. Some key questions that were explored are:

What are the key advantages and disadvantages of different urban design patterns in terms of the ability to achieve high quality urban performance and the 15-Minute City quality standards? What mathematical distributions best describe the urban performance KPIs for each city and typology? How can we strengthen the degree of Urban Form Fractality in a city? How can we achieve optimal values of urban form entropy in a city? How can we identify urban design and placemaking strategies tailored to each city in pursuit of increasing the quality of life of citizens, achieving the 15-Minute City standards, raising the material urbanization efficiency/sustainability, and fostering a vibrant economy propelling inclusive growth?

City science modeling techniques enable us to describe and evaluate the systems-level impact of different city design typologies on urban dynamics and performance with respect to social interaction, economies of agglomeration, innovation and wealth creation, talent attraction, accessibility and mobility, energy and water efficiency, and access to urban services and amenities, among others.

Network of Urban Design

City Typologies Impacting Urban Performance: Rationale

Each city typology exists within a specific family of networks based on its topology, morphology, and scale. Such network features shape how we live, interact, and work with one another. Hence, urban performance patterns depend intrinsically on how urban form types impact human behavior. Every city typology, then, is associated with network types. Through network theory modeling, we can measure the expected dynamics and performance levels for critical urban systems. Generally speaking, every city typology presents some advantages and disadvantages. However, overall, some urban growth models present qualitatively superior qualities compared to others.

- Namely, fractal cities tend to present high performance results in terms of both value creation and capturing. Their main strategic advantage relies on a nested hierarchy, enabling both a relatively even distribution of services and activity hubs, hence capturing both the benefits of the geographic concentration of activities with a harmonic distribution of services and minimizing average travel times while maximizing urban experience diversity.
- Radial or concentric cities, for example, tend to present the benefits of agglomeration in the central core areas; however, those positive effects are increasingly mitigated as you travel farther from the center.
- Linear cities present strategic advantages in terms of time minimization to access the central mobility network; however, there are physical limitations to linear cities in terms of functionality and pragmatic deployment of urban infrastructure and design types. Beyond a certain threshold, a linear model may present internal inefficiencies.
- Organic networks tend to present diverse urban environments, thus contributing to a lively urban experience. However, the organic nature of the network tends to create relatively inefficient urban performance patterns.

The 15-Minute City Standards

The 15-Minute City concept proposes the possibility of a completely decentralized city that provides each individual with equal access to housing, places of work, recreation, and efficient transport within locally oriented neighborhoods defined by proximity. It is believed that this model can provide a higher quality of life, with decreased travel times and greater opportunities for social interaction. In addition, cities can benefit from reduced congestion, lower costs associated with road maintenance and pollution, and potential opportunities regarding employment creation and innovation.

The 15-Minute City formalizes a set of urban design criteria and performance goals; however, to date, most approaches only address this theory through speculative and mainly qualitative analysis.
The Aretian team developed a methodology to provide urban and economic development guidelines to achieve the 15-Minute City. The core goal is to capitalize both the superlinear surplus from a geographic aggregation of urban density and activities, and a relatively evenly spread distribution of urban services and amenities across the territory.

Our proven framework enables us to evaluate different cities, estimate their projected urban performance KPIs and confidence levels, and identify the key ingredients and dynamics for urban development success.

City Form Characteristics

The city form characteristics are a set of custom KPIs to quantitatively describe a city's urban features. The KPIs are universal and allow any geographic region, district, or neighborhood to be assessed and benchmarked against similar or different areas of interest. Below are summaries of each KPI with examples to illustrate the results of the analysis.

The urban design and infrastructure metrics are composed of several factors. The first factor is Urban Topology, which describes layouts and network design for streets and highways. The network analysis is used to predict intermodal traffic, pedestrian flows, and social interaction patterns.

The second, Urban Morphology, serves to describe the shape and layout of buildings. The hubs are divided into three categories: Tier 1, 2, and 3, which have different effects on urban performance. In addition, the analysis focused on the optimal size of buildings and their location for services based on the industry.

Third, Urban Fractality defines the level of city form self-similarity, as a measure of harmonic polycentrism. Urban fractality estimates the degree of morphological clustering and fragmentation of urban patterns; the higher the fractality, the better for urban performance.

Fourth, Urban Entropy describes the structural rigidness/order and behavior of different urban systems. For Urban Entropy, an intermediate level of entropy – balancing and harmonically integrating freedom and efficiency – is optimal for urban systems.

Fifth, Urban Scale describes the optimal density, scale, concentration, and distribution of buildings with regard to their location within the city. Based on the long-term urbanization goals, recommendations are provided for where to increase the scale of specific neighborhoods.

Urban Performance: The 15-Minute City KPIs

Zoning and Placemaking describes the space programming quality and inner balance of a given city district. This reflects the potential for activities, or new activities, if the zoning changes. Often the recommendations can inform new zoning codes and guidelines to allow for new development trends.

Urban Amenities and Services describes how each neighborhood performs within the city based on the amenities and services for the local population. Metrics for this study describe the attractiveness of each district for quality of life and business.

Network of Industries

Economic Development Strategy: Industries with a Global Comparative Advantage

An Economic Development Strategy involves identifying and applying a series of specific smart specialization and placemaking interventions at the local level aiming to propel the prosperity of a brand new city development or urban regeneration plan. More precisely, a successful Economic Development Strategy can benefit from performing advanced analytics on economic and innovation data gathered at the sub-municipal, territorial scale, including information on production, exports, spending in innovation, patent creation, and firm-level data on production, employment, and innovation. The main goal of an Economic Development Strategy is to provide a roadmap and recommendations to shape and nurture the local economies of a given city, conforming its growth with clear goalposts and benchmarks with other comparable cities and districts. The main components of the Economic Development Strategy are the Innovation Pipeline Strategy and the Smart Specialization Strategy.

Smart Specialization Strategy

The successful development of a given city requires taking into account the contributions that different industries and skills bring into the mix to create a fruitful innovation ecosystem. In this regard, analyzing the levels of diversification and economic complexity of the district and broader region can provide precise estimates to predict and shape the future diversification path. In addition, risk mitigation strategies can be informed to provide an assessment of potential pitfalls in the diversification strategy. Risk mitigation strategies should focus on potentially promising sectors that nevertheless are exposed to failure, and industries that seem safe but have an underestimated risk component.

The analysis of the network of industries and economic complexity starts from the perspective that economic growth requires the accumulation of capabilities. The typical Neoclassical theory of economic growth assumes that these capacities can be aggregated in an additive fashion forming a stock. The larger the stock, the larger the flow of output in a given period. This theory has some drawbacks. In the first place, the data shows that sustained economic growth is explained, for the most part, by technological improvements instead of factor accumulation. Secondly, the stock of knowledge is more complex than an additive theory and must consider the complementarities in the accumulation of human capital.

One solution to this puzzle comes from the application of network theory. Knowledge is distributed across people. Technology is not an aggregate value but a combination of this distributed knowledge. As a result, countries or regions with more knowledge can produce a larger variety of products. They will be more diversified. In the same fashion, few countries and regions will be able to produce complex products. These regions will have more knowledge and higher diversification than those producing less complex products. As a result there is an inverse relation between the diversification of a region and the complexity of its exports. We can observe this inverse relation in the figure below. Regions with a larger stock of knowledge have more diversity and produce goods that are more complex and less ubiquitous (produced by few regions). As a result, countries or regions with more knowledge can produce a larger variety of products. They will be more diversified. In the same fashion, few countries and regions will be able to produce complex products.

These regions will have more knowledge and higher diversification than those producing less complex products. As a result there is an inverse relation between the diversification of a region and the complexity of its exports. We can observe this inverse relation in the figure below. Regions with a larger stock of knowledge have more diversity and produce goods that are more complex and less ubiquitous (produced by few regions).

We can observe the relationship between economic complexity and prosperity growth in the figure on the right. Countries that were above the trend in 2008, such as Greece, reverted back to the trend over time, and countries that were below, such as China, grew remarkably over the following years. We use these insights in the analysis of the urban region to analyze and forecast economic growth and economic complexity.

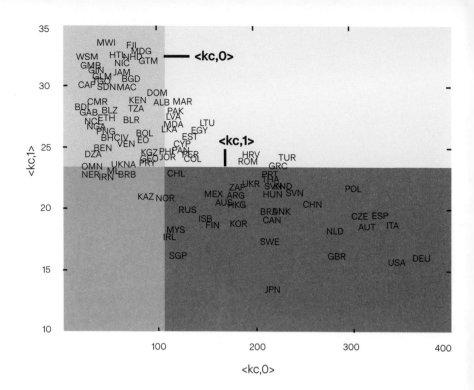

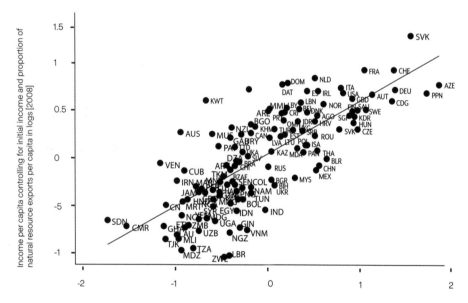

Inverse relation between diversity (how many products are exported by a region) and ubiquity (how many regions export a given product).
Source: Atlas of Economic Complexity (2011).
Source: The Atlas of Economic Complexity

Export Basket Barcelona

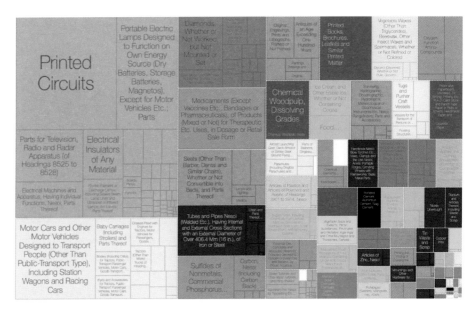

Modeling the Network of Industries

Urban innovation performance is the main driving force behind sustained economic growth. There have been many attempts to quantify innovation performance in order to guide decision making, promoting investment and innovation projects. Most studies do not accurately describe innovation in terms of how knowledge-intensive activities develop over multiple phases, how they are distributed geographically, and the ways in which agglomerated urban innovation efforts can enhance economic growth. Primarily, they fail to effectively combine urban practice and economic findings through data science efforts to design quantitative innovation performance metrics.

This chapter presents a novel database and analytical methodology to measure and describe the nonlinear benefits of the geographic aggregation of knowledge-intensive activities within urban environments.

The results of this research demonstrate empirically that innovation districts, characterized by the geographic concentration of knowledge-intensive activities, benefit from the superlinear growth of innovation, both in terms of innovation output per employee (new patents, new products, new services, R&D, scientific papers) and in terms of innovation-related employment creation per resident.

The geospatial, analytical framework has been applied to the study of 50 notable innovation districts to benchmark them against a baseline of all districts in the U.S. We have extracted the most salient features of these districts that illustrate the value of investing in the geographic concentration of innovation activities. The analytical framework can then be applied to any geographical area to evaluate the economic performance of knowledge-intensive activities within urban environments. The work expands on general knowledge of how cities operate as complex systems and how they shape the collective knowhow of urban communities. Further research may identify the key factors, features, and dynamics underlying the success of innovation districts, such as urban design criteria and smart specialization strategies, and apply them to specific communities to support the economic growth of urban environments.

Recent research in the study of economic development and urban phenomena has applied insights of economic complexity to provide a reliable methodology to describe industry comparative advantage at the national level. This strand of research applies network theory to study the linkages between knowledge producing agents in an economy (Hidalgo and Hausmann, 2009). This methodology enables a systematic understanding of collective knowhow advancement and knowledge diffusion at the national scale, as well as the identification of smart specialization and diversification strategies. However, the current literature presents two major limitations: on the one hand, it primarily focuses on international trade of physical goods, thus lacking the analysis of high-value-added intangible services; on the other hand, the national level of aggregation does not permit a deeper understanding of geospatial dynamics, hence precluding a detailed understanding of territorial dynamics and the nonlinear benefits of the geographic aggregation of knowledge-intensive activities. As a result, the economic complexity models tend to come up short in terms of identifying sub-national and city-level dynamics of collective knowhow, and in illustrating urban development recommendations at the regional, urban, and local level (Hausmann, Hidalgo et al., 2014).

There is a research gap in the urban innovation literature when it comes to understanding the links between good practices in urban design and the main factors, features, and underlying dynamics of successful cities. By combining city science techniques with insights from economic complexity, we can provide a higher resolution methodology to measure, evaluate, and better understand innovation systems at the urban scale.

The geospatial analysis of innovation and knowledge-intensive activities within urban environments will (1) enable a deeper understanding of the dynamics of the nonlinear benefits of the strategic geographic aggregation of knowledge-intensive activities; in order to (2) identify the key ingredients and dynamics facilitating economic growth and stable employment creation; thus (3) propelling regional growth, and distributed prosperity by means of providing urban development decision-making recommendations for the purpose of improving urban economic performance.

Previous research by Bettencourt, Lobo, Strumsky, and West (2010), as well as Barabási (2017), shows that the scale of cities has a superlinear or sublinear impact on social measures such as patents, crime, and sustainability. In this section, we quantify the superlinear effects of the geographic aggregation of knowledge-intensive activities within innovation districts and provide quantitative measures of the multiplying effects and the derived economic surplus in terms of knowledge advancement, wealth, and employment creation for the surrounding communities. The novel framework used in this chapter will allow readers to understand these relationships by modeling knowledge-intensive activities from a network theory perspective.

The city science modeling of the network of industries contributes to four main strands of the literature linking economic development and innovation. First, the literature of economic complexity and collective knowhow tries to model the relationship between the stock of knowledge in a region and economic outcomes (Hidalgo, Hausmann, 2009). Our work incorporates these intuitions but places the scope of analysis at the city and district level and incorporates higher quality data such as firm-level data. Second, the study of power laws in urban scenarios, as proposed by Bettencourt, Lobo, Strumsky, and West (2010), looks at the universal relation between scale and urban phenomena by using graphical descriptions of sublinear or superlinear effects with larger and larger scales of aggregation. We contribute to this literature by focusing the analysis on innovation districts in urban settings. Third, the study of agglomeration economies by Ellison and Glaeser (2009) tries to disentangle the effect of local comparative advantage and endogenous spillovers to explain the geographic distribution of economic activity. The literature finds that intra-industry externalities play an important role, and local natural advantages have a limited explanatory power. We build upon these findings to concentrate on the powerful externalities driven by innovative activities in urban settings. Finally, the city-level evidence-based approach to increase urban performance, developed by Kent Larson and Andres Sevtsuk, serves as a source of inspiration to bridge the gap between economic geography, economic complexity studies, and urban design (Ekmekci, Kalvo, and Sevtsuk, 2016).

Economic Complexity as a Measure of Collective Knowhow

The study of how people collaborate to add value in the economy dates back to the writings of Adam Smith (1776), who studied the division of labor. People and firms specialize in different activities, increasing economic efficiency and the impact of the interactions between them. Hidalgo and Hausmann (2009) applied this insight at a national scale to study the relation between the human and physical capital resources in a given country and the type of goods that they export. Basing their work on the study of Scale-Free networks by Barabási (2016), they modeled the structure of an economy as a bipartite network in which countries are connected to the products they export and showed that it is possible to quantify the complexity of a country's economy by characterizing the structure of this network. Furthermore, this measure of complexity is correlated with a country's level of income, and deviations from this relationship are predictive of true growth (Barabási, 2017). This suggests that countries tend to converge to the level of income dictated by the complexity of their productive structures. The level of complexity is modeled as the combination of capabilities available in a given country or, more broadly, as a measure of collective knowhow.

This body of work spurred further research including by Hartmannet et al. (2017), who expanded the scope of analysis of economic complexity to study implications on institutional design and income distribution. Youn et al. (2016) use a similar motivation to investigate how the diversity of economic activities depends on city size.

The limitation of this approach as usually applied is that it lacks the level of detail to be implemented at an urban scale. In addition, it is mainly tailored for the analysis of export data, which tend to lack measures of service industries. We contributed to these two dimensions by focusing the analysis of collective knowhow at the urban scale and making use of firm-level data to incorporate the production of services. In addition, we believe that a less indirect and more precise approach to measuring collective knowhow is through the output of the innovation process, as measured by patents and innovation-related metrics.

Barcelona Area: Four Quadrant Analysis by Industry

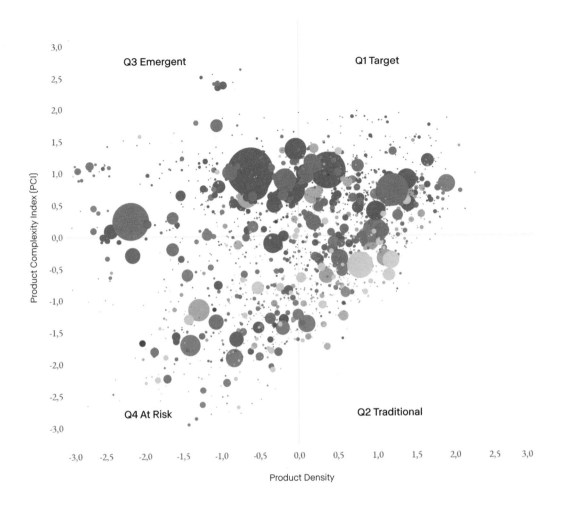

Q3 Emergent

Q1 Target

Q4 At Risk

Q2 Traditional

Product Complexity Index (PCI)

Product Density

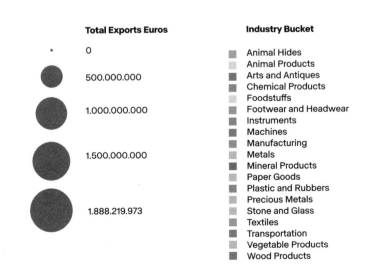

Total Exports Euros

0

500.000.000

1.000.000.000

1.500.000.000

1.888.219.973

Industry Bucket

- Animal Hides
- Animal Products
- Arts and Antiques
- Chemical Products
- Foodstuffs
- Footwear and Headwear
- Instruments
- Machines
- Manufacturing
- Metals
- Mineral Products
- Paper Goods
- Plastic and Rubbers
- Precious Metals
- Stone and Glass
- Textiles
- Transportation
- Vegetable Products
- Wood Products

Network of Talent

Innovation Pipeline Strategy

The Innovation Pipeline is a diagrammatic representation of how knowledge is conceived, generated, transmitted, and ultimately materialized as a new product or service. Modeling aesthetically and mathematically the networks of talent and the seven phases of innovation for each of the research centers, technology transfer centers, and industry value chains of a given city allows for performing network diagnostics and identifying concrete recommendations to elevate the quality of a knowledge economy ecosystem. Research Centers typically include but are not limited to academic centers and universities, technology transfer centers, startup incubators and accelerators, coworking spaces and industrial parks. Industry Value Chains and Industrial Liaison Strategy need to be assessed across the metropolitan area.

By completing the Innovation Pipeline Strategy Analysis, the strengths, weaknesses, risks, and opportunities can be evaluated for any given city or Metropolitan Area, in order to envision, design, chisel, build, shape, nurture and strengthen a successful knowledge economy ecosystem. The analytical results can then be deployed to strengthen the innovation pipeline in a data-driven, evidence-based manner.

Propelling the Network of Talent

The analysis of the socio-demographic profiles of a broader urban area, in terms of demographic features, level of education and specialization, and professional expertise should be combined with the evaluation of the needs for the Smart Specialization Strategy to succeed. Measuring the distance between the desired skills and professional proficiency required to consolidate the new industries and startup companies enables urban development leaders will be able to shape the programs for the academic and professional training necessary to bridge the gap between the local capabilities and the upskilling and reskilling strategies needed for the community to succeed. The shared vision can also help strengthen the sense of community and ethos across the different people and stakeholders involved in leading the new development.

The Seven Phases of Innovation

The Seven Phases of Innovation provide a framework for organizations to create support systems to promote innovation efforts among startups and young companies. Creating startup competitions, accelerators, boot camps, and conferences will help to increase excitement and provide opportunities for the creation of new companies. In addition, providing legal, IP, and financial advice and mentorship during the startup process will help to remove obstacles and make it easier for individuals and teams to achieve their goals. Successfully nurturing this innovation-friendly environment will require the support of innovative organizations associated with the leading research institutions, co-working spaces, and industry professionals, as well as state sponsorship to achieve its full potential.

During the innovation journey, organizations and communities such as the leading research institutions need to enable innovators by providing adequate support. The three platforms enabling that journey are University Applied Research Lab, Innovation Centers & Labs/Technology Transfer, and Startup Incubators & Accelerators. Below we discuss how the platforms can be developed.

The first platform, University Applied Research Lab, focuses on the first four phases of innovation (Human scale): Idea Creation Inception, Data Gathering, Hypothesis and Prototype. These University Applied Research Labs help researchers formulate ideas and lead them towards a prototype.

The second platform, Innovation Centers & Labs/Technology Transfer, covers the fourth, fifth and sixth phases of innovation: Prototype, Validation & Calibration, and Minimum Viable Product. Those Innovation Centers & Labs/Technology Transfers accompany researchers who have established a prototype in order to help them polish those prototypes into minimum viable products (MVPs).

The third platform, Startup Incubators & Accelerators, covers the last two phases of innovation: Minimum Viable Product and Mass Production & Diffusion. These Startup Incubators & Accelerators help entrepreneurs grow their companies from a mere startup with one minimum viable product to the mass production and diffusion of this product, as well as helping with the development of new products and the development of the companies themselves to reach the following stage.

Seven Phases of Innovation
in the Network of Talent:

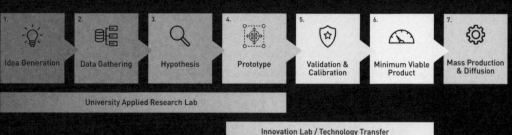

| 1. Idea Generation | 2. Data Gathering | 3. Hypothesis | 4. Prototype | 5. Validation & Calibration | 6. Minimum Viable Product | 7. Mass Production & Diffusion |

University Applied Research Lab

Innovation Lab / Technology Transfer

Startup Incubators & Accelerators

01

Idea Creation Inception corresponds to the different research areas leading to the inception of creative ideas with a potential for innovation development.

05

Validation & Calibration are the steps during which the prototypes are consolidated, validated, and calibrated before the launch of the product.

02

Data Gathering is the step following the idea; it corresponds to the development of processes to gather data with the aim of confirming the validity of the idea itself.

06

Minimum Viable Product is the first truly entrepreneurial step. It corresponds to the creation of startups based on the product that has been previously developed.

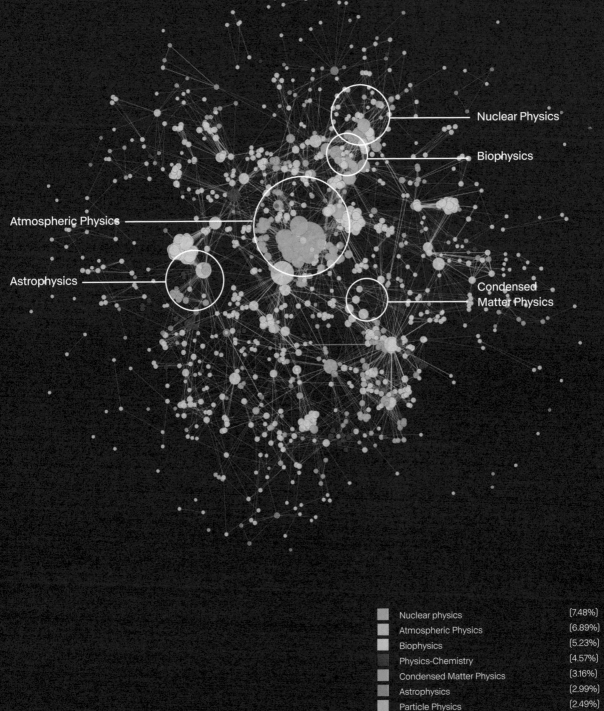

Nuclear Physics

Biophysics

Atmospheric Physics

Astrophysics

Condensed Matter Physics

Nuclear physics	(7.48%)
Atmospheric Physics	(6.89%)
Biophysics	(5.23%)
Physics-Chemistry	(4.57%)
Condensed Matter Physics	(3.16%)
Astrophysics	(2.99%)
Particle Physics	(2.49%)
Cosmology	(2.41%)
Physics	(2.24%)
Plasma Physics	(2.08%)
Nanoparticles	(1.83%)
Galaxy Agglomerations	(1.83%)
Molecular Physics	(1.58%)
Magnetic Materials	(1.5%)

University of São Paulo (USP)
Institute of Physics Research Network

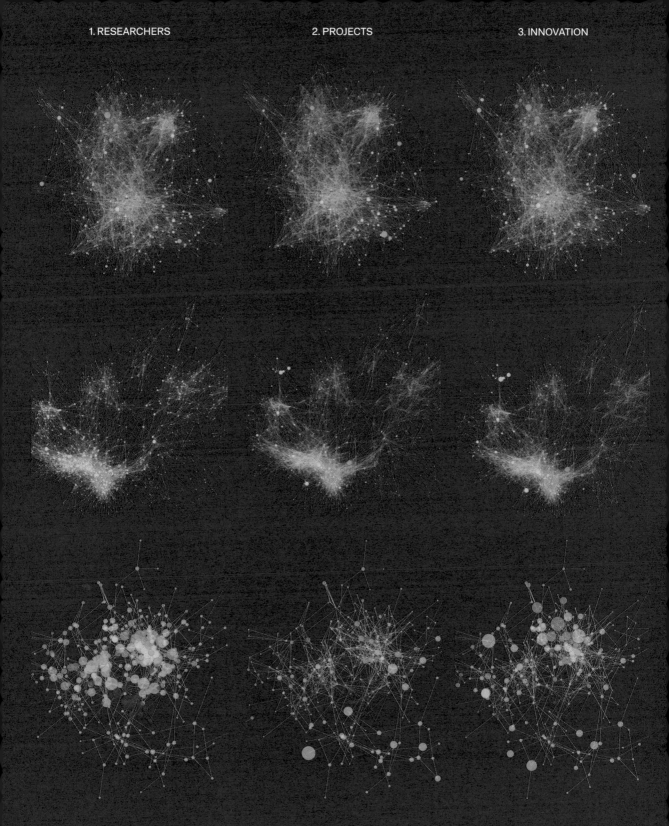

BarcelonaTech-UPC Research Network
Universitat de Barcelona Research Network
Universitat Ramon Llull Research Network

Innovation KPIs by Phase

City science research developed by Aretian Urban Analytics and Design at Harvard presents a series of key performance indicators (KPIs) in order to gauge the maturity of a district and its innovation potential to become a true anchor for its environment. In this case, our Harvard-based team studied the KPIs of multiple knowledge intensive ecosystems by following the Seven Phases of Innovation to the letter. The descriptive statistics gathered from leading universities, research centers, knowledge transfer centers, startups, and geospatialized industries enable us to describe the following proxies for those seven phases: (1) Researchers by School & Department, (2) Researchers by Focus, (3) Scientific Publications, (4) Scientific Articles, (5) Patents and Inventions, (6) Startups, and lastly (7) Innovative Companies.

The first two phases of innovation, (1) Idea Creation Inception, and (2) Data Gathering, are related to the effort carried out by Researchers by School & Department and Researchers by Focus Area.

Those metrics serve as the basis for the KPI of Innovation Intensity, a variable measuring the collective effort deployed to create knowledge networks. Innovation Intensity is measured as a percentage of employees working on knowledge-intensive activities per geographic unit. Our research shows that the average community in the United States has an Innovation Intensity of less than 12%, while innovation districts typically operate at or above 25%. The top-performing innovation districts are high-intensity environments: the top 10% have an Innovation Intensity of 50% and above, while the top 1% reach 85- 95%.

The following three phases of innovation (3) Hypothesis, (4) Prototype, and (5) Validation & Calibration describe the knowledge advancement output in terms of Scientific Publications, Scientific Articles, and Patents and Inventions, respectively. Those metrics serve as the basis for the Aretian Key Performance Indicator of Innovation Performance, a KPI measuring the tangible results of the collective effort deployed to create knowledge advancement. Innovation Performance measures the tangible outputs of innovation created on an annual basis by the innovation community, preferably at the smallest possible census geographic aggregation level. Innovation Performance measurements reflect the output of new products, services, and production processes, new patents and their associated revenues, scientific research papers, and other R&D outputs.

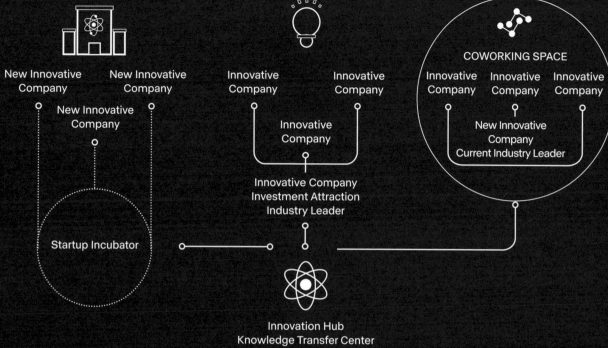

New Innovative Company

New Innovative Company

New Innovative Company

Innovative Company

Innovative Company

Innovative Company

COWORKING SPACE

Innovative Company

Innovative Company

Innovative Company

Innovative Company

New Innovative Company
Current Industry Leader

Innovative Company
Investment Attraction
Industry Leader

Startup Incubator

Innovation Hub
Knowledge Transfer Center

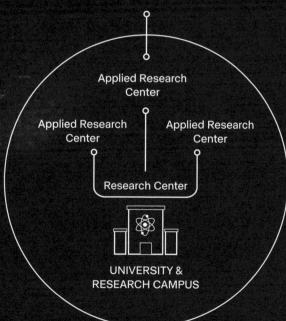

Applied Research
Center

Applied Research
Center

Applied Research
Center

Research Center

UNIVERSITY &
RESEARCH CAMPUS

Boston Area Businesses
and Innovation Phases

EMPNUM

0
5.000
10.000
16.999

Innovation Type

Research and Academia
Design, Engineering and Technology
Production
Regular

The last two phases of innovation, (6) Minimum Viable Product and (7) Mass Production & Diffusion, describe the positive societal impact generated by innovation activities in terms of startup creation, and knowledge advancement in innovative companies. These metrics serve as the basis for the Aretian Key Performance Indicator of Innovation Impact, a KPI measuring the societal benefits of the collective effort deployed to create knowledge and innovation networks. Innovation Impact describes the benefits to the broader community that result from the development of knowledge-intensive activities. Innovation Impact is measured through a variety of contributing indicators, including the number of innovation-intensive employees in the district, the meritocracy index, the prosperity index, the inequality index, measurements of indirect employment generation, measurements of diversity, and industry alignment with the broader metropolitan area.

Network of Talent Diagnostics

The Network of Talent diagnostics includes the review and processing of data that describes how the knowledge economy system operates in a given urban area in terms of demographics, educational programs, research specialization, and professional expertise. The evaluation of the research and innovation networks of universities throughout the seven steps of the innovation process revealed the knowledge areas that present the most promising prospects for developing fruitful synergies with the local industries in the broader metropolitan area.

Thus, it is paramount to shape a city planning zoning strategy so that the urban design, activity programming, and placemaking enables a given community to evolve from a system where there is a remarkable disconnect between applied research and industry into a thriving innovation ecosystem where there are spaces, centers, activities, and management programmes facilitating the fruitful and seamless connection between academia and the most dynamic economic sectors in any metropolitan area.

City Form Characteristics

**City Form:
Urban Topology,
Morphology, Scale,
Entropy, Fractality**

The city form features reveal the underlying design patterns patterns that characterize the urban fabric of every city. The topological network describes the underlying bidimensional transport and communications infrastructure that connects any given location and facilitates the territorial relationships between individuals and communities. The morphological system characterizes the three-dimensional architectural properties, features, and characteristics such as location, building shape and form, building height, space programming, capacity, and connectivity to nearby activities. The scale describes the orders of magnitude of city size and density levels. Finally, entropy is a holistic measure for regularity of the overall urban form composition, while fractality describes the quality or self-similarity of a three-dimensional system, and to what extent it is characterized by harmonic polycentrism and virtuous properties.

A casual wanderer exploring the old quarter of the city of Brugge in Belgium may inadvertently become in awe whilst admiring its human scale, highly walkable, and pedestrian-friendly streets; appreciating the sense of proportion, beauty, and harmony of its gorgeous buildings; and the charming and welcoming atmosphere exuded by its family-friendly, reasonably sized city form configuration and accessible services. Similar feelings and subjective perceptions may stimulate the spirit of anyone who shows an appreciation for the beautiful, the good and the sublime whenever they step on the streets of the old quarters of Tallinn, Kyoto, Venice, Buenos Aires, Tarragona, or Downtown Boston.

What all these beautifully crafted urban environments share in common are the subtle underlying design properties that we -whether consciously or unconsciously- perceive, appreciate, and experience. Understanding the specific properties, system dynamics, and functional implications of different design configurations unleashes a new world of possibilities in terms of raising the quality bar of architectural design and city building

Urban Topology

Amsterdam, The Netherlands

METRIC	DESCRIPTION
Avg. streets per node	Average count of streets per node.
Street density	Street length total per sq km.
Avg. length of street segments	Average length (normalized) of street segments within the building group, as a proxy for network edge connectivity
Density of intersections	Density of intersections per building group (BG)
Density of street segments	Density of street segments per standardized building group (BG)
Avg. circuity of street network	Average ratio between network distance to Euclidean distance, a reciprocal concept to network directness, as a proxy for detour ratio
Avg. intersection connectivity	Average number of street network connections colluding in the same urban network node/intersection within a given census tract, as a proxy for intersection connections
Avg. straightness centrality	Average Euclidean distance between two points, as a proxy for network node connectivity
Avg. betweenness centrality	A measure of centrality in a street network based on shortest paths

The study of network relationships within cities, their components, agents, and dynamics, whether physical (roads, highways, streets and general layout, boulevards, avenues, walkways and pathways) or interpersonal.

Urban Morphology

Los Angeles, United States of America

METRIC	DESCRIPTION
Avg. area of building footprints	Average area of building footprints within a given building group (BG), as a proxy for space utilization within a given urban unit
Avg. area of tessellations	Average area of tessellations or polygons composing a given building group (BG), as a proxy for sub-unit space utilization
Avg. building orientation	Building orientation optimization
Avg. tessellation orientation	Average building parcel orientation, as a proxy for urban parcel orientation efficiency
Avg. street alignment	Efficiency of street alignment, as a measure of street layout efficiency
Avg. building compactness	Building compactness as an indirect measure of Architectural efficiency

The study of physical characteristics and form of cities, their components, buildings, streets and layout. The morphology of a city also determines the efficiency of architectural space use and building arrangement which has a spatial and experiential effect on the user. The city form morphological pattern will also affect accessibility to amenities, as well as housing and jobs as it measures the types of buildings and their arrangement throughout the land.

Urban Fractality

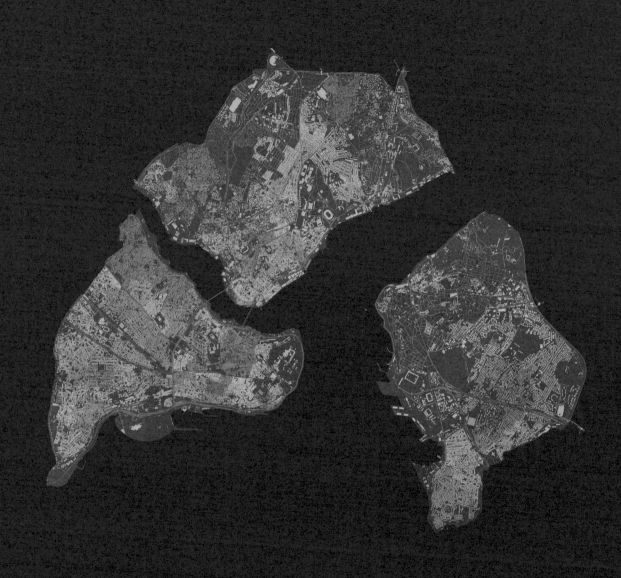

Istanbul, Turkey

1st percentile

100th percentile

METRIC	DESCRIPTION
Urban Fractality	A measure of City Form self-similarity from 0-1: Urban form is organized in a self-similar, hierarchical nested fashion whereby there are large central features surrounded by a second tier and then interspersed with Tier 3 and subsequent tiers' features. Features can include residential spaces, economic activity, hospital and educational systems, parks, transportation hubs, etc. The higher the number, the greater the fractality and, subsequently, the higher the economic performance.
Urban Compactness	A measure from 0-1, which is a ratio between the total area of the shape and the length of the perimeter boundary. A polygon has a low compactness score if the perimeter length is high and the shape area is low.

Urban Fractality measures the degree of urban form harmony or self-similarity, composed of hierarchical nodes structured in a nested fashion whereby there are large central features, surrounded by a second tier and then interspersed with tier three and subsequent tiers' features. Features can include residential spaces, economic activity, hospital and educational systems, parks, transportation hubs etc. The higher the number the greater the fractality and subsequently the higher the economic performance, urbanization efficiency, and access to services and amenities. Fractality or self-similarity is equivalent to harmonic polycentrism and is the best predictor for urban design efficiency and high levels of achievement of the 15-Minute City standards. High urban fractality levels present a combination of a decentralized, distributed urban network with local hubs or leading nodes enabling the multiplying effects of concentration.

Area Compactness is a measure from 0-1, which is a ratio between the total area of the shape and the length of the perimeter boundary. A polygon has a low compactness score if the perimeter length is high and the shape area is low.

A brilliant French-Polish mathematician, Benoît Mandelbrot, developed the concept of the fractal dimension, and contributed to bridge the gap between art and science, proving that these two worlds are not mutually exclusive. Mandelbrot observed that self-similar structures could be frequently observed in nature, as well as in art, and that morphological self-similarity properties presented an unusual combination of formal beauty and empirical efficiency. In his own words: "The form of geometry I increasingly favored is the oldest, most concrete, and most inclusive, specifically empowered by the eye and helped by the hand and, today, also by the computer ... bringing an element of unity to the worlds of knowing and feeling ... and, unwittingly, as a bonus, for the purpose of creating beauty. [...]. Clouds are not spheres, mountains are not cones, coastlines are not circles, and bark is not smooth, nor does lightning travel in a straight line". City form fractality can be measured by means of the Hausdorff-Besicovitch dimension.

Highly fractal or self-similar design patterns can be perceived both in world class architectural masterpieces, such as Cattedrale di Santa Maria del Fiore, Sagrada Família in Barcelona, the Real Chiesa di San Lorenzo in Turin, the Boston Back Bay Area, Ely Cathedral, Frauenkirche, Dresden, the City of Blois in France, Frederiksberg Denmark, the Hofburg Palace in Vienna as well as in global examples of vernacular architecture such as Castle Combe in England.

Urban Entropy

QUEENS

STATEN ISLAND

BRONX

BROOKLYN

MANHATTAN

CIUTAT VELLA

EIXAMPLE

GRÀCIA

HORTA-GUINARDÓ

SANTS-MONTJUÏC

SARRIÀ-SANT GERVASI

LES CORTS

NOU BARRIS

SANT ANDREU

SANT MARTÍ

ALTO DE PINHEIROS

BARRA FUNDA

BELA VISTA

BUTANTÃ

CASA VERDE

CONSOLAÇÃO
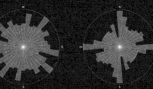

FREGUESIA DO Ó

ITAIM BIBI
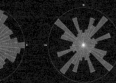

JAGUARA

JAGUARÉ
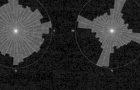

JARDIM PAULISTA

LAPA

LIMÃO

MOEMA

MORUMBI

OSASCO

PERDIZES
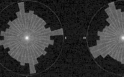

PINHEIROS

New York, Barcelona, São Paulo

METRIC	DESCRIPTION
Street Orientation Order (Shannon Entropy)	Average area of building footprints within a given building group (BG), as a proxy for space utilization within a given urban unit
Topology (Boeing)	Average area of tessellations or polygons composing a given building group (BG), as a proxy for sub-unit space utilization

The street layout orientation patterns show the diverse urban design patterns across a specific metropolitan area. The street orientation shows multiple orientations, with a few districts having specific axes. Street Orientation Entropy: a measure of the orderliness of a street network orientation. Entropy is minimized when all streets run in parallel and maximized when they follow no discernible pattern. This has implications for land use, transportation, access to amenities, and energy efficiency.

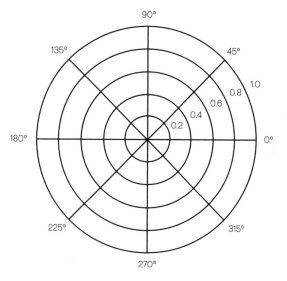

The concept of information entropy was introduced by Claude Shannon in his 1948 paper "A Mathematical Theory of Communication", and is also referred to as Shannon entropy. Geoff Boeing, an urban planner and spatial analysis professor at USC - Sol Price School for Public Policy conceived a visualization technique to describe in a visually succinct manner the street orientation patterns of a city, hence summarizing, among other aspects, the dominant axes, growth patterns, and the degree of regularity observed in a given urban area.

Urban Performance: Measuring the Quality of Urban Life

Network of Urban Design: Urbanization Efficiency and Social Interaction Patterns

The morphological design and activity programming that characterizes our cities impacts our perception of the urban landscape and induces certain types of human behaviour. A series of network theory based indicators and Key Performance Metrics help us measure, quantify, describe, evaluate and comprehend the nature of the conditions under which citizens operate on a daily basis. Fundamental urban life aspects such as intermodal accessibility to critical services, mobility and logistics efficiency, space capacity and architectural efficiency, construction materials cost and lasting environmental impact, energy and water consumption patterns, human and economic network connectivity, and innovation ecosystem dynamism can be evaluated by means of complex systems modeling.

Network of Urban Infrastructure: Urbanization Efficiency

Reach Index: The urban network science Reach measure (Sevtsuk, 2010) captures how many surrounding points (e.g., buildings, doors, bus stops, etc.) each building reaches within a given search radius on the network. The reach centrality, $R^r[i]$, of an origin i in a graph G describes the number of destinations in G that are reachable from i at a shortest path distance of at most r. The Reach index is defined as follows:

$$Reach[i]^r = \sum_{j \in G - \{i\}, d[i,j] \leq r} W[j]$$

Where $d[i,j]$ is the shortest path distance between origin i and destination j in G and $W[j]$ is the weight of a destination j. The Reach index corresponds to the number of destinations j that are found from the origin within the search radius on the urban network.

Gravity Index: Whereas the Reach metric simply counts the number of destinations around each origin within a given search radius (optionally weighted by destination attributes), the Gravity measures additional factors in the travel cost required to arrive at each of the destinations. First introduced by Hansen (1959), the Gravity index remains one of the most popular spatial accessibility measures in transportation research.

The Gravity measure assumes that accessibility at the origin is proportional to the attractiveness (weight) of destinations and inversely proportional to the distances between i and j:

$$Gravity[i]^r = \sum_{j \in G-\{i\}, d[i,j] \leq r} \frac{W[j]^\alpha}{e^{\beta \cdot d[i,j]}}$$

where $Gravity[i]^r$ is the Gravity index at the origin within the graph G at the search radius r; $W[j]$ is the weight of destination j; $d[i,j]$ is the geodesic distance between i and j; α is the exponent that can control the destination weight or attractiveness effect; and β s the exponent for adjusting the effect of distance decay. The Gravity index thus captures both the attraction of the destinations $(W[j]'\alpha)$ as well as the spatial impedance of travel required to reach those destinations $(d[i,j])$ in a combined measure of accessibility. If no weight attributes are given, then the weight of each destination is considered to be "1". The default value for alpha is also set at "1", so that the destination weight has a linear effect.

Average Betweenness Index (or Average Betweenness Centrality) is a measure of centrality in a road network based on the shortest paths between intersections. For every pair of intersections in a connected street network, there exists at least one shortest path between the intersections such that the number of streets that the path passes through is minimized. The average betweenness centrality for each intersection is the average number of these shortest paths that pass through a given intersection. Betweenness centrality (or shortest-path betweenness) is a measure of accessibility in terms of the number of times a node is crossed by shortest paths in the urban graph. Anomalous centrality is detected when a node has a high betweenness centrality and a low order (degree centrality), as in air transport.

The Betweenness index approximates by-passing traffic or footfall at particular locations in a spatial network. The Betweenness of a building is defined as the fraction of shortest paths between pairs of other origins and destinations in the network that pass by a particular location (Freeman 1977). If more than one shortest path is found between two nodes, as is frequently the case in a rectangular grid of streets, then each of the equidistant paths is given equal weight such that the weights sum to unity. The Betweenness measure is defined as follows:

$$Betweenness[i]^r = \sum_{j,k \in G-\{i\}, d[i,j] \leq r} \frac{n_{jk}[i]}{n_{jk}} \cdot W[j]$$

where $Betweenness[i]^r$ is the betweenness of location i within the search radius r (specified in the search radius box); $njk[i]$ is the number of shortest paths from origin j to destination k that pass by i; and njk is the total number of shortest paths from j to k. Betweenness for location i is computed by considering all pairs of buildings that are within a distance from each other.

Closeness Index: The Closeness of an origin is defined as the average distance required to reach from that origin to all the specified destinations that fall within the search radius along the shortest paths (Sabidussi 1966). Similar to Gravity, the Closeness measure indicates how close an origin point is to destinations within a given distance threshold, but the distance that is used is a simple linear distance and the result is given as an average closeness between all destination points. The Closeness measure is defined as follows:

$$Closeness[i]^r = \frac{\sum\limits_{j \in G-\{i\}, d[i,j] \leq r} \frac{W[j]}{d[i,j]}}{n}$$

where $Closeness[i]^r$ is the Closeness of origin i within the search radius r; $d[i,j]$ is the shortest path distance between nodes i and j; $W[j]$ is the weight of the destination; and n is the number of destinations found.

Straightness Index. The Straightness metric (Vragovic, Louis, et al. 2005) illustrates the extent to which the shortest paths from origins to destinations resemble straight Euclidian paths. Put alternatively, the Straightness metric captures the positive deviations in travel distances that result from the geometric constraints of the network in comparison to straight-line distances in a featureless plane. The Straightness measure is formally defined (Porta, Crucitti et al. 2005) as:

$$Straightness[i]^r = \sum\limits_{j \in G-\{i\}, d[i,j] \leq r} \frac{\delta[i,j]}{d[i,j]} \cdot W[j]$$

where $Straightness[i]^r$ is the Straightness of node within the search radius r; $delta[i,j]$ is the straight-line Euclidian distance between i and j; and $d[i,j]$ is the shortest network distance between the same nodes. The Straightness index illustrates how long the shortest path connections from each origin to the surrounding destinations j are in comparison to the as-a-crow-flies distance. Naturally, as the distances between nodes get longer, the differences between the network distance and as-a-crow-flies distance start diminishing.

Network of Urban Design Urban Development Efficiency

METRIC	DESCRIPTION
Total Urbanization Efficiency	Urban Development Material Efficiency
Total Built Area Efficiency	Global Closeness Centrality
Total Street Length Efficiency	Area_km2 / total_street_length
Urban Flow Centrality	Avg. Betweenness Centrality
Urban Node Centrality and Opportunity KPI	Avg. Closeness Centrality (Local) Avg. Closeness Centrality (Global)
Urban Mobility Efficiency	Circuity Efficiency

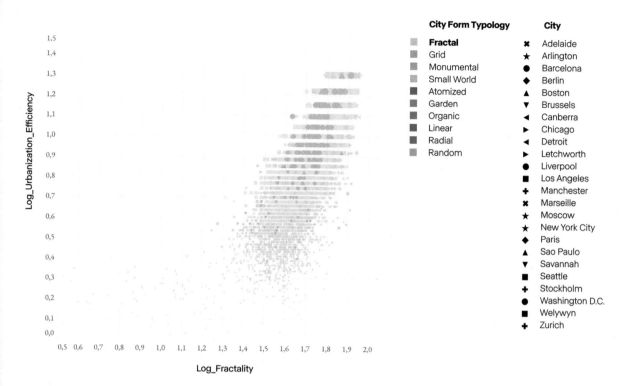

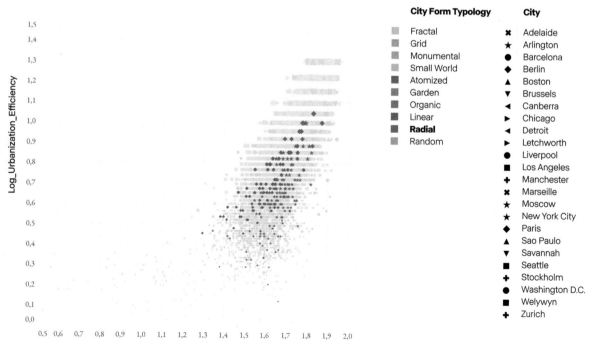

City Form Fractality Urbanization Efficiency Superlinearity (Log-Log)

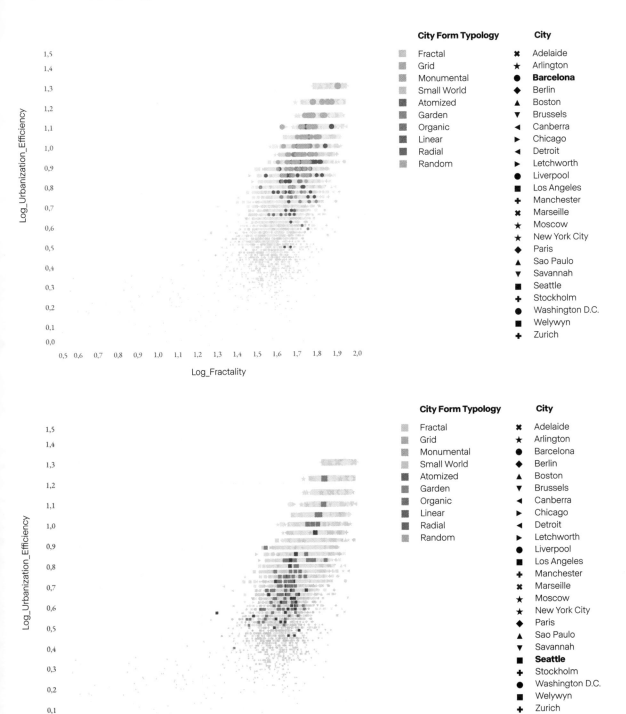

Network of Industries: 15-Minute City Standards and Economic Complexity

Access to Urban Amenities: Measurements to evaluate how easy or difficult it is to access various urban amenities from residential nodes or offices, weighted by number of employees, or from residents, and population numbers. Distance is measured by willingness to walk standards, which vary based on the type of amenity and local urban conditions. Amenities are gathered from Open Street Maps, GIS files from the client, or websites that describe the amenities of a given region.

DESCRIPTION	METRIC
Number of representative facilities within a given polygon of analysis. This can also be calculated by the number of representative facilities from any given point and search radius.	**Mobility and Public Transit per Km2:** bus stations, taxis, metro stations, commuter rail stations, tramway stations, bicycle parking and rental, car rental and sharing.
	Education Centers per Km2: kindergarten, primary schools, high schools, private schools, professional centers, universities, research centers
	Healthcare Amenities per Km2: clinics, dentists, doctors, hospitals, nursing homes, pharmacies, urgent care, mental health and addiction treatment centers.
	Sustenance Amenities per Km2: bars, cafes, fast food establishments, food courts, pubs, restaurants, and convenience stores.
	Entertainment Amenities per Km2: art centers, cinemas/concert halls, cinemas, concert halls, general theaters, community centers, conference centers, events venues, nightclubs, social centers, theaters.

Urban Services
Access to education
Academic training

Urban Amenities
Access to sustence
Restaurants and cafes

Urban Experience
Access to entertainment
Culture and leisure

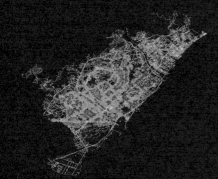

Mobility
Access to public transit
Bus Network

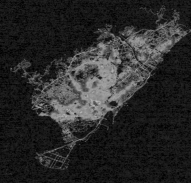

Mobility
Access to public transit
Metro / Underground Network

Mobility
Access to public transit
Tramway Network

Barcelona network analysis:
access to amenities and mobility services

The heatmaps display the gradient of accessibility to amenities, segmented by type of service: sustenance (restaurants and cafeterias), education, healthcare, leisure, culture, commerce, mobility services, etc. The more intense red areas show the hotspots of the city, whereas the blue and green areas describe the zones with limited to access to amenities within walkable distance.

Access to Urban Amenities: Sustenance (Restaurants and Cafeterias)
Number of representative facilities within a given polygon of analysis: bars, cafes, fast food establishments, food courts, pubs, restaurants.

Access to Urban Amenities: Education
Concentrations of libraries, schools and kindergartens are relatively high around the new development. This aligns with the fact that many of the neighborhoods are residential. The expansion of the innovation district can maintain these levels to continue to promote education in the neighborhoods.

Access to Urban Amenities: Healthcare services
Number of representative facilities within a given polygon of analysis: clinics, dentists, doctors, hospitals, nursing homes, pharmacies.

Access to Urban Amenities: Entertainment
Number of representative facilities within a given polygon of analysis: arts centers, cinemas, community centers, conference centers, events venues, nightclubs, social centers, theaters.

Access to Urban Amenities: Mobility and Transportation
Number of representative facilities within a given polygon of analysis: bus stations, taxis, bicycle parking, bicycle rental, car rental, car sharing.

Access to Urban Amenities: Minimum Distance to the 1st Amenity
Describes the minimum distance to the closest amenity (sustenance, healthcare, education, culture and leisure, entertainment, urban services) within a walkable radius

Access to Urban Amenities: Minimum Distance to the 5th Amenity
Describes the minimum distance to the 5th closest amenity (sustenance, healthcare, education, culture and leisure, entertainment, urban services) within a walkable radius.

**Network of Talent:
Innovation KPIs**

Innovation Metrics: A set of metrics that describe measurable innovation activities in a given geographic area.

Innovation Intensity: The ratio of innovative jobs to regular or service jobs. Based on Aretian's proprietary tagging of industry codes.

Innovation Performance: Total output from innovation activities including number of patents, papers and publications as well as total sales and revenue from such activities.

Innovation Impact: An imputed metric to predict the projected impact that innovation activities will have in a given geographic area. For every innovative job there are approximately five regular service jobs created.

Knowledge Economy: A system of consumption and production that is based on intellectual capital. Specifically, it refers to the ability to capitalize on scientific discoveries and applied research. The knowledge economy represents a large share of the activity in most highly developed economies.

Network of Talent Knowledge Economy
(SC) (percentiles)

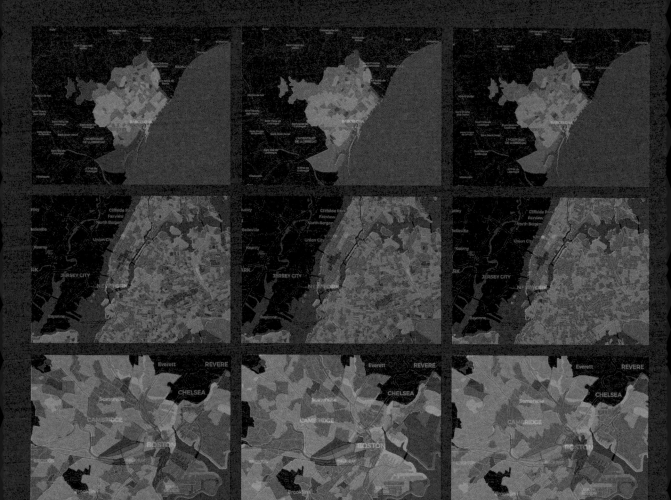

Innovation Intensity
Percentage of people working in knowledge-intensive jobs, whether in research, technology transfer, or advanced production

Innovation Performance
Number of sales per new patent, product or service, as well as R&D projects

Innovation Impact
Economic benefits to the surrounding community based on Innovation Intensity: knowledge-intensive employment creation, increased wages

Barcelona, New York, Boston   1st percentile   100th percentile

Scope of Geospatial Analysis of Innovation Systems

We proceeded to develop a countrywide analysis of the Innovation KPIs to measure the surplus achieved by the geographic concentration of knowledge intensive businesses. The territorial scope of the analysis consisted of the 48 contiguous U.S. states (plus the District of Columbia) for the year 2017. The analysis has been deployed in other regions of the world with similar results. Within the US geographic area, 50 of the most well-known innovation districts were identified and tagged within our database, as depicted in as depicted in the map below. The tagging process identified census block groups, in which businesses known to make significant contributions to innovation within the neighborhood were located. Due to their irregular shapes, the block groups were chosen as close to the center of research or business activity of the neighborhood as possible. It was important to choose innovation districts based on the geographic area of the block group so that the data could be combined with social demographic information from the United States Census. It was also a relevant criterion that block groups could be compared to one another in an apples-to-apples comparison and describe how businesses and industries cluster together in high-performing areas.

01 ■ 20th Century Fox Entertainment Cluster, LA, CA
02 ■ Aerospace Cluster, Wichita, KS
03 ▣ Ames Research Center, NASA, CA
04 ■ Apple Software Cluster, Silicon Valley, CA
05 ▣ Atlanta Midtown Innovation District, GA
06 ■ Boeing Aerospace Cluster, Los Angeles, CA
07 ■ Boeing Aerospace Cluster, Seattle, WA
08 ■ Boston Seaport, MA
09 ■ Boulder Innovation District, CO
10 ▣ Capital City Innovation, Austin, TX
11 ■ Cornell Tech, NYC, NY
12 ■ Cortex Innovation Community, MO
13 ▣ Downtown Detroit, MI
14 ▣ Downtown San Jose, Silicon Valley, CA
15 ▣ Dumbo Innovation District, NY
16 ▣ Durham.ID, NC
17 ■ Facebook Software Cluster, Silicon Valley, CA
18 ■ Fulton Market Innovation District, IL
19 ■ Google Software Cluster, Silicon Valley, CA

20 ▣ Harvard Enterprise Research Campus, MA
21 ▣ Harvard Square, MA
22 ■ Houston Innovation District, TX
23 ■ Houston Medical, TX
24 ▣ Innovate Carolina, NC
25 ▣ Jefferson National Accelerator, VA
26 ■ Kendall Square, MA
27 ■ Keystone District, KS, MO
28 ■ Longwood Medical Area, MA
29 ▣ Los Alamos National Laboratory, NM
30 ■ Microsoft Software Cluster, Redmond, WA
31 ▣ NC State, NC
32 ▣ Norfolk Naval Shipyard Tech. & Inno. Lab, VA
33 ▣ Oak Ridge National Laboratory, TN
34 ▣ Pittsburgh Innovation District, PA
35 ▣ Portland Innovation Quadrant, OR
36 ▣ Purdue Innovation District, IN
37 ▣ Red Hook, NY
38 ▣ Research Triangle Park, NC

39 ■ San Jose Boomerang, Silicon Valley, CA
40 ▣ Sandia National Labs, NM
41 ▣ Silicon Alley, NY
42 ■ Sony Entertainment Cluster, Culver City, CA
43 ■ South Lake Union, WA
44 ■ South of Market (SOMA), CA
45 ■ SpaceX Aerospace Cluster, LA, CA
46 ▣ Stanford Research Park, Silicon Valley, CA
47 ■ Tech. Cluster, Los Gatos, Silicon Valley, CA
48 ▣ University City District, Philadelphia, PA
49 ▣ University of California, San Diego, CA
50 ▣ University of Colorado Boulder, CO

■ Entrepreneurial (12)
■ Industry Cluster (9)
■ Local Government (6)
▣ Research & Academia (17)
▣ Strategic Governmental (6)

Geographic distribution of 50 Innovation Districts

Definition of Key Performance Metrics for Measuring Urban Innovation

The Key Performance Metrics for measuring Urban Innovation enable quantitative descriptions of key factors concerning knowledge-intensive activities across the U.S. territory, at the smallest census unit (the census building group), while also illuminating the correlations and potential causation between them. Innovation Intensity describes the societal effort in supporting innovation in terms of the percentage of employees per geographic unit working on knowledge-intensive activities. Innovation Performance describes the business revenue generated as a result of knowledge-intensive activities (patents, new products, new services, scientific articles, R&D). Innovation Impact serves as a proxy for the societal benefits of the multiplying effect of knowledge-intensive activities in terms of accessibility to innovation-related employment per unit of resident, as a proxy for attractive, well-paid, stable employment opportunities and the indirect benefits derived therefrom.

Notation:
$i \in [1,n]$; domain of values describing each geo-located business in the U.S.
β_i = Business Employment (i); Number of employees working in the business location (i)
ρ_i = Business Revenue (i); Annual revenue for each business location (i)
κ_i = Innovation clasification; Boolean value describing whether the business is knowledge intensive
$g \in [1,m]$; domain of values describing each building group in the U.S.
δ_g = Building Group Residents; Number of residents within a building group (g)

Innovation Intensity: describes the percentage of employees working on knowledge-intensive activities, broken down by each of the three innovation phases: research, technology transfer, production. It is computed as the sum of all the employees working in geo-located businesses belonging to one of three innovation categories (research, technology transfer, advanced production), divided by the total number of employees per building group.

$\alpha_{int}(g)$ = Innovation Intensity. For each building group g:

$$\alpha_{int}(g) = \frac{\sum\limits_{i=1}^{i=n} (\beta_i \cdot \kappa_i) \cdot 100}{\sum\limits_{i=1}^{i=n} \beta_i}$$

Innovation Performance: describes the business revenue per building group generated by measurable innovations: new patents, new products, new services, new processes, R&D, scientific papers.

$\alpha_{per}(g)$ = Innovation Performance = Total Innovation Revenue per Employee per BG (g). For each building group g:

$$\alpha_{per}(g) = \frac{\sum_{i=1}^{i=n}(\rho_i \cdot \kappa_i) \cdot 100}{\sum_{i=1}^{i=n}\beta_i}$$

Innovation Impact describes innovation employment per resident for each BG, as a proxy for availability of knowledge-intensive employment opportunities within the community.

$$\alpha_{imp}(g) = \frac{\sum_{i=1}^{i=n}(\beta_i \cdot \kappa_i)}{\sum_{g=1}^{g=m}\delta_g}$$

Innovation Districts are defined as urban neighborhoods or districts purposely designed, nurtured, and supported to concentrate and promote innovation-related activities in dense urban areas, to leverage the nonlinear effects of the geographic concentration of knowledge-intensive activities. By comparing representative statistics on the Urban Innovation Performance KPIs from those 50 notable Innovation Districts with those of the average block groups, we can provide a tangible understanding of the positive, superlinear effects of such strategies in terms of job creation, wealth creation, knowledge advancement and standards of living.

The three core innovation KPIs are the building blocks of the analysis. They allow us to quantitatively measure the differential impact of Innovation Districts and benchmark different typologies of Innovation Districts against one another and other non innovation-intensive districts. Finally, we analyzed the superlinearity of innovation-related activities in a regression framework against population, city size, and other variables to benchmark our results against previous studies.

The business database covered the entire contiguous United States for a given year with approximately 12.5 million businesses. It is understood that the largest, most well reported firms were included in the dataset. The NAICS codes were six digits long and used for the industry / sub-industry and company classification. The dataset was cleaned with.imputed data observations where there were trivially incorrect or missing values. Addresses were already geolocated so there was no need to compute the latitude and longitude of each business. Key inputs included: employment, revenue, and industry code. The United States demographic data came from ESRI's imputed database of the United States Census for the year. Data was used from the smallest geographic area of roughly 2,000 people per building block group to provide the most granular level of analysis for the study. Key inputs for the model included variables that described employment, income, wealth, education, and employment density.

Industry innovation metrics were used from data gathered by a survey conducted by the National Science Foundation in 2014. The data was gathered through interviews and surveys, which covered topics such as the total number of patents per company and revenue generated from the patents, and total spent on R&D, new products, new services, and new processes. The data was then aggregated at various levels of industry codes, from 2-4 digit NAICS codes, to provide an understanding of innovation activity per industry.

Classification methods of analysis were conducted by tagging specific industries as "innovative", "innovation-related", and "other" based on the NAICS code per industry. The tagging originated from previous classification methods determined by the Brookings Institute's Advanced Manufacturing Industry List and the BERD survey from the National Science Foundation. The final set of industry codes then became drivers of the innovation performance metrics used for further analysis, and the tagging process is continually updated and refined as new data and technology continuously change industry operations throughout the United States.

The final list of tagged NAICS Codes were translated to HS Codes through a crosswalk table. Through this industry code system, information about innovation performance was combined with each business entry from the INFO Group Database, thereby creating a proxy for the level of innovation for that specific business.

Urban Innovation Performance Dataset Creation

Each business entry was then tagged with the specific block group in which it was located, through a spatial merge command. With every business associated with its own block group, it was then possible to aggregate all businesses to provide highly accurate totals for business and innovation metrics at the block group level and associate the data with the U.S. Census. Therefore, the U.S. Census block group dataset was expanded with private business and innovation metrics, which allowed each block group to be compared to the others because they all have the common feature of roughly 2,000 residents. For example, if a block group had close to no businesses, it was clear that innovation activity is low; whereas blockgroups that contained high numbers of businesses, with strong innovation performance metrics from the National Science Foundation, were ranked highly in our model.

The block group level of detail was chosen given that it is the smallest administrative geographic area used by the U.S. Census, therefore, allowing for the most granular analysis of high-density urban environments. In addition, it is possible to use the same attribution method and apply metrics in larger census areas such as census tracts, metropolitan statistical areas, counties, states, regions, and divisions of the U.S. However, there is less and less actionable information at higher levels due to the high amounts of aggregating business activity. With the standardization of variables across the United States, it is now possible to create mathematical distributions describing the ranges of possible values for urban performance. New boolean variables were also introduced to describe how new knowledge, which is then designed and engineered, is finally mass produced for the general public. We denote this process through the Three Phases of Innovation, where businesses are tagged based on their NAICS code, according to their category: Research and Academia, Technology Transfer, and Production, based on previous research from research institutions, National Science Foundation surveys and analysis, as well as the advanced manufacturing industries listed by the Brookings Institution. In addition, another new variable allowed for the assessment of how central innovation was to each industry. For each phase, a new variable column was created, where boolean values were added, first if the industry code was innovative, innovation-related, or other. This tagging system allowed for specific innovation metrics to be associated with each business in the database. This process is generalizable and scalable and illuminates the strengths and weaknesses of a given innovation ecosystem.

Business - Innovation Phases	NAICS	SIC	NAICS & SIC Businesses
Research	9 (0.72%)	121 (1.12%)	2.08%
Technology Transfer	40 (3.19%)	692 (6.39%)	5.45%
Advanced Production	209 (16.65%)	1,747 (16.13%)	2.42%
Innovation Total	258 (20.56%)	2,560 (23.63%)	9.95%
All Businesses - Total	1,255 (100%)	10,833 (100%)	

Number of businesses within each innovation phase – U.S

Number of business classification categories within each innovation phase

Ten City Design Typologies

Geospatial Analysis Framework: Defining City Typologies and Their Urban Form Characteristics

Every city typology can be described by the layout of the street network and underlying structural patterns. It is important to consider that the historical evolution of cities often results in a tapestry of multiple grid and layout types that nest together, overlap, and morph into one another. Therefore, in our process we have picked cities for this study that contain as many "pure typologies" as possible within their municipal boundaries. Below is a list of the 10 city types we have identified based on their urban form and design characteristics. In addition to their relation to typological categories from architecture and urban planning/design history, our core set of typologies are closely related to network theory typologies, which describe categories of networks with distinct structural layouts.

Each of the 10 city types is placed in a circular diagram that organizes each type by pattern and category. Since many cities are composed of multiple different types, in different neighborhoods for example, this chart helps to illustrate how each type is similar and different from one another. Fractal and Small World city types are a subset of Scalar and Harmonic patterns. Radial, Monumental and Garden types have hierarchical patterns. Organic, Random and Atomized are irregular. Linear and Grid are distributed. By moving clockwise or counterclockwise, each city type is next to its closest neighbor in terms of street layout (topology), building form (morphology) and city order (fractality, scale, and entropy).

Defining City Typologies: Identifying Empirical Examples
Aiming to prove our core hypothesis that each urban form typology described above is intrinsically characterized by certain urban form features, which in turn shape the urban dynamics, we have developed a geospatial methodology for systematically collecting and calculating metrics that describe features of urban form and then using these metrics to classify areas within cities that correspond to our set of 10 typologies.

Selection of Geographic Units for Analysis

In order to collect metrics that describe urban form accurately and consistently, it is critical to define a minimal statistical unit of urban space for each empirical city. The criteria for selecting this minimal statistical unit is that it must be large enough to contain a non-trivial amount of infrastructure (e.g., more than a few roads or buildings) and also must contain a relatively consistent population. This means that the size or shape of this unit of space can change depending on population density. A clear example of such a unit is the census tract, which is a census geography used by the U.S. Census Bureau. The Census Tract is below a municipal boundary in the hierarchy of administrative divisions but is not the smallest urban unit (e.g., block group) and therefore contains a significant amount of infrastructure from which a discernible pattern may be observed.

Looking at the different global cities we have identified for this analysis, we have endeavored to select sub-municipal units of urban space that meet these criteria and are comparable in size or level of hierarchy across examples. These units of urban space will henceforth be referred to as geographic units.

Selection and Calculation of Metrics for Describing Features of Urban Form

There are many measurements of urban complexity and many features of infrastructure that make up the urban form of a city. We have determined a subset of metrics related to three primary categories describing three essential aspects of urban form that ultimately relate to the layout of urban spaces. The first category is related to design harmony and order. This category encompasses metrics that aim to determine the level of order or disorder in the layout of urban space, as well the degree to which space is systematically organized across many scales (e.g., fractality). The second category relates to urban topology, the two-dimensional layout of city streets and transportation infrastructure. Metrics included in this category are network theory measurements that describe aspects of connectivity and complexity of the topological layout of urban space. Lastly, the third category relates to urban morphology or the characteristics of buildings and other non-transportation infrastructure. The metrics within this category describe the qualities of the spaces and places that individuals inhabit and build in concert with the connective networks of streets and transportation infrastructure.

In order to discern which "pure typologies" are contained within real empirical cities, we apply spatially constrained multivariate clustering in order to produce groups of geographic units based on their quantified features within the three categories of urban form we have defined previously. These agglomerations of geographic units represent larger units of urban space that are defined entirely by urban form. Therefore, each of these agglomerations represents a common structural pattern that can be translated into one of the 10 typologies we have defined that most closely resembles its qualities.

As such, we have applied a supervised tag to each agglomeration of geographic units indicating which of the 10 typologies it best represents. Additionally these agglomerations of geographic units can be clustered in a non-spatially constrained supervised manner across many cities to discern data-driven typological patterns underlying the 10 typological categories we have defined from architectural and urban design/planning intuition and network theory based concepts.

Given a set of typological tags for each agglomeration of geographic units, we are then able to propagate this tag back down to the level of each geographic unit, thus resulting in a dataset of geographic units assigned to a typological group with quantitative metrics describing the urban form contained within its respective geographical boundaries.

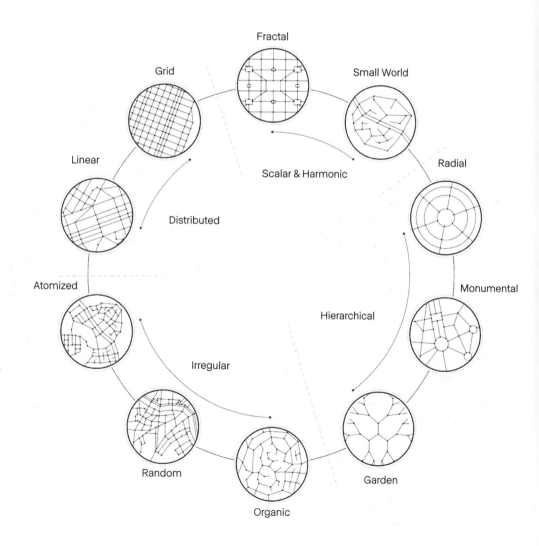

Small World City

The European cities that emerged after the collapse of the Roman Empire, during the early Middle Ages, presented a number of shared characteristics: they were typically fortified and self-sufficient from a food and energy perspective, experienced continuous yet gradual growth patterns, and displayed a combination of hierarchical activity programming (churches, political and military centers, markets, guild workshops, homes) and a relatively egalitarian distribution of wealth compared to more rural civilizations. Their consolidation coincided in time with the virtual disappearance of slavery as it was understood during ancient times and the widespread hegemony of Christianity. From a morphological viewpoint, European medieval cities followed a traditional Small World Network pattern, a tightly knit network of interwoven connections or streets, where every node or building is easily accessible from any other corner in town, social interaction is highly enhanced across the town, and the architectural landscape integrates both vernacular design patterns and monumental spaces for institutional purposes. The probability density function associated with Small World Networks is the Normal distribution.

Small World Networks are characterized by a high degree of local clustering, or intense interpersonal social interaction and communication patterns, and very short average path lengths, hence allowing for relatively universal access to services and amenities, and a hub-and-spoke internal hierarchy. Small World City facilitates a more personal, face-to-face, and more egalitarian pattern of socialization. The social classes coexist within physical proximity, and the division of labor allows for a remarkable increase in sophistication and diversity of products and services. One of the most remarkable features of Small World Cities is their ability to shape and nurture successful economic clusters, where a merit-based incentive scheme permits young professionals to learn the craft from their peers and supervisors, progress through the artisan workshop organizational structure, and eventually create their own *atelier*. The medieval craft guilds were the seed and the cradle that allowed the development of the great Renaissance and Baroque workshops, characterized by the excellence of their creations, and the foundations of the Enlightenment and the Industrial Revolution.

Representative cases of Small World Cities include Bruges, Tallinn, Brussels, Hallstatt, and Siena, among others. Their main disadvantages are the difficulties in scaling the social network schemes beyond certain thresholds, and the difficulty in adopting and absorbing mass-production technologies.

Bruges, Belgium
© travelism

Radial City

A radial city design plan is shaped by a series of concentric rings combined with axial streets that extend from the center outward to the urban edges. Radial cities are a constantly observed pattern since the beginning of the Agrarian Revolution, throughout ancient times across the globe, and up until the present. The concentric circles are a manifestation of a highly hierarchical system, often fueled by authoritarian regimes characterized by a thirst for centralized power, in a worldview where a relative position in the social sphere matters more than an individual's personal merit. It must be noted that radial systems present an internal logic, and the hierarchy tends to facilitate the concentration of power, wealth, and the surpluses associated with the exponential benefits of the geographic concentration of knowledge-intensive activities, which can be exploited more efficiently than in distributed networks. Notorious examples of radial or concentric cities include Paris, Milan, Moscow, certain areas in Dubai, Shanghai, Abu Dhabi, or the Plaza del Ejecutivo Area in Mexico City, among others.

The probability density function associated with Radial or Concentric Networks is the Weibull-Gumbel distribution, or the skewed Lognormal distribution. However, concentric cities present two major setbacks. First, radial or concentric cities tend to benefit from the advantages of agglomeration in their central hub or core, although these effects decrease dramatically as you move away from the city center and disappear altogether in most outlying neighborhoods, hence contributing to social stratification and potentially the sclerotization of ghettos and structural classism. Second, given the arbitrary nature of the distribution of citizens through the network, the ability to deliberately extract the surplus and multiplying effects of reinforced network centrality is diminished the farther a node is from the core center. Therefore, while it is true that radially designed cities tend to amalgamate an extraordinary surplus within their core areas, it must be noticed that both the quality of social interaction opportunities and the financial case behind infrastructure and amenities diminishes dramatically beyond a certain radial distance from the center. Such pernicious effects can be perceived most notably, for example, in the Banlieues of Paris.

Paris, France
© Jeffrey Milstein Photography

Reticular / Grid City

Grid-like urban designs characterized by orthogonal street layout patterns can be found in numerous civilizations since the Agrarian Revolution. Examples range from the reconstruction of Babylon directed by Hammurabi, all the way through workers' villages in Giza, Egypt, multiple major cities from the Indus Valley Civilization, several regional capitals across China, the great city of Teotihuacan in Mesoamerica, the prosperous city of Miletus in Greece/Asia Minor, and most notably the Roman military camp tessellation, shaped along the lines of the *cardo* and *decumanus* axes. Orthogonal grids, whether shaped around squares or rectangles, present a number of strategic advantages: they facilitate highly efficient and widespread movement of people and distribution of goods by multiple transport modes in coexistence; they increase the cognitive legibility of the urban fabric and the internal navigation across neighborhoods; and they provide a relatively egalitarian distribution of services. The grid city pattern presents a perfect analogy with reticular or distributed networks.

Reticular cities often characterize emergent powers during rapid growth periods, in need of accommodating the complex logistics associated with new settlements, diverse populations, and brand new colonies with a highly efficient distribution of residential and commercial activities. Some recent examples in history include a number of cities that experienced their most radical growth during the Industrial Revolution in the United States, such as New York City, downtown Philadelphia, Chicago, San Francisco, and Detroit, among many others. The low levels of urban form entropy observed in grid cities tend to increase the efficiency of internal mobility. However, urban grids tend to facilitate the organic emergence of radical wealth disparities, income inequality, and demographic atomization over long periods of time, hence contributing to social segregation and ghetto formation. Representative examples of reticular cities include New York City - Manhattan, Chicago, Toronto, Melbourne, Karachi, and downtown Cape Town, among others.

New York, USA
© Jeffrey Milstein Photography

Linear City

Linear cities are structured around a one-dimensional longitudinal axis, presenting various degrees of developmental growth on both sides of the urban spine. There are primarily three main types of linear cities. Traditional linear cities were typical of rural communities around the globe, typically a series of rows of houses stemming from a longitudinal axis and situated along a linear object such as a riverbank, road, valley, or stream. They have been known as Reihendorf in Germany, ribbon or strip farms in Anglo-Saxon Countries, and linear communities in Japan and Eastern Asia. Ribbon or strip farms were prevalent in diverse areas of the world along rivers; locations where these farms appear include parts of Ireland, Central Europe, West Africa, and Brazil. In North America, ribbon farms are found in various places settled by the French explorers, particularly along the Saint Lawrence River, the Great Lakes, the Detroit River and its tributaries, and parts of Louisiana.

A second type of linear city was conceived during the early stages of the Industrial Revolution by socialist utopian thinkers and urban designers, aiming to take advantage of the wonders and benefits of mass transportation by means of railroad systems. The civil engineer and urban designer Arturo Soria conceived a transcontinental linear city crossing Europe from Cádiz to Saint Petersburg; however, only a small stretch was ultimately completed in Madrid: the Ciudad Lineal. Other fundamentally linear cities were built during the heyday of the Industrial Revolution, including Turin, Karlsruhe, Volgograd, Quito, Las Vegas, the Nice-Cannes-MonteCarlo urban continuum, and the Linear City designed by Michael Graves and Peter Eisenman for a 34-kilometer-long linear settlement in New Jersey.

Finally, a series of futuristic cities, including The Line in Saudi Arabia, adhere to the linear typology, aiming to maximize the combined benefits of linear and vertical cities. The probability density function typically associated with Linear Cities and networks is the Poisson distribution. A fundamental advantage of linear cities is minimizing the time it takes to access the main transport network, but they also suffer several major scalability limitations. Once population density reaches a certain point, the main roads require such a high capacity that they tend to divide the city into several poorly interconnected parts, thereby diminishing the efficiency of the network.

Las Vegas, USA
© The Speedy Butterfly

Organic City

One of the most widespread types of urban development is the organic city. Organic growth patterns emerge whenever there is primarily informal, bottom-up, private-sector-driven growth without a more cohesive top-down design. Organic cities tend to be driven by the short-term demand and conspicuous impulses of the *laissez faire* economy, hence lacking a sense of formal, functional and quality consistency. While it can be asserted that organic growth patterns tend to naturally compensate for the utmost urgent needs and deficiencies experienced by the city as it grows, it must be noticed that such compensation dynamics tend to operate like a pendulum law. The probability density function typically associated with Organic Cities and networks is the Poisson - Lognormal distribution. Lognormal distributions typically describe oligarchic power structures, where a tiny segment of the population concentrates the majority of the wealth, political power, social influence, and access to premium products and services. Oligarchic networks with a Lognormal node degree distribution typically damage the quality of social life in two ways: they both hinder the ability of the most brilliant citizens to succeed and contribute to the broader society, and remarkably damage the opportunities of the most vulnerable demographic sectors of a given society.

As for organic cities, these tend to contain a wide variety of urban settings, increasing the diversity of the urban experience, but they also present a series of inefficiencies in terms of infrastructure costs per resident, making them undesirable on the whole. The high degree of entropy observed in organic cities contributes to creating unique street layout patterns and architectural forms, albeit also a much higher degree of urbanization inefficiency and higher energy and water consumption per citizen. One such inefficiency is the randomness of the organic urban layout, which renders mobility systems less efficient, increasing average commuting times and costs. Moreover, their irregularity makes it difficult to evenly distribute services. Finally, due to the lack of a more efficient pattern, organic cities tend to have poor accessibility between different neighborhoods and districts, with higher levels of social and financial inequality. Notable examples of cities composed to a large extent by organic growth patterns include São Paulo, Mexico City, Damascus, Jakarta, and Nairobi.

Manchester, United Kingdom
© Chunyip Wong

Atomized City

Atomized or fractured cities typically share a blessing and a curse: on the one hand, they tend to depict intermodal logistics hubs, usually around a major maritime or river port infrastructure, and benefit from a local vibrant ecosystem and the dynamism associated with regional and global commerce and knowledge exchange. On the other hand, atomized or fractured cities usually suffer from difficult and challenging orographic conditions, hence impacting the street layout patterns, generating meandering road systems and atypical transport networks connecting the different urban areas in spite of the environmental constraints and limitations. The probability density function equation of Atomized or fractured cities follows the skewed Lognormal distribution.

The fractured nature of the maritime coastal façades, riversheds, mountainous areas, and other environmental accidents constitutes a series of major constraints through which the urban settlements of atomized cities expanded. Consequently, the underlying topological network of interwoven roads, avenues, boulevards, streets, and walkways of Atomized or Fractured cities usually result in neither the utmost harmonic, balanced, efficient, and fluent of urban fabrics, nor the most beautiful or logistically rational architectural landscapes. However, a myriad of high-spirited, economically dynamic, culturally rich and hectic metropolitan areas have arisen around major ports and intermodal freight crossroads. Representative examples of primarily atomized or fractured cities include Istanbul, Hong Kong, Bilbao, Seattle, Osaka, Singapore, Venice, Amsterdam, Liverpool, Mumbai, Cartagena de Indias, São Luís de Maranhão, central Tokyo, Busan, Rotterdam, Antwerp, Bremen, as well as a number of the cities that composed the Hanseatic League.

Historically, major port cities such as Singapore and New York City have dramatically benefited from their privileged locations as trade hubs, and investment magnets. The opening of the Erie Canal in the 19th century allowed New York to become the foremost destination for Europeans migrating to the United States during the latter decades and at the turn of century, hence allowing the Big Apple to grow exponentially and surpass Boston and Philadelphia as the referential city of the nascent republic. For their part, Singapore and Panama became some of the most dynamic city states within their respective regions thanks to their flourishing intermodal logistics trade networks. Despite their limitations, fractured cities present a number of unique characteristics that often position them as commercial and cultural hubs on a global scale.

Hong Kong, Hong Kong
© ahei

Random City

The random growth pattern typically describes urban settlements that developed with neither significant planning efforts nor the required time and resources to shape a sustainable community. The rushed nature of their inception and early-stage development makes them particularly vulnerable to malpractice in terms of morphological design, infrastructural quality, placemaking rationale, and satisfactory activity programming needs. On that account, random cities usually represent manifestations of informal, bottom-up urbanization, often constituting a provisional solution to mass migration from rural areas to urban centers under duress, scarcity of resources, and characterized by fragile, if not marginal, social networks. Random networks are a well-known archetypal system, one that presents unique configurations, but not necessarily the most attractive, safe, or prosperous communities. The probability density function intrinsically associated with random cities is the one associated with random networks: the Binomial / Poisson.

A notable form of random urban developments is the slum development, typically built on a series of squalid and overcrowded urban streets or districts inhabited by very poor people, often on the verge of social marginalization. Representative examples of random growth patterns and slums can be found in New Delhi, Rio de Janeiro (favelas), São Paulo, Mexico City, Jakarta, Marseille, Orangi Town in Karachi, Pakistan, Ciudad Neza in Mexico, Dharavi in Mumbai, India, Kibera in Nairobi, Kenya, and Khayelitsha, Cape Town, in South Africa.

Delhi, India
© Westend61 / Amazing Aerial

Monumental City

Monumental cities are primarily envisioned, conceived, designed, and built aiming to aesthetically communicate the worldview, power structure, and values of a community. The quintessential monumental city is the imperial or national capital, host to the foremost administrative, managerial, cultural, and religious institutions of a nation or a region. Monumental cities are typically filled with majestic avenues, splendorous palaces, and public buildings, stunning churches, temples, synagogues, mosques, and other religious institutions, and august public parks and other recreational open spaces and facilities. Their most notable characteristic is that the beauty and sublimity pursued by grand spaces and magnificent sites is a formidable manifestation of political power, hence under this specific pattern, aesthetics and ideological messages outcompete certain urban design and economic considerations. Representative examples of monumental cities include Washington DC, Rome, Vienna, Prague, Budapest, Saint Petersburg, Brasilia, the Habsburg area in Madrid, Beijing, Ottawa, Jerusalem, and Berlin. The probability density function typically associated with Monumental Cities and networks is that of the hierarchical network: the Skewed Power Law.

Hierarchical network models are iterative algorithms for creating networks that are able to reproduce the unique properties of the Scale-Free topology and a high clustering of nodes at the same time. These characteristics are widely observed in nature, from biology to language to some social networks. Monumental cities tend to gather a juxtaposition of political layers, from local to regional to national or imperial governmental spheres of power, in addition to hosting significant religious sites and spiritual centers. Often, regional or state capitals reproduce elements of monumental cities at a smaller scale.

Rome, Italy
© 4FR

Garden City

The concept of the Garden City was originally formulated by Utopian thinkers and city planners as a humane solution to shape healthy and desirable residential communities for industrial workers, geographically separated from industrial manufacturing, mining, and port environments. The goal pursued by means of programming segmentation was to dramatically increase the quality of life, hygiene, and sanitary conditions of working-class and middle-class households during the early stages of the Industrial Revolution. The Garden city vision conceived by the likes of Ebenezer Howard, Robert Owen, Charles Fourier, Edward Bellamy, Henry George, and Raymond Unwin aimed to mitigate the undesirable living conditions experienced by most factory workers as a result of Manchesterian capitalism and the alienating conditions imposed on them by shaping a city in which people could live harmoniously together with nature.
The probability density function typically associated with Garden Cities is the tree-shaped hierarchical network. Quintessential examples of garden cities include Letchworth, Welwyn, Canberra, Brøndby Haveby in Denmark, Forest Hills Gardens in NY, Radburn, Ciudad Jardín de el Palomar near Buenos Aires, Butantã, Jardim América, Goiânia, Sant Cugat del Vallès, and Pozuelo de Alarcón.

Although, throughout history, most urban settlements from ancient civilizations included different forms of extramural single-family housing such as villas, domus, mansions, chateaus and country houses, they were routinely devoted to the upper classes, the social and economic elite demographics. Spurred by the Cold War dynamics, the Garden City movement experienced a strong revival, particularly in Anglo-Saxon countries. The initial push towards suburban single-family housing areas was predominantly led by the upper middle classes. Geopolitical motivations, such as the convenience of forcing the USSR to dramatically invest exponentially more in their nuclear technology to potentially retaliate and annihilate the same amount of citizens pushed the Garden City agenda way beyond the original plan. Subsequently, a lower quality version of Garden Cities was popularized across the Western world after WW2, and across the globe since the 1960s, hence diminishing dramatically the average population density of most metropolitan areas and creating a series of mostly isolated communities often designated as "tapestries of banality"—where neither the aesthetic charm nor the quality of life of the original and more luxurious Garden Cities is manifested.

Canberra, Australia
© IIIShutter

Fractal City

City science research efforts reveal interesting patterns and performance results. One city type that is worth looking at more closely is the Fractal City, intrinsically defined by its Scale-Free network structure, aesthetic self-similarity, and harmonic polycentrism. The fractal city is constructed with a series of hubs (city/neighborhood centers) that are strategically spread throughout the city, providing access to important amenities for residents and businesses alike. Mathematically, we describe this distribution as having positive, Power Law-driven, non-linear benefits through the aggregation of urban infrastructure and activities. More so than any other type of city, the fractal structure provides equitable access to critical services and mobility within walkable distances. After analyzing hundreds of metropolitan areas across the globe, we found that only one of the 10 urban design typologies is capable of meeting the standards of quality associated with the Sustainable Development Goals and the 15-Minute City' model: the fractal city. The harmonious hierarchy of hubs found in fractal urban layouts tends to facilitate high levels of urban performance in terms of value creation (productive human collaboration to propel the knowledge economy), maximization of access to services and amenities, and urban design beauty and efficiency. The probability density function typically associated with Fractal Cities and networks is the Power Law / Pareto function, with a topology and morphology shaped by Scale-Free networks.

Fractal structures can be perceived in nature, science, art, and architecture, and are often associated with beauty, harmony, and highly efficient and balanced systems. Fractal cities combine the multiplying, non-linear benefits of the geographical concentration of knowledge-intensive activity with a polycentric, decentralized layout, where every corner of the city is within a 20-minute walk of all essential services: education, healthcare, shops, employment, recreational and cultural opportunities, etc. This makes the most of the multiplying benefits of the geographical concentration of uses in the city center, while also facilitating a polycentric distribution of second-, third-, and fourth-tier hubs around squares and intersections scattered across the length and breadth of the urban fabric. Representative examples of highly fractal cities include Boston's Back Bay Area, La Plata in Argentina, Barcelona's Eixample and Sant Martí districts, Savannah, certain areas in Washington DC, and Stockholm.

Boston, USA
© Gray Malin

Performance Follows Form: Relationship between City Form and Quality of Urban Life

Network of Urban Design: Relationships

The application of a scientific approach to analytically evaluate the relationship between city form patterns and their impact on urban performance by means of combining network theory principles with evidence-based, data-driven observations has been proven to be a fruitful and rewarding endeavor, providing highly revealing yields that illuminate the complex yet structural dynamics between quality of urban life and morphological design. The results of the analysis of 100 global metropolitan areas not only point in the direction of statistically significant correlations, but also suggest deeper causal relationships that can be modeled and better understood.

A thorough, systematic, and generalizable model emerges, presenting the foundation for a universal city science model to be further developed and refined. The empirical validation of a series of hypotheses evaluating the hidden dynamics between city design, human relationships, and the subjective experience of citizens and visitors alike solidifies the integration of top-down ontological concept models with bottom-up empirical observations.

First, city form features can be defined as measurable indicators, and the evaluation of topological, morphological, scale, entropy and fractality-related features reveals that certain archetypal patterns tend to present similar characteristics. Second, we conclude that there is a structural relationship between such design characteristics and urban performance indicators, most notably fractality, entropy and density. Finally, we see a finite number of fundamental network growth patterns with an infinite number of variations. Those fundamental typologies tend to induce certain types of behavior and display universal patterns of performance.

A number of highly insightful sets of learnings can be derived when evaluating the relationship between city form and urban performance.

Discovery 1

City form typologies and their representative features (urban topology, morphology, entropy and scale) have an effect on urban performance, with respect to urbanization efficiency, access to urban amenities, and the knowledge economy. The city form characteristics are a set of custom KPIs to quantitatively describe a city's urban features. Each of the 10 city form typologies presents distinct, universal features and characteristics

The KPIs are universal and allow any geographic region, district or neighborhood to be assessed and benchmarked against similar or different areas of interest. A selected group of morphometric parameters holds a strong predictive power in terms of urbanization and architectural efficiency: maximizing city form fractality combined with intermediate levels of urban form entropy tend to present the highest performing design combination. By way of example, from an urban compactness perspective, there is a sublinear relationship between city density and urban performance, with a log-log trend line slope of 0.81: every time we double Population Density (2x growth), we appreciate 19% sublinear increase in economies of scale in terms of access to amenities, all else being equal.

Urban Form Fractality Urbanization Efficiency Superlinearity (Log-Log)

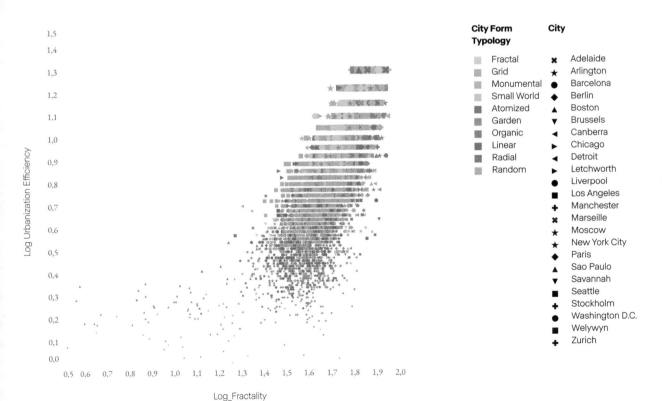

The Cost Savings realized due to increased Density/Scale are manifested in the form of architectural and urban design efficiency: doubling density values enables material and cost savings to the order of 19% and remarkably diminishes the carbon footprint overall. Hence, denser cities tend to outperform lower density cities, but present a wide range of efficiency levels, with most not attaining the 15-Minute City standards below certain lower bound density thresholds, given their internal urban form and programming inefficiencies. Subsequently, desirable average ranges for density can be estimated for each municipality and urban area. The desirable ranges for critical city form parameters aiming to maximize sustainable urbanization efficiency (material savings), access to services and amenities, and the multiplying effects of the knowledge economy are:

City form KPI	Desirable Range of Values
Urban Form Fractality	> 0.7 Normalized Fractality > 1.25 City Form Fractal Dimension (absolute value)
Shannon Entropy	0,45 - 0,55 (0 - 1 scale) Average area of tessellations or polygons composing a given building group (BG), as a proxy for sub-unit space utilization
Avg. Betweenness Centrality	> 0.15
Avg. Global Closeness Centrality	> 0.085
Avg. Circuity Centrality	> 0.05
Avg. Straightness Centrality	Between 0.85 and 0.95
Avg. Building Tessellation Area	Approx 10 - 15
Avg. Building Tessellation Orientation	Approx 10 - 20

The street layout orientation patterns show the diverse urban design styles across a specific metropolitan area. The street orientation shows multiple orientations, with a few districts having specific axes. Street Orientation Entropy: a measure of the orderliness of a street network orientation. Entropy is minimized when all streets run in parallel and maximized when they follow no discernible pattern. This has implications for land use, transportation, access to amenities, and energy efficiency.

Each urban design typology presents a series of universally manifested common features and characteristics, denoting the urban performance commonalities derived from inducing certain human behavior patterns by means of city form physical and psychological conditioning.

Discovery 2

The urban form fractality index is positively correlated with urban infrastructure efficiency, and the fractal city typology is the most efficient out of the 10 types in terms of urban infrastructure economies of scale and superlinear social interaction patterns.

City Form Fractality is the most salient and analytically informative urban design feature when it comes to predicting urbanization efficiency. The city science-based analysis of urban development patterns around the world reveals a positively nonlinear, exponential relationship between city form fractality and urbanization efficiency, in terms of higher urban performance for social interaction patterns, access to urban services and amenities, access to mobility / transportation stations and services, and infrastructure efficiency per resident. Thus, contributing to increasing the overall urban design fractality may enable a city to become an attractive environment to live and work in, as soon as it reaches its maturity state.

The higher the fractality levels, the higher the urban development efficiency, the access to urban services and amenities, the connectivity between architectural spaces, and the social interaction patterns, including those facilitating the success of the knowledge economy.

Urban topology (2D street layouts) and morphology (3D architectural features) can be combined to increase self-similarity or fractality and to attain desirable entropy values. We observe that when we double City Form Fractality (2x growth) we attain on average a 31% superlinear increase in efficiency in terms of social interaction superlinearity, access to amenities, and urbanization efficiency, all else being equal. A combination of 2D topological and 3D morphological features can help achieve highly fractal architecture and urban design configurations.

In the first figure we appreciate a 31% superlinearity index between city form fractality and social interaction surplus or multiplying effects. In the second one, we appreciate a 19% sublinearity index in terms of economies of scale between population density and material infrastructure efficiency.

Global Cities Analysis:
Urban Form Fractality - Access to Urban Services (Log-Log)
Urban Density - Access to Urban Services (Log-Log)

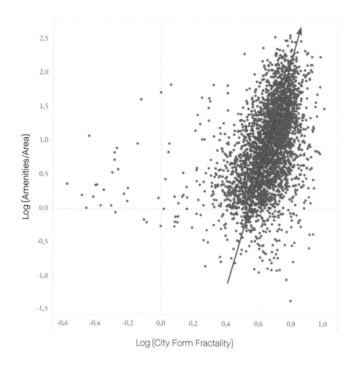

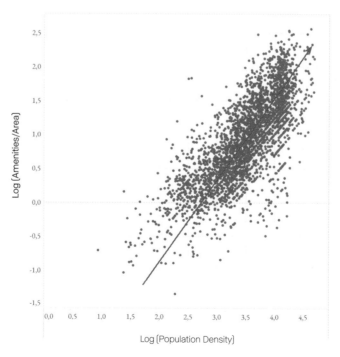

City Form Fractality
Network Closeness, Cicuity, and Betweenness Centrality

Center_point

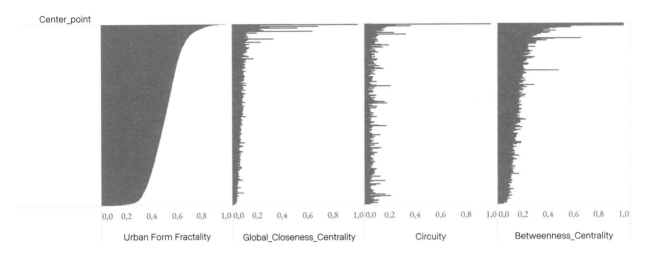

| Urban Form Fractality | Global_Closeness_Centrality | Circuity | Betweenness_Centrality |

City Form Urban Fractality Index
Superlinear Urbanization Efficiency and Street Length Efficiency

Center_point

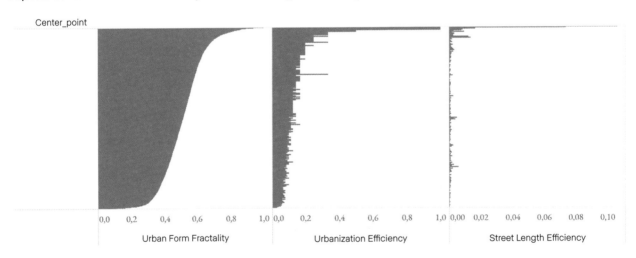

| Urban Form Fractality | Urbanization Efficiency | Street Length Efficiency |

City Form Fractality Gradient by Typology

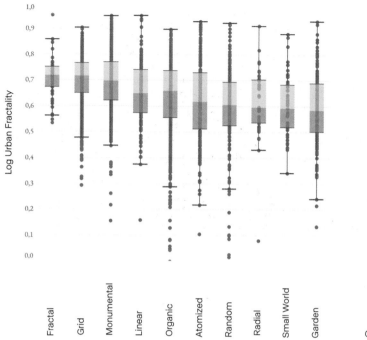

Log Urban Fractality

Fractal · Grid · Monumental · Linear · Organic · Atomized · Random · Radial · Small World · Garden

Global Cities

City Form Typology

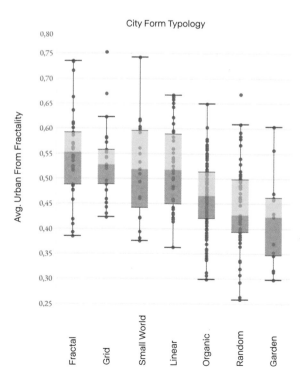

Avg. Urban From Fractality

Fractal · Grid · Small World · Linear · Organic · Random · Garden

(Boston)

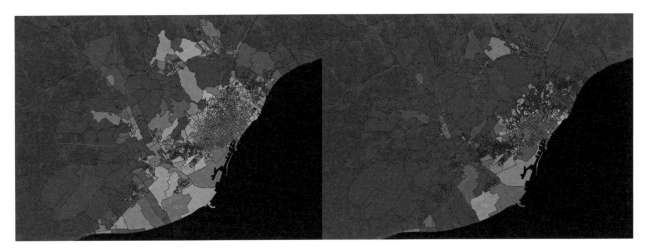

Discovery 3

The urban form fractality index is positively and superlinearly correlated with the access to urban services and amenities, and fractal grids achieve a more egalitarian distribution of services than other network types. The positive, nonlinear relationship between urban form fractality and urban performance metrics reveals a clear gradient across city form typologies within any metropolitan area: the higher the fractality, the higher the urbanization efficiency.

A key takeaway is that doubling City Form Fractality or design quality allows for increasing to the order of 31% the ability to access urban services and amenities, hence boosting the chances of attaining the 15-Minute City standards. A combination of high density and high fractality would help a city achieve the 15-Minute City standards throughout the urban continuum. Urban Design Efficiency dramatically increases the access to amenities.

In the following figures, each data point is an urban unit of approximately 1,000 residents of a city throughout the world, each data point is a neighborhood of a city throughout the world. There is a clear trend that, as the fractality increases, so too do urban material efficiency and betweenness centrality. In addition, as the Shannon Entropy as the Shannon Entropy reaches intermediate values, so too do urban efficiency and betweenness centrality. By using these measures it is possible to understand where a city lies in comparison to others around the world. This city science approach can help to guide investment, policy, and design decisions to increase performance and economic output.

City Form Fractality: Superlinear Urbanization Efficiency and Social Interaction

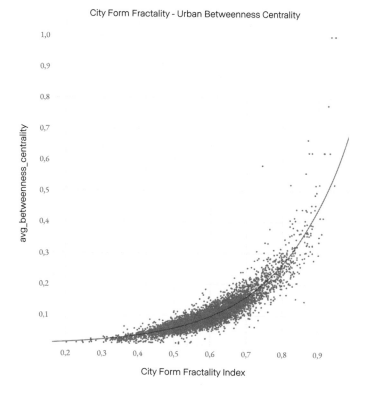

City Form Fractality - Urban Betweenness Centrality

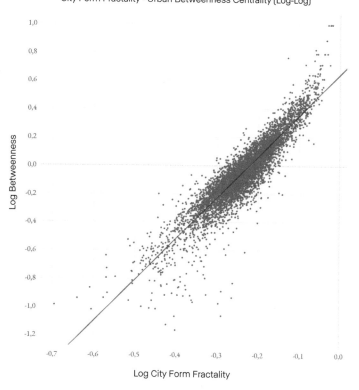

City Form Fractality - Urban Betweenness Centrality (Log-Log)

Discovery 4

The urban form entropy index is correlated with urban development efficiency metrics, and intermediate levels of city form entropy achieve the maximum/optimal degrees of urbanization efficiency. The street layout orientation patterns show the diverse urban design patterns across any given metropolitan area. The street orientation shows a very wide range of typologies, from the essentially reticular / gridded patterns to the most organic or random models. Intermediate levels of street and walkway orientation entropy provide highly harmonic urban spaces, combining a certain degree of regularity (efficiency) with circulation freedom (flexibility).

City Form Entropy
Network Closeness, Circuity, Betweenness Centrality, Urbanization Efficiency

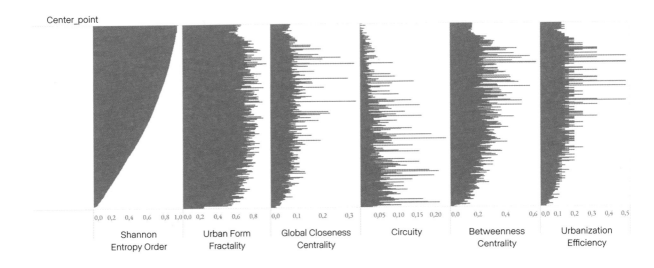

Average Distance to 1st and 5th Amenity vs Amenities/Area (Entropy Gradient)

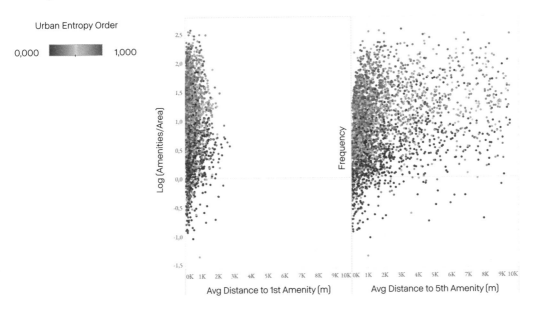

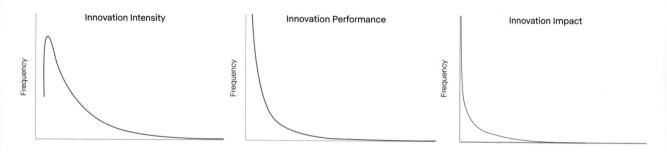

Innovation Intensity measures the collective effort deployed to create knowledge networks. Innovation Intensity is measured as a percentage of employees working on knowledge-intensive activities per geographic unit. The average community in the West has an Innovation Intensity of approximately 12%, usually ranging between 5% and 20%, while Innovation Districts typically operate at or above 35%. Top-performing Innovation Districts are high-intensity environments: the top 10% achieve values of 50% and above.

Innovation Performance measures the tangible outputs of innovation created on an annual basis by the innovation community. Doubling Innovation Intensity and concentrating it produces an average output of 4x more new products, services, patents, inventions, scientific research papers, and R&D projects and their associated revenues per employee.

Innovation Impact describes the benefits to the broader community resulting from the development of knowledge-intensive activities. By doubling Innovation Intensity and concentrating it geographically, we can realize 15x time more quality employment per capita, and 25x higher business revenue per resident.

The geographic aggregation of knowledge-intensive activities within physical proximity to an innovation network logic tends to facilitate fruitful interaction, hence producing multiplying effects benefitting the overall urban economy. The strategic combination of doubling Innovation Intensity whilst geographically concentrating the core knowledge-intensive activities by means of a Scale-Free, hierarchical urban design fractal network dramatically increases the superlinear benefits of clustering intellectual activities and social collaboration.

Boston Area Innovation Districts:
Innovation Intensity per Building Group (0-1, weighted by abs)

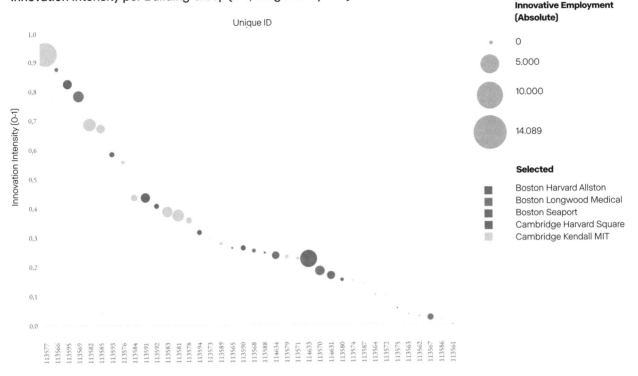

Fractal-shaped urban design networks tend to facilitate the emergence of Scale-Free knowledge economy networks, where a hierarchical structure deliberately connects idea generators (such as universities and research centers) with innovation catalysts (innovation centers, technology and knowledge transfer centers, startup incubators and accelerators) all the way to industry verticals (leading innovative companies, industry-specific suppliers and service providers). Scale-free urban knowledge systems present two major advantages: (1) they connect all the nodes in the system, thus creating a more egalitarian and connected network; and (2) they maximize the high-performing nodes by creating merit-based *hubs*. A combination of highly fractal urban design strategies with hierarchical network-led space programming techniques can help nurture more egalitarian and merit-based ecosystems where liberty and recognition are harmonically integrated, hence creating more prosperous and humane workplaces and cities.

The identification of the 10 main urban form or design typologies, all of which can be modeled as complex network systems, is based upon their two-dimensional topology, three-dimensional morphology, level of urban entropy and scale. We subsequently found that the formal properties of a city have an impact on the dynamics of urban systems, which in turn structurally condition urban performance indicators. Therefore, each type of city can be described, both visually and mathematically, by means of networks in constant flux. Through modeling based on network theory and validated by empirical data, we can measure the performance level of each part of a city or metropolitan area in great detail, in terms of their principal urban systems: talent network, economy and creation of wealth, value chains by business sector, efficiency of mobility, energy and water systems, etc. Among other things, this modeling allows us to assess the extent to which each of the 10 urban design types affects, facilitates, or hinders efforts to capitalize on the multiplying benefits of the strategic aggregation of knowledge-intensive activities.

In summary, the most efficient urban development patterns tend to present a combination of high degrees of city form fractality, intermediate degrees of entropy, dense/compact environments, mixed use space programming enabling high levels of access to urban amenities and services, a self-similar distribution of third places fostering high quality socialization patterns, and unique architectural qualities creating a sense of belonging and community.

In summary, the most efficient urban development patterns tend to present a combination of high degrees of city form fractality, intermediate degrees of entropy, dense/compact environments, mixed use space programming enabling high levels of access to urban amenities and services, a self-similar distribution of third places fostering high quality socialization patterns, and unique architectural qualities creating a sense of belonging and community.

Urban Design and Hierarchical Network Building Strategies to Nurture Successful Innovation Ecosystems

Shaping a successful urban innovation ecosystem vision requires that the urban design strategy takes advantage of insights and learnings extracted from a network theory framework: a strategy to deploy a harmonious, polycentric fractal urban plan that will allow existing and new companies, institutions and residents to enjoy a thriving neighborhood that promotes social interaction, quality of life, and a strong knowledge-based economy.

A possible Innovation District within a broader Metropolitan Area has the potential to benefit from strengthening its harmonic polycentrism by designing new urban development layouts in a fractal urban morphology. The key design criteria to achieve the proposed objectives include the deployment of:

1. the fractal urban form (topology, morphology, entropy, self-similarity) and
2. a distribution of services in a "self-similar" nature, where services are reproduced on different scales through space.

This assumes a balanced or harmonious distribution of the services offered to the population that can help optimize and maximize the creation of value (freedom, interaction, opportunity) and the capture of value (equal distribution of critical services and sustainable development).

In addition, urban topology design criteria can help reinforce the mobility and accessibility strategy, thus increasing the shares of sustainable mobility. Urban morphology will be measured to strategically design nested hierarchies of architectural spaces based on intermediate levels of entropy and high compactness, in order to combine the efficiency of urbanization with the flexibility of socialization. This will help support the knowledge economy based on innovation value chains rooted in comparative advantage and wider access to critical services, and it will increase sustainable development practices by reducing air pollution, travel time, and car dependency, and promoting more efficient energy/water systems.

The proposed urban design vision combines a predominantly fractal street layout and activity programming, serving the needs in terms of future capacity for the core knowledge areas presenting a comparative advantage in a given area. A networked space programming model allows for accommodating different Node Tier activities within physical proximity: from applied research to technology transfer, via innovation hubs and startup incubators, connecting with advanced production industries and their supporting value chains. In the next page we present an: Urban Design Strategy to enhance the multiplier effects and synergies of a new urban development for a knowledge economy ecosystem or Innovation District.

City Design Strategies and Best Practices to Increase the Quality of The Urban Experience Around The World

TOPOLOGICAL STRATEGY (2D NETWORK)
Establishment of a self-similar or fractal network, with Tier 1Edges (metropolitan avenues), Tier 2 Edges (metropolitan streets), Tier 3 Edges (a basic reticular grid), Tier 4 Edges (local district streets) and Tier 5 Edges (pedestrian grids)

MORPHOLOGICAL STRATEGY (3D ARCHITECTURAL SPACES)
Harmonic distribution of architectural spaces, designed to accommodate the uses of the 7 node hierarchies, with the appropriate capacity (employees, m2, plans) specific to each case

SCALE STRATEGY
scale optimization that allows for growth from the preexisting network of researchers up to the fullest potential of the community employees in its maturity phase

ENTROPY STRATEGY
achievement of intermediate levels of urban entropy

FRACTALITY STRATEGY
Harmonic network of nodes on the order of 1 to 7 based on the strategy of innovation, on a grid of axes on the order of 1 to 5 of the self-similar type, maximizing efficiency and fruitful interactivity

Fractal Nodes	Fractal Edges
Tier 1 Nodes: Research and academic centers	Tier 1 Edges: Metropolitan avenues Global accessibility
Tier 2 Nodes: Knowledge and Technology Transfer Knowledge areas and their respective innovation and technology transfer centers, fields of innovation	Tier 2 Edges: Metropolitan streets Boulevards that reinforce the centrality of the main nodes of the knowledge network
Tier 3 Nodes: Innovative Companies Private business hubs, by knowledge area	Tier 3 Edges: Partially reticulated access and distribution network for essential services
Tier 4 Nodes: Startups Incubators and startup accelerators	Tier 4 Edges: Street network at neighborhood / district scale
Tier 5 Nodes: Pre-existing companies and Coworking spaces Coworking centers for small and medium-sized companies Suppliers and providers	Tier 5 Edges: Local network of the innovation district connecting architectural spaces that present synergies Pedestrian areas

Network of Industries: Relationships

The analysis of the structural impact of city form features and typologies on the network of industries presents two major sets of learnings: on the one hand, city form features such as density, fractality, and entropy directly impact the ability for cities to attain the 15-Minute City quality standards. On the other hand, urban design aspects such as city form, density, and strategic geographic activity programming, combined with evidence-based smart specialization policies, can help dramatically propel the degrees of prosperity experienced by a given city and district.

City Form and Placemaking Strategies and the Ability to Attain the 15-Minute City Standards

The 15-Minute City quality standards are rarely met by cities and urban areas today, although they are feasible, attainable, and desirable. A key take away from our analysis shows the power of how mathematical modeling can help to address specific design challenges of urban environments by evaluating each component of cities individually and finding common patterns between different city types. This allows us to understand and learn from the diagnostics technique and use it for recommendations in the future. Because no city is exactly of a single type, it is therefore important to have a tool that can respond to the complexity of real-world examples, where cities are made of multiple types blended together. Therefore, this type of analysis can be helpful for us to better understand how our cities perform and the best way to make interventions to improve the quality of life in each context.

The descriptive statistics after evaluating thousands of submunicipal units representing hundreds of millions of citizens worldwide reveal highly heterogeneous patterns when it comes to assessing the ability of cities and urban areas to adhere to the 15-Minute City quality standards.

Variable	Global Cities (Avg)	Urban Design Target
Avg. Population (Estimate)	7034 residents and approx 3,165 employees	> 10,000 residents and approx 5,000 employees / Km2
Avg. All Amenities	8.05 amenities per Km2 (all types combined)	Approx 80 - 100 amenities per Km2
Avg. Amenities / Population	0.002986 amenities per resident	0.0080 amenities per resident
Avg. Avg Distance to 1st Amenity (m)	279 m	< 150m
Avg. Avg Distance to 5th Amenity (m)	1,568 m	< 500m
Avg. education_count	0.42 education centers per Km2	> 3 education centers per Km2
Avg. entertainment_count	0.14 entertainment centers per Km2	> 1.5 entertainment centers per Km2
Avg. healthcare_count	1.05 healthcare centers per Km2	> 7 healthcare centers per Km2
Avg. sustenance_count	4.92 sustenance centers per Km2	> 50 sustenance centers per Km2
Avg. transportation_count	1.89 transportation nodes per Km2	> 35 transportation nodes per Km2
Avg. area_km^2	2.49 Km2, with approx 3,200 residents/Km2	

The desirable ranges for urban amenities to achieve the 15-minute city standards are presented in the table above.

Moving forward, a core challenge will be to identify what types of urban design and placemaking interventions can reinforce the fractal condition of any given city type, as well as what types of network science analyses (such as geographic clustering, reach and gravity indexes, triadic closure, strength of weak ties, catchment area analyses, betweenness, etc.) can inform exogenous shocks in the system to raise the overall quality of life. This will boost the chances for cities to increase their ability to serve their citizens by achieving the quality standards of the 15-Minute City.

Hierarchical Network Urban Design and Smart Specialization Strategies to Propel Prosperity

The successful development of a new innovation area or district should take into account the contribution that different industries and skills bring into the mix to create a fruitful innovation ecosystem. The levels of diversification and economic complexity of the city and broader metropolitan area will provide a path to economic diversification. Risk mitigation strategies will guard against providing an assessment of potential pitfalls in the diversification strategy. This will include industries that are promising but have a high risk of failure and industries and sectors that seem safe but have an underestimated risk component.

The complex systems analysis of export sectors of a city can be succinctly summarized by means of the Product Space, showing a given city's main strengths by sector. In the Product Space, each economic sector is depicted by a bubble or node, which is color-coded according to the industry it represents. Economic sectors are related if they are linked to one another by a line or edge. Central nodes or sectors, in the graph, have more connections. They generally correspond to sophisticated and high-value industries such as auto-parts manufacturing and electrical equipment, while peripheral nodes correspond to less complex industries such as agricultural products and natural resources. When a node is highlighted, this implies that the region has a comparative advantage in that sector. Implicitly, it shows that the economy has the skills, knowledge, resources, and infrastructure for the specific economic sector to thrive.

For instance, the Product Space of the State of São Paulo has 529 active nodes out of a total of 775 available nodes. This high number makes sense, as São Paulo is the largest city in South America and a center of education and industry. This allows for a critical mass of talent and resources to develop in multiple different industries, from auto manufacturing and electrical equipment to creative industries and information technology.
A city science-led Smart Specialization Strategy illuminates strategic sectors within São Paulo as desirable targets for the foreseeable future. To that end, we classify industries according to two main metrics described above: Economic Complexity and Proximity, which will allow for the identification of successful and high-performing industries. As explained above, Economic Complexity is a measure of sophistication and value added by industry.

A firm with a high value in economic complexity produces a product that is internationally competitive and exports more than other competitors. As a result, economic complexity correlates strongly with niche and sophisticated products and is a predictor of future growth. In the case of the figure below, there is a subset of industries in the textile sector that ranks high in terms of economic complexity.

The second measure, Proximity, conveys the distance between the current portfolio of industries surrounding the project and those industries that are "within reach" of currently activated nodes within the network. For example, a subgroup of industries in the textile sector has a high ranking on the complexity axis and is relatively close to the current set of comparative advantages of São Paulo. Hence, we can rank the manufacturing industries available in a city according to these two metrics and select the subset of industries that are both high in economic complexity and proximity in order to tailor to a given Innovation District's needs. The results are shown in the figure and table below. A majority of the industries listed in the table are both present in a municipality and also in other neighboring cities. What is strategic about them is that they actively use many of the capabilities and resources that are abundant in the area and also provide high value added for the economy due to their economic complexity. As a result, these are attractive sectors to consider both from a growth but also a low-risk perspective.

It is important to note that the x-axis represents the proximity and the size of the critical mass in each industry; the farther to the right the data point is, the bigger the critical mass is for this industry. The y-axis represents an industry's level of sophistication (which also happens to show how promising the industry is); the farther toward the top the data point is, the more sophisticated and promising the industry. When applying this framework to a city such as São Paulo and selecting the industries within the top right quadrant, we observe that at the highest level of aggregation, the selected sectors cluster mainly around the industries of chemical products, plastics, and machinery and electrical equipment. Across all industries, we identify for the São Paulo Metropolitan Area around 18% of industries in the high opportunity sector, 14% belonging to the low-hanging fruit quadrant, and 35% corresponding to strategic bets.

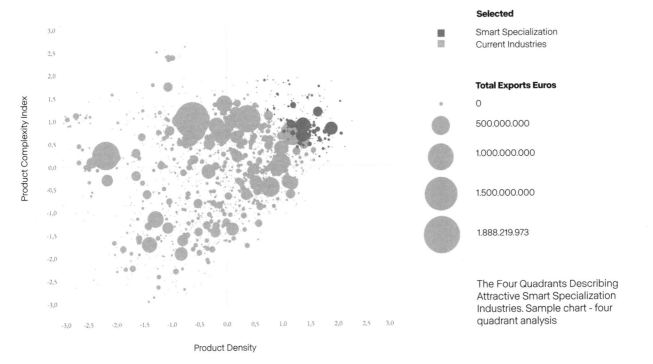

Product Complexity Index

Product Density

Selected
■ Smart Specialization
□ Current Industries

Total Exports Euros
· 0
○ 500.000.000
○ 1.000.000.000
○ 1.500.000.000
○ 1.888.219.973

The Four Quadrants Describing Attractive Smart Specialization Industries. Sample chart - four quadrant analysis

This categorization corresponds to a ranking that equally ponders economic complexity and proximity. We can alternatively ponder economic complexity higher than proximity for a more aggressive strategy that targets sophisticated industries that might not be as close to the current export portfolio. Inversely, we can weigh proximity more heavily than complexity, which implies the prioritization of sectors that are less risky from a diversification standpoint even though they are not as sophisticated. The smart specialization results provide an analytical and globally valid framework to inform by means of combining urban design and policymaking.

Network of Talent: Relationships

Innovation Ecosystems: Superlinear Effects of Geographic Concentration in Urban Innovation

How can we deliberately inform urban development strategies to strengthen the local knowledge economy? In recent years, a rising number of innovative firms and talented workers have chosen to congregate and co-locate in compact, amenity-rich urban settlements in the cores of central cities. Professor Miquel Barceló coined the term innovation district and proposed a series of complex systems-infused strategies to foster vibrant knowledge economy ecosystems where creativity and rigor can flourish and generate distributed prosperity. Innovation districts are geographic areas where leading-edge anchor institutions and companies cluster and connect with start-ups, business incubators, and accelerators. They are also physically compact, transit-accessible, and technically wired and they offer mixed use housing, office, and retail. These patterns are described in Katz and Wagner (2014) as well as Burke, Gras, and Yu (2019, 2022).

Analyzing the economic prosperity of a city through this lens has revealed that building Innovation Districts in cities can lead to distributed wealth for the people who live and work there, unlocking the latent potential of a community. The most effective Innovation Districts intentionally develop 3 kinds of networks: networks of talent from composed of individual workers collaborating within the labor force, networks of organizations collaborating together, and networks of the physical urban environment these organizations are distributed across, which host and support the economic fabric. Organizational structures layered on top of intelligent infrastructure can optimize innovation interactions among workers. Unlocking these synergies creates ecosystems that run on virtuous cycles of innovation. Optimizing the coordination of these networks can add significant value to the communities in which they operate.

Innovation and Economic Geography

We evaluated the urban innovation phenomenon across the entire United States to illuminate the ingredients and dynamics required to conform successful innovation ecosystems. Within the economic geography literature, there has been a large body of work focusing on agglomeration economics. Why do industries agglomerate? How much of this agglomeration is explained by local advantages and how much is a result of endogenous intra-industry spillovers? Ellison and Glaeser (2009) try to tackle this fundamental question by disaggregating the effect of economic agglomeration between natural advantages and intra-industry spillovers in a sample of four-digit manufacturing industries in the US. They study the determinants of agglomeration based on cost of inputs (electricity, gas, coal, agricultural products), cost of labor inputs (relative wage differences), relative price of skill, transportation costs, and unobserved spillovers. They find that natural advantages have a limited explanatory power, accounting for only 20% of observed agglomeration. The implication is that agglomeration effects are an important force driving the geographic distribution of economic activity. As noted by the authors, this effect is particularly extreme in manufacturing industries, in particular the automobile manufacturing sector.

We build upon these insights to carry over the question of the agglomeration of manufacturing industries to the more general understanding of innovation activities. How much of the agglomeration in innovation activities can be explained by local comparative advantage, and how much is an endogenous spillover effect that can be replicated in different regions? This is a fundamental question since, as we will show below, the spillover effects of innovative activities appear to be systemic and exponential. Based on the body of work described above, we expand the analysis to narrow the scope from a regional level to a city and district level, incorporate new granular data on innovation activities, and provide theoretically based measures to analyze the agglomeration of innovation efforts. In the following sections we aim to explain how and to what extent innovation districts outperform other urban areas in knowledge and wealth creation and how to measure the impact.

A key insight from the research revealed that the geographic concentration of knowledge-intensive activities tends to enable the liberation of multiplying effects of the innovation clustering, thus creating increasingly superlinear results. By way of example, when we double the concentration of Innovation Intensity and we cluster it geographically, professionals tend to create four times more inventions (new products, new services, patents, inventions) per capita, and 15 times more new quality jobs over a given period of time. A thorough city science diagnostic can inform the types of design and management decision-making processes or exogenous shocks for a given urban innovation ecosystem to succeed.

Measuring the Surplus or Superlinear Benefits of Geographically Concentrating Innovation

The purpose of this section is to define a conceptual and methodological framework for performing a geospatial analysis of innovation performance metrics within urban environments. By building an urban economic performance database describing geographically distributed innovation variables, we can design and compute geospatially detailed urban economic variables across the US, while also tracking their evolution over time. Building the database requires knowledge and testing of different methods for combining data using specific joining keys, tagging methods, and geospatial join and merging commands to create the specific key performance indicators (KPIs). The brand new KPIs will enable the measurement of economic performance metrics by describing the nonlinear benefits of the strategic aggregation of knowledge-intensive activities. The main hypothesis is that certain types of urban development and geographic clustering of innovation-related activities, usually observed in Innovation Districts, tend to generate sustainable prosperity and superlinear economic growth patterns.

The methodology will enable the identification of strengths and weaknesses in the geospatial network of urban infrastructure and collective knowhow, hence illustrating both the local comparative advantage of specific industries and knowledge areas, and the economic growth prospects. The empirical research will describe the analysis of the entire US territory, in addition to highlighting the economic performance metrics for 50 notable innovation districts with respect to the rest of the national territory.

The contribution of the novel theoretical and methodological framework is to create a geospatial model illuminating best practices in economic development to evaluate the impact of urban design and knowledge-intensive economic activity concentration. Applications of the model may include the evaluation of the adequateness of different types of urban topology, morphology, density, fractality and entropy for a given city and region.

Urban Innovation Ecosystems as Complex Dynamic Networks

The current stream of work integrates city science and network theory and applies this framework to urban design and the knowledge economy. On the empirical side, there is heavy emphasis on the measurement of innovation activity in knowledge-intensive urban ecosystems. These data points are combined to identify the main trends and relevant patterns. The theoretical framework and empirical analysis are then combined to evaluate the performance of alternative urban design and economic activation strategies. The analytical rationale is based upon the assumption that cities operate as dynamic complex systems, susceptible to be analyzed by means of network science. Thus, by analyzing the nature of the underlying networks supporting knowledge creation, we can compare, contrast, and extract best practices in terms of economic and innovation agglomeration dynamics and city design (urban topology, morphology entropy). Hence, by analytically identifying the nature and potential of a specific city or region, we can extract insights and guidelines to increase urban performance by determining the key ingredients and dynamics to propel economic growth and prosperity.

The Multiplying Effects of Physically Concentrating and Connecting Innovation Activities

The first innovation KPI corresponds to Innovation Intensity and measures the share of people working in knowledge-intensive activities in a given geography, broken down by innovation phase. The second innovation KPI, Innovation Performance, tracks the revenue generated by measurable innovations in the form of new patents, products, services, processes, R&D, scientific papers, and startup companies. Finally, the last set of indicators corresponds to the Innovation Impact, which encompasses the societal benefits, knowledge-intensive employment, wages, unemployment metrics, and housing affordability. Additional performance measures include quantitative surplus of good practices, urban design characteristics, urban typologies and their associated positive and negative externalities.

We conclude that the Innovation Intensity distribution follows a Lognormal pattern, the Innovation Performance indicator adheres to a Pareto (Power Law) distribution, and the Innovation Impact metric can be best described by a Gamma distribution.

Multiplying Effects of Knowledge-Intensive Activity Concentration in Innovation Districts

Innovation KPIs	Multiplying Factor
Innovation Intensity	2.8 times higher innovative employment per total employment (%)
Innovation Performance	4 times higher inventions and creations per capita
Innovation Impact	15 times higher innovation employment opportunities per resident 25 times higher business revenue per resident

The comparison between Innovation Intensity, Innovation Performance, and Innovation Impact depicts the amplifying effects of clustering knowledge-intensive activities: on average, innovation districts present 2.8 times higher concentration of knowledge-intensive activities per employee, 4 times higher innovation output per employee in terms of patents, new products, new services, new processes, and R&D, and 16 times higher creation and availability of knowledge-intensive employment opportunities per resident.

These results reveal that Innovation Districts systematically benefit from structural nonlinear innovation patterns as a result of the geographic aggregation of knowledge-intensive activities within urban environments. These results also apply for medium-sized Innovation Districts such as Boston Seaport, Silicon Alley and the Pittsburgh Innovation District.

Finally, we want to decompose this finding between a scale component and an innovation component. As we observed above, the municipal scale as measured by daytime residents also correlates strongly with total employment. We run the above regression again, this time taking into account total employment in addition to innovative employment. We find that the coefficient on total employment is 1.108, which explains 59% of the total effect found for innovation. This implies that there are two contributing factors to the superlinear result. The first factor is purely due to agglomeration economics of total employment: larger municipalities concentrate more employment opportunities. The second and most important factor is innovation externalities: even when we take into account the agglomeration of total employment, innovative employment tends to concentrate even more.

Measuring Superlinear Innovation in Innovation Districts

The analysis of the over 267,000 building groups in the continental US reveals the amplifying effects of investing in knowledge-intensive activities. The goodness of fit analysis of the distributions describing innovation effort (intensity), tangible knowledge advancement (performance), and societal benefits (impact) present increasingly nonlinear mathematical distributions. By comparing the representative descriptive statistics for the Urban Innovation Performance KPIs of 50 notable Innovation Districts with those of the rest of the US territory, we observe that systematic amplifying effects of investment in knowledge-intensive activities take place.

The statistical distribution describing the best goodness of fit for the Innovation Intensity (%) PDF follows a Lognormal (Power Lognormal) distribution, where c = 2.14 (scaled), and s= 0.446 (scaled):

The results of performing a geospatial analysis framework to model and measure urban innovation performance illuminate the evaluation of urban economic systems at the smallest census unit scale: the building group. The novel methodology allows for measuring the nonlinear benefits of the geographic aggregation of knowledge-intensive activities. Three new key performance metrics have been designed to measure the societal effort or investment supporting knowledge-intensive activities (Innovation Intensity), the tangible outcomes of such innovations (Innovation Performance), and the societal benefits derived from knowledge advancement activities (Innovation Impact).

The goodness of fit adjustment for the Probability Density Function (PDF) of the three KPIs reveals the increasingly nonlinear nature of the amplifying effects of investing in knowledge-intensive activities. The Innovation Intensity (societal effort) metric follows a Lognormal distribution, the Innovation Performance Metric (knowledge advancement and wealth creation) follows a Scale Free / Power Law / Pareto distribution, and the Innovation Impact Metric (societal benefits) follows an extremely skewed Gamma distribution.

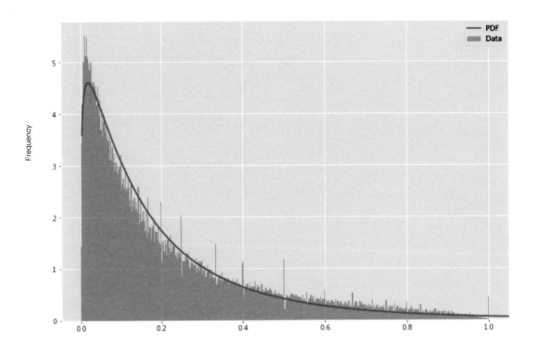

Innovation Intensity

The statistical distribution describing the best goodness of fit for the Innovation Intensity (%) PDF follows a Lognormal (Power Lognormal) distribution, where c = 2.14 (scaled), and s= 0.446 (scaled):

$$f(x, c, s) = \frac{c}{xs}\Phi(\frac{log(x)}{s})(\Phi(\frac{-log(x)}{s}))^{c-1} = \frac{2.14}{x \cdot 0.446}\Phi(\frac{log(x)}{0.446})(\Phi(\frac{-log(x)}{0.446}))^{2.14-1}$$

The Goodness of Fit to best describe the Probability Density Distribution for the Innovation Intensity metric follows a Lognormal shape. On average, the top 50 Innovation Districts in the US concentrate 2.8 times more Innovation Intensity (34%) than the national average (12%).

Goodness of Fit analysis of the Innovation Performance PDF.
Power Law distribution

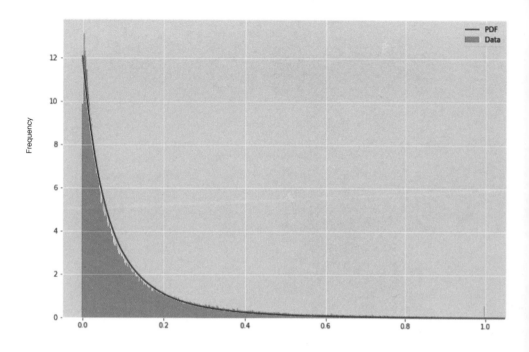

Innovation Performance   The statistical distribution describing the best goodness of fit for Innovation Performance PDF follows a Pareto / Power Law distribution, where b = 2.62, loc = 0.21, scale = 0.21:

$$f(x) = \frac{b}{x^{b+1}} = \frac{2.62}{x^{2.62+1}}$$

The function describing the best Goodness of Fit for the Probability Density Distribution regarding the Innovation Performance metric follows a Pareto-shaped Power Law function. On average, the 50 notable Innovation Districts produce up to four times more business revenue per employee than the national average, as a result of inventions and knowledge advancement in the form of patents, new products, new processes, scientific articles, and R&D projects.

Innovation Employment. with best fit distribution gamma
(a=0.65, loc=0.00, loc=0.00, scale=0.20)

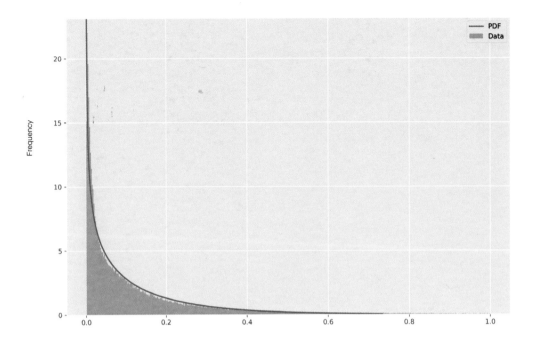

Innovation Impact

The statistical distribution describing the best goodness of fit for Innovation Impact PDF follows a Gamma Distribution, where: a=1.99:

$$f(x) = \frac{x^{a-1} e^{-x}}{\Gamma(a)} = \frac{x^{1.99-1} e^{-x}}{\Gamma(1.99)}$$

The function describing the best Goodness of Fit for the Probability Density Distribution regarding the Innovation Impact metric follows a Gamma-shaped distribution. The 50 notable Innovation Districts outperform by a factor of 16 in terms of availability of knowledge intensive job opportunities per resident.

The comparisons between 50 notable innovation districts and the average descriptive statistics for building groups across the US enables the extraction of revealing insights regarding the amplifying effects derived therefrom. The superlinear effects of the geographic concentration of knowledge-intensive activities can be described when observing that Innovation Districts systematically outperform regular districts.

The multiplying factors are 2.8 (Innovation Intensity), 4 (Innovation Performance), and 16 (Innovation Impact) on average. This illustrates the strong agglomeration economies present in urban innovation and reinforces the current efforts in understanding innovation patterns and their implications for urban performance. Finally, we observe that agglomeration in innovation activity is due to two factors. The growth of total employment is linear, but the growth of innovative employment is superlinear, which is amplified in Innovation Districts.

Innovation Pipeline Strategy

The Innovation Pipeline is an analysis of the networks of talent and the seven phases of innovation to describe the research center, technology transfer center, and industry value chain. Research centers are departments within universities that conduct research on a specific topic or domain and can be visualized through the innovation pipeline. Technology Transfer Centers include, but are not limited to: Technology Transfer Programs, Startup Incubators and Accelerators.

Industry Value Chains and Industrial Liaison Strategy should be assessed throughout a given city. By completing the Innovation Pipeline Strategy analysis, the strengths, weaknesses, risks, and opportunities of the city were evaluated for selected urban regeneration projects. The results of the study will constitute the recommendations to strengthen the development of new innovations in a data-driven, evidence-based manner.

When a nascent innovation ecosystem reaches its maturity state, it tends to realize the multiplying effects of the geographic concentration and clustering of the knowledge economy dynamics. On average, the comparison between Innovation Intensity LogNormal, Innovation Performance (Pareto/Power Law), and Innovation Impact (Gamma) depicts the increasingly nonlinear amplifying effects of clustering knowledge-intensive activities: on average, innovation districts present 2.8 times higher concentration of knowledge-intensive activities per employee, thus producing 4 times higher innovation output per employee in terms of patents, new products, new services, new processes, and R&D, 16 times higher creation and availability of knowledge-intensive employment opportunities, and 25 times higher business revenue per resident.

Superlinear relationship between population, employment, and innovation (All USA Municipalities)

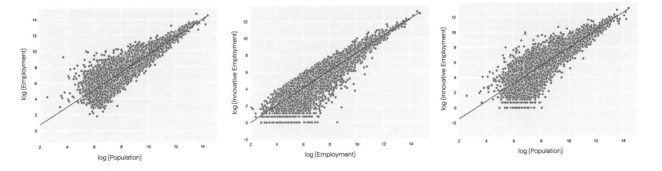

These results reveal that Innovation Districts systematically benefit from structural nonlinear innovation patterns as a result of the geographic aggregation of knowledge-intensive activities within urban environments. Representative examples of successful Innovation Districts include Kendall Square in Cambridge, Silicon Alley in NYC, 22@ in Barcelona, the Grand Canal Innovation District in Dublin, and the Pittsburgh Innovation District.

In order to strengthen the knowledge economy, Innovation District leaders need to chisel a new vision that focuses on an innovation strategy. There are many ways to increase the output of innovation materials within the Innovation District Area, but a key ingredient for the success of a given innovation district will be to consider how to better connect the sources of innovation (universities and research centers) with industry to help boost the internal production of new products and services. By completing an assessment of the strengths, weaknesses, risks and opportunities it is possible to create a strategic plan for how to move forward with the new vision for the city.

One key tool to assist with this process is Aretian's Innovation Pipeline. By linking the research activities in nearby universities with local industry it is possible to map out the connections between academic outputs of new innovation and how they can plug into the current economic performance of the city. This will also show the gaps that might be filled by new industry or startups that might help diversify the economic performance of the city.

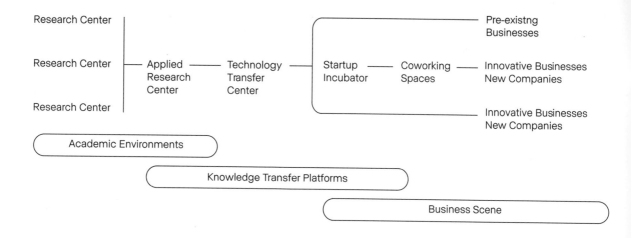

Innovation pipeline diagrams help identify the most critical needs of a given community. On the left hand side of the diagrams and quantitative measures we present the representative university research centers, whereas on the right hand side we locate the startups, most dynamic businesses, and high value added industries. Between them are the connecting institutions that can support the technology transfer process. The goal of this exercise is to determine what types of physical and intangible support would be most beneficial to the community based on the identification of promising new research and the design of buildings and architectural spaces, tailored to the industry and activity needs, to help transfer that new knowledge into a product aligned with market needs.

To best identify the key drivers of innovation within the community, the creation of research network graphs allows for the visualization of publications and patents within the academic community. By describing each innovation production process step by step, the natural hierarchies will emerge and help to inform the knowledge economy vision. Below is a representative network map of researchers throughout the University Research community. Such a generalizable framework allows for identifying the strengths, weaknesses, risks and opportunities of the research community, whilst informing space design, location intelligence, activity programming, and organizational strategies aiming to propel the local knowledge economy ecosystem.

The increasing superlinearity of innovation associated with population growth is further exacerbated by local urban and economic development interventions such as nurturing well-though-out innovation districts.

Conclusions and Insights

Urban Design Is a Plastic Manifestation of an Underlying Worldview

The perceived scaffolding of urban, architectural, and engineering design that makes up the built environment of urban settlements is a plastic, aesthetic, and functional manifestation of the underlying worldview of every society.

On the one hand, the morphological composition (city form) of an urban space reveals the *Weltanschauung*, values, and sense of beauty of a given society. The architectural forms, structural shapes, selected materials, street layouts, and activity programming constitute an ever-evolving dynamic system that can be analyzed through the lens of complex systems and network theory principles. The urban phenomena is the result of the dynamic relationship between city dwellers and the built environment they shape around them to inhabit. We can classify the creative class of a given society between artists and artisans. Artists combine the objective techniques and scientific approaches required to incept a work of art with the creative and subjective perception and sensitivity embedded in their design, by which they metaphorically communicate a sense of purpose, relationships, and values. In other words, artists create and advance culture, whereas artisans diffuse, propagate and convey an existing, inherited culture. In the realm of urban design, the resulting artifact is an always dynamic complex system where citizens interact, collaborate, and communicate with one another to solve the complex problems facing society.

On the other hand, the development of a network theory-based City Science analytical methodology enables us to evaluate the relationship between city form and space programming and the quality of life of citizens in an evidence-based, data-driven manner. By creating a series of measurable, benchmarkable, universal key performance metrics describing the urban design efficiency and sustainability, the accessibility to urban services and amenities from any given point of a city, and the economic dynamism enabling prosperity, we can ascertain the empirical relationships and point in the direction of potential underlying causal mechanisms. Such an approach permits not only an ontological classification of different urban development patterns based on their shared features and idiosyncratic characteristics, but also the development of predictive power, making it possible to reduce uncertainty and increase the quality of urban design, space programming, and economic development decision-making processes.

The analysis of the structural, causal relationships between city form and urban performance reveals to what extent and how a given urban design model contributes to or hinders the living opportunities, talents, and quality of life of citizens. The City Science methodology presented in this book is grounded on network theory and complex systems modeling, and it allows for disentangling the complex and subtle, delicate yet structural and causal relationship between the quality of a given urban space and the subjective experiences of people living within it.

The processes by which we can model any given city in terms of its networks of urban infrastructure design, industries, and talent can equip urban leaders with thorough analytical tools to inform accurate and insightful territorial diagnostics. They can also hint at both the types of best practices that, once tailored for a specific context and urban setting, can inform quality urban design solutions and the malpractice decisions that should proactively be avoided.

The establishment of a series of analogies between archetypal network growth patterns and urban design strategies illuminates not only the morphological properties and dynamics inherent to each type of development, but also the aesthetic personality and subjective impact on the individual and social psyche. The Small World City, the Radial City, the Linear City, the Reticular City, the Organic City, the Atomized City, the Random City, the Garden City, the Monumental City, and the Fractal City tend to present a myriad of topological, morphological facets, which crystallize in their fractality, entropy, and overall aesthetics.

Great masters of thought such as Kant, Schopenhauer, Heleno Saña, and Georges-Louis Leclerc, Comte de Buffon, already suggested the intimate yet subtle and nontrivial relationship between aesthetics and ethics. Kant's *Beobachtungen über das Gefühl des Schönen und Erhabenen* deliciously unravels the subtle differences between beauty and sublimity and traces the delicate connection between the intrinsic nature of a person, collective, or space and the aesthetic manifestation it projects outwards. For its part, Schopenhauer's *Die Welt als Wille und Vorstellung* doubles down on Kant's intuition and asserts that behind any aesthetic projection there is an underlying worldview grounded on certain ethical principles, even if assumed as a matter of fact. Heleno Saña enriched that hypothesis by hinting in the direction of suggesting that every person exudes a particular vibe or aura, which, more often than not, vocalizes in a visual manner his or her personality and values. Finally, we can cite the Comte de Buffon, postulating in his celebrated proposition that "Le style c'est l'homme même". Similar conclusions can be drawn when we observe the intimate, yet often shared, subjective impression that a façace, a solemn column structure, a beautiful window, a thriving street, or a beautifully designed city projects onto the people who visit a particular site.

Moreover, the ontological classification of city development patterns and the ability to measure their impact on the quality of life of citizens does not only present material consequences, such as inducing or facilitating certain types of relationships and socialization; it also enlightens the subjective experiences that people perceive when they visit or live in a city, district, borough, or architectural space. The systematic analysis of 100 global cities presented in this book portrays the specific strengths, weaknesses, risks, and opportunities of different patterns of urban and economic development strategies and how to extract generalizable, global insights that can illuminate any given urban development problem.

Cities as Three Dimensional Complex Systems

Modeling the Underlying Urban Networks Impacting the Quality of City Life

Three core urban networks define the idiosyncratic nature of cities and the quality of the human networks that inhabit and operate within them: the networks of talent, industries, and urban design. The first two urban systems summarize the nature and qualities of the structural relationships between citizens and visitors alike. The last one describes the physical properties of the built environment that surrounds us and subtly conditions our individual and social psyche. The higher the quality of those three urban networks, the higher the chances of a given person to fruitfully thrive within the community. The resulting qualities of such society can be indirectly estimated by means of urban performance metrics, which quantitatively measure the quality of the three urban networks, in terms of their urbanization efficiency and quality, the collective knowhow and ability to access critical services and amenities, and the underlying social networks enabling for the knowledge economy to advance, hence creating new products and services that propel the prosperity, the human potential, and the quality of life of the community.

Generally speaking, each archetypal urban development pattern embodies a set of aesthetic, moral, and functional values that can be modeled and better understood. However, two of those systems deserve close attention: the Lognormal-based model and the Scale-Free urban network. Lognormal and Poisson-based urban development patterns are the most frequently observed city design typology, since they describe organic growth patterns that do not require substantial skill or design qualities. Organic growth models tend to respond to hyperlocal needs at the expense of the overall urban system quality, and generally speaking they embrace and induce an oligarchic worldview and relationship pattern. Oligarchic systems are very often encountered, yet they tend to replicate inherited inequalities and present two major setbacks: they tend to both marginalize the most vulnerable segments of society, whilst hindering the potential of the most virtuous and capable citizens. Scale-Free urban networks, on the contrary, present two major advantages: they both inclusively integrate the most vulnerable segments of a given society, while empowering the most talented and promising individuals. Scale-Free urban networks tend to be structured around highly fractal, self-similar systems, composed of nested hierarchies of individuals dynamically collaborating within a merit-based system.

The stronger the self-similar features of an urban network, the higher the chances a city will produce the conditions that facilitate the development of a fulfilled and free human existence. Conversely, the stronger the organic features, the more oligarchic a specific society will tend to be. In order for a society to excel at its duty to create the conditions for citizens to thrive, urban leaders can contribute to introduce design interventions and decision-making management principles aiming to reinforce the self-similar, fractal, Scale-Free like nature of the three urban systems: the networks of talent, industries, and urban infrastructure. Whenever we introduce subtle yet deliberate changes in an urban system, aiming to increase the self-similar properties of the 3 urban networks, we are indirectly contributing to raise the standards of living and human potential of the broader community. The juxtaposition of highly fractal networks of talent, industries and urban design maximizes the chances of broadening the set of possibilities and conditions enabling each and every citizen to achieve his or her fullest potential.

The deployment of network science-based City Science modeling techniques permits to illuminate the analytical diagnostic of an urban system, and discern the inherent strengths, weaknesses, risks, and opportunities affecting such society. Whereas the universality of the methodology is solvent to illustrate the challenges and potential solutions of any community, the ultimate design and management solutions will need to be tailored for each community, context, and time.

The novel geospatial City Science methodology presented in this book allows us to evaluate the relationship between city form, urban dynamics, and urban performance. By analyzing the impact of urban topology, morphology, and scale on human behavior, we can infer how the different city form typologies impact the performance of every urban area. Our city science mathematical model enables us to evaluate two-dimensional architectural space systems (street layouts, orientation patterns, network hierarchies), three-dimensional systems (building form, height distributions), and scale/density levels, as well as other time-based urban form and placemaking factors that impact the human experience and the overall success and enjoyment of a city, with a particular focus on the knowledge economy.

City Design: Urban Performance Insights and Learnings

When evaluating the structural relationship between city form features and urban performance, the formulation of five core hypotheses led to analogous discoveries illuminating the causal mechanisms behind design and function, and reveal new pathways to be explored in integrating art/creativity and analysis/rational, scientific studies.

1) City form typologies and their representative features (urban topology, morphology, entropy and scale) have a distinct and structural effect on urban performance, with respect to urbanization efficiency, access to urban amenities, and the knowledge economy. The systematic analogy between city form archetypes (Small World, Radial, Linear, Reticular, Garden, Monumental, Organic, Random, Atomized and Fractal City) and their respective network types allows for performing specific network theory-based studies, evaluating aspects such as average node degree, node tier hierarchy levels, triadic closure mechanisms, clustering effects, betweenness and connectivity, node and edge/street centrality, reach, and gravity, network circuity and legibility, urbanization and architectural efficiency, and the sublinear and superlinear advantages associated with urban density and compactness. For example, urban compactness tends to have vast structural effects on the subjective urban experience. Every time we double population density, we obtain on average 19% gains in urbanization efficiency by means of economies of scale, and higher access to urban services and amenities. Thus, by doubling urban density, we attain the same quality standards of living whilst observing a reduction of material infrastructure expenditure and costs down to 81% compared to the original investment.

2) Fractality as a proxy for urban design quality and architectural harmony: urban form fractality index is positively correlated with urban infrastructure efficiency, and the fractal city typology is the most efficient out of the 10 types in terms of urban infrastructure economies of scale and superlinear social interaction patterns. City Form Fractality is the most salient and analytically informative urban design feature when it comes to predicting urbanization efficiency. The fractal layout is the most sublinear of all typologies in terms of material infrastructure. This implies that it is the most efficient in terms of use of space and materials for construction. We observe that when we double City Form Fractality (2x growth), there is on average a 31% superlinear increase in urbanization efficiency and social interaction superlinearity, including the multiplying effects of the knowledge economy, all else being equal. Hence, highly self-similar urban design patterns (urban fractality >70%, and ideally >85%) are recommended in order to foster highly fruitful and fertile human dynamics within urban environments. A combination of 2D topological and 3D morphological features, as well as thoughtful space programming and zoning strategies can help achieve highly fractal architecture and urban design configurations.

City Form fractality presents a superlinear relationship with urban betweenness (centrality and connectivity), circuity, straightness, closeness, as well as average node intersections.

3) Fractal urban form patterns achieve a more egalitarian distribution of amenities than other network types. Worldwide, only 4.5% of urban areas within global cities tend to satisfy to some extent the 15-Minute City standards. However, these quality standards are a desirable, realistic and attainable goal. The self-similar properties of fractal urban design patterns tend to provide a harmonic polycentrism morphology capable of presenting the utmost efficient and desirable geospatial distribution of amenities, in terms of education, healthcare, sustenance, culture, leisure, entertainment, mobility and public transit. The optimal urban performance is achieved whenever the most basic services tend to be ubiquitous and within walkable reach, whereas the more sophisticated activities and services tend to be clustered, hence realizing the multiplying effects associated with highly complex human networks. A self-similar urban fabric and space programming rationale benefits from the embedded, nested programmatic hierarchies of Fractal cities, where citizens experience a broader sense of opportunity, diversity, and quality of services. Every time we double urban design fractality, we obtain approximately 31% gains in terms of access to amenities, from sustenance, to healthcare and education, all the way through public transit, cultural and urban services.

4) Entropy as a proxy for a balanced equilibrium between urban design liberty and regularity / efficiency: intermediate levels of urban form entropy present the optimal urban development efficiency performance overall. The overall degree of city form regularity or specificity can be estimated by means of the urban form entropy metric. Highly rigid three dimensional urban design patterns characterized by simple replicable patterns present low levels of entropy, whereas highly idiosyncratic, unique and unpredictable city design morphologies present high entropy levels. Optimal values of urban form entropy tend to be observed in the bracket between 45% and 55%.

5) The geographic aggregation of knowledge-intensive activities in physical proximity and structured with a hierarchical innovation network logic tends to facilitate fruitful interaction, hence producing multiplying effects benefitting the overall urban economy. Generally speaking, the average Innovation Intensity tends to oscillate between 5% and 20% in developed countries, with an average around 12%. Those values fluctuate around 5% or less within developing countries. The combination of urban renewal and smart economic development strategies can help attain Innovation Intensity values of over 35% in innovation districts, potentially reaching upwards of 85% around their core area. A hierarchical clustering strategy, based upon connecting within physical proximity applied research centers,

innovation centers, startup incubators, headquarters of leading knowledge intensive firms, and their core network of suppliers can help amalgamate the appropriate combination of critical mass & hierarchical network logic that is required to unleash very potent multiplying effects: on average, innovation districts achieve 4x more innovations per capita (new products, services, articles, books, patents, inventions, artistic creations), 15x higher access to knowledge intensive employment opportunities, and 25x higher business revenue per capita, hence contributing to raise the quality standards of living for nearby citizens and visitors alike.

Those discoveries open the door to deliberately inform urban development strategies by inducing network mutation and upgrade decisions and urban system quality rising through exogenous shocks and local interventions. Further research can illuminate how network science strategies such as average node degree increase, node tier leap, urban node clustering, and triadic closure dynamics can contribute to consummate the deliberate transition from Poisson and Lognormal-based urban systems towards high quality, virtuous self-similar Scale-Free urban networks, characterized by their harmonic polycentrism.

Fractal Metropolis: How to Incept Inclusive Distributed Prosperity by Means of Harmonic Polycentrism

The recent advances achieved in the realm of City Science research allow us to identify 10 main urban form or design typologies, all of which can be modeled as complex network systems. Each type of city belongs to a family of urban networks, depending on its two-dimensional topology, three-dimensional morphology, level of urban entropy, and scale. We subsequently found that the formal properties of a city have an impact on the dynamics of urban systems, which in turn structurally condition urban performance indicators. Therefore, each type of city can be described, both visually and mathematically, by means of networks in constant flux.

Through modeling based on network theory and validated by empirical data, we can measure the performance level of each part of a city or metropolitan area in great detail, in terms of their principal urban systems: talent network, economy and creation of wealth, value chains by business sector, efficiency of mobility, energy and water systems, etc. Among other things, this modeling allows us to assess the extent to which each of the 10 urban design types affects, facilitates, or hinders efforts to capitalize on the multiplying benefits of the strategic aggregation of knowledge-intensive activities.

In general, each type has advantages and disadvantages inherent to its structure. However, some urban models possess properties that are qualitatively superior to others.

Ten core urban form design typologies have been identified based on similar city form features, which helped to establish urban performance metrics that were used to define a set of urban performance KPIs. Research results show that (1) City typologies have a structural effect on urban performance, (2) City form fractality or self-similarity is a key urban form component when evaluating the relationship between urban form and urban performance KPIs. Highly fractal urban design patterns are the most efficient in terms of material infrastructure, (3) Fractal grids achieve a more egalitarian distribution of amenities than other network types, (4) intermediate degrees of urban form entropy present the optimal urban development efficiency performance overall, and (5) Hierarchical space programming strategies for innovation-related activities operating within physical proximity and medium-high levels of density tend to facilitate the creation of thriving knowledge economy ecosystems, hence creating distributed prosperity and higher standards of living for citizens.

Fractal Metropolis: Incepting Inclusive Prosperity by Means of Harmonic Polycentrism

In summary, the urban and economic development quality standards that enable the inception of distributed prosperity are rarely met by cities and urban areas today, although they are feasible, attainable and desirable. A key takeaway from our analysis shows the power of how mathematical modeling can help to address specific design challenges of urban environments by evaluating each component of cities individually and finding common patterns between different city types. This allows us to understand and learn from the diagnostics technique and use it for recommendations in the future. Because no city is exactly of a single type, it is therefore important to have a tool that can respond to the complexity of real-world examples, where cities are made of multiple types blended together. Therefore, this type of analysis can be helpful for us to better understand how our cities perform and the best way to make interventions to improve the quality of life in each context. Moving forward, a core challenge will be to identify what types of urban design and placemaking interventions can reinforce the fractal condition of any given city type, as well as what types of network science analyses (such as geographic clustering, reach and gravity indexes, triadic closure, strength of weak ties, catchment area analyses, betweenness, etc.) can inform exogenous shocks in the system to raise the overall quality of life. This will boost the chances for cities to increase their ability to serve their citizens by incepting inclusive growth, thus benefiting the broader society.

In conclusion, by harmonically integrating evidence-based city science insights with traditional urban design and economic development strategies, urban leaders can shape innovative and resilient metropolitan areas, thus increasing the quality of life of citizens by means of combining three articulated strategies: (1) an **Urban Design Vision for a Fractal Metropolis Strategy**, aiming to increase the quality of life of citizens and achieve universal access to services, while capitalizing on the exponential benefits of the geographic concentration of knowledge-intensive activities; (2) **an Economic Development Vision, grounded on an evidence-based Smart Specialization** to activate the dormant capabilities of collective knowhow by strengthening industry-specific value chains and informing product diversification and sophistication strategies; and (3) a network-theory-driven **Innovation Strategy based on envisioning, designing, building, and nurturing a Network of Innovation Districts**, liberating the potential of the local talent by geographically clustering knowledge-intensive activities and linking research with knowledge transfer and production at scale.

The great challenge we now face is to determine, for each city and context, what kind of urban layout design interventions, density levels, building form, capacity, and heights, smart location and design of innovation hubs for boosting the knowledge economy, geographical distribution of services, and mobility model structures should be prioritized to reinforce this fractal condition, consolidate the standards of quality of the '15-Minute City' model and, ultimately, outline strategies that will allow us to achieve a sustainable development pattern. Such goals can be achieved by harmonizing a vibrant knowledge economy able to ignite prosperity cycles, with a resilient urban development model, thus increasing the quality of life of citizens. A deeper understanding of the underlying properties of an urban system enables us to identify the types of interventions that can potentially transform the nature of the structural properties of the networks that systematically impact our lives. By integrating art and science in city design and urban development, we can tailor the design and decision making for every city and cultural context, hence deliberately chiseling the built environment so that we subtly yet solvently contribute to unleash the most noble latent forces in society, thus contributing to raise the quality of life of citizens, and create more prosperous, egalitarian, and freer communities around the world.

Atlas of Global Cities

City Population

City Area

City Density

Metropolitan Population

Metropolitan Area

Metropolitan Density

City Form Typologies

City Profile describing the urban planning and social evolution of a given city, as well as the cornerstones defining its personality, values, economic character, and aesthetic culture.

1st percentile

100th percentile

Topology:
The topological features dictate mobility patterns and influence the relative centrality and connectivity of every node within a city.

Morphology:
The morphological features condition the urban experience, social interaction, access to services, and human dynamics.

The urban topology and morphology combined structure the urban fabric of the built environment, and shape city-wide human dynamics and performance such as the level of self-similarity or fractality, the entropy, and urbanization efficiency indicators such as centrality, straightness, closeness, betweenness, circuity, and compactness.

Fractality:
The higher the values, the higher the urbanization efficiency, access to services, and multiplying effects of the knowledge economy.

Entropy:
Intermediate entropy values tend to achieve the most desirable urbanization efficiency, access to services, and multiplying effects of the knowledge.

Betweenness:
The higher the betweenness, the higher the urban centrality, and the most vibrant and fruitful the social interaction patterns.

Amsterdam

North Holland
Netherlands

City Population
921,402

City Area
219 km²

City Density
4,201.18 /km²

Metropolitan Population
2,480,394

Metropolitan Area
2,580 km²

Metropolitan Density
961.30 /km²

City Form Typologies
**Small World / Radial,
Atomized, Organic, Garden**

Amsterdam was originally founded as a modest fishing village along the banks of the Amstel River, eventually growing into a thriving fluvial port. A radial-organic canal network enabled the consolidation of an efficient hub for freight trade, thus cementing the future prosperity of the city and allowing for its sophistication and embellishment. The pragmatic political stance adopted by its citizens, and their openness to international trade and knowledge exchange, permitted the emergence of a global naval thalassocracy. Amsterdam's port became a global trade hub, fueling the urban expansion beyond its original walls due to accelerated population growth. A network of canals was dug, and the beautifully crafted gabled houses became the emblem of Dutch architecture. Amsterdam's canal belt was extended to make way for the industrial-era neighborhoods (Jordaan). The hydric/orographic conditions surrounding Amsterdam required the development of sophisticated design techniques to build the intricate network of bridges, dams, roads and stations required to overcome the flooding risks. The Amsterdamse Bos provided a major green corridor, connecting a series of residential suburbs as the population continued to grow amid the post-war repair efforts. Contemporary Amsterdam has embraced an ambitious urban agenda, aspiring to position the vibrant Dutch city as a technology and sustainable development champion.

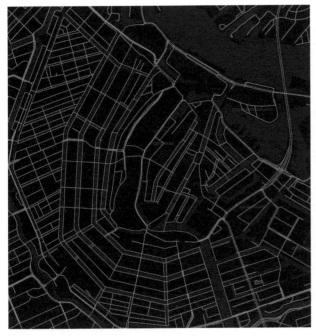

Athens

Attica
Greece

City Population
643,452

City Area
39 km²

City Density
16,514.01 /km²

Metropolitan Population
3,154,463

Metropolitan Area
2,929 km²

Metropolitan Density
1,077.08 /km²

City Form Typologies
Monumental, Reticular, Organic, Linear

Before becoming the urban cradle of Western civilization, the ancient city of Athens grew around the majestic Acropolis, crowned by iconic architectural structures such as the Parthenon and the Erechtheion. The Hellenic city became the leader of Greek civilization, adopting a distinct combination of Small World and Monumental urban design typologies, such as its narrow streets, open marketplaces (Agora) and residential areas. Athens emerged as the foremost center for culture, education and democracy across the Hellas, eventually becoming one of the very first European cities to adopt Christianity and remaining a leading city throughout the Roman and Byzantine periods. The combination of Greek, Roman, and Byzantine architectural elements created a synthesis of European Mediterranean urban styles, populated by theaters, religious temples, aqueducts and public baths. After the fall of Constantinople, the city experienced urban decline under Ottoman rule, suffering infrastructure damage and neglect, hence leading to population decrease and suburban sprawl. Elected as the new capital of independent Greece, Athens underwent an intense modernization process, and remarkable planning efforts were conducted to transform the city into a European-style capital via the construction of grand boulevards filled with modern style buildings. Contemporary Athens is experiencing renewed urban expansion, involving suburban garden city growth and state-of-the-art transportation.

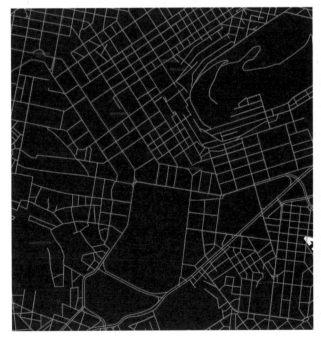

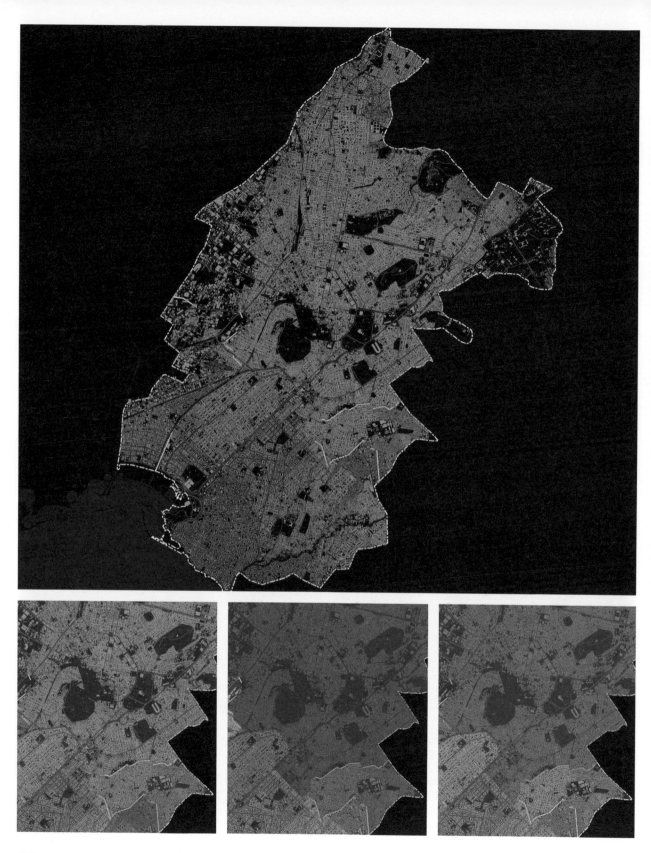

Atlanta

Georgia
United States of America

City Population
490,270

City Area
350 km²

City Density
1,398.85 /km²

Metropolitan Population
6,222,908

Metropolitan Area
22,489 km²

Metropolitan Density
276.72 /km²

City Form Typologies
Random, Organic, Garden

Atlanta, Georgia, founded in 1837 as Terminus, has exhibited a rich tapestry of economic and urban evolution. Initially conceived as a terminus point for the Western & Atlantic Railroad, Atlanta's economic inception was deeply intertwined with rail transportation. The Civil War accelerated its prominence when General William T. Sherman's infamous 1864 siege illuminated Atlanta's strategic significance. Reconstruction saw Atlanta rise, metaphorically, from its ashes as it embraced manufacturing and commerce, becoming a regional economic hub. In the 20th century, Atlanta burgeoned as a national center for commerce. The establishment of Hartsfield-Jackson International Airport in 1926, which would eventually become the world's busiest airport, exemplified its deepening connection to global trade.

Civil Rights movements of the 1960s further intensified Atlanta's national prominence as figures like Martin Luther King Jr. underscored the city's importance in advocating for racial justice. By the turn of the 21st century, urban renewal projects such as the BeltLine — an initiative to repurpose old railway tracks into trails and parks — highlighted Atlanta's continued commitment to urban innovation and sustainable development. Atlanta's trajectory from a railroad terminus to an international beacon of commerce and civil rights epitomizes its adaptive economic and urban dynamism.

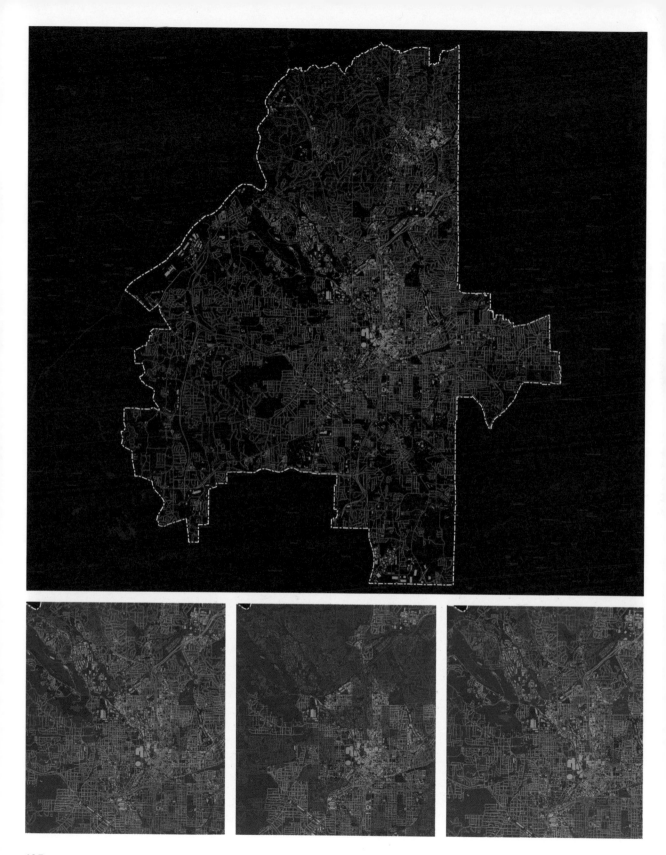

Auckland

Auckland
New Zealand

City Population
1,440,300

City Area
607 km²

City Density
2,372.43 /km²

Metropolitan Population
1,673,220

Metropolitan Area
4,941 km²

Metropolitan Density
338.63 /km²

City Form Typologies
Atomized, Random, Organic, Reticular, Garden

European explorers and traders arrived in Auckland in the late 18th century, where they found indigenous Māori settlements amid a privileged environment composed of the Auckland isthmus and the natural harbors of Waitematā-Manukau. Officially founded as a British colony in 1840, Auckland soon became New Zealand's capital. The infrastructure needs associated with the region's maritime trade potential resulted in a strongly atomized urban growth pattern devoted to providing preferential access to transportation routes. Queen Street became the main artery of the city, hosting critical governmental institutions . Taking advantage of its privileged location, Auckland canalized the leading commerce flows in the region and become a major maritime trading hub. The waterfront façade was rapidly populated by warehouses and docks, reinforcing the atomized nature of the city. The housing scarcity brought about by the rapid development was addressed by expanding the city's footprint into the harbor and suburbs (Ponsonby, Parnell). The Post-War intense suburbanization process and the articulation of a series of motorways and bridges promoted automobile-centric development and lifestyles (Auckland Harbour Bridge). Recently, Auckland has been embellished with modern architecture and reinvigorated with high-rise buildings, and areas like Wynyard Quarter and Britomart have been revitalized thanks to improvements in public transportation.

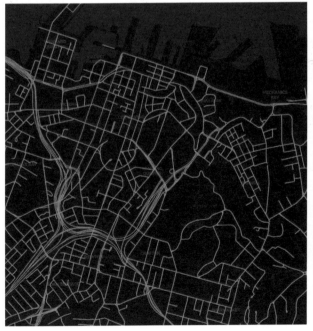

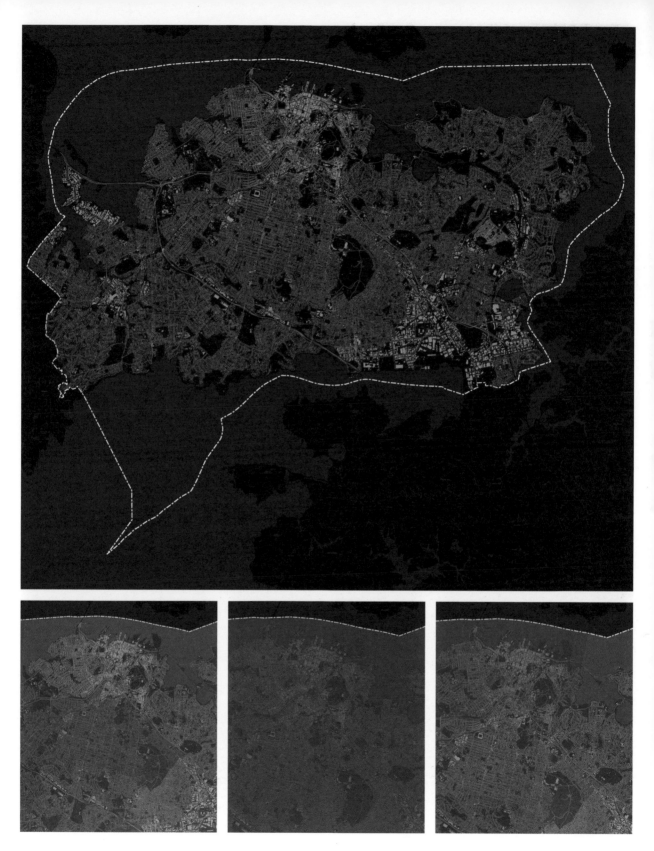

Austin

Texas
United States of America

City Population
974,447

City Area
829 km²

City Density
1,175.96 /km²

Metropolitan Population
2,421,115

Metropolitan Area
11,100 km²

Metropolitan Density
218.12 /km²

City Form Typologies
Reticular, Organic, Atomized, Random, Garden

Austin, situated along the Colorado River, has seen a multifaceted trajectory in its urban and economic development. Originally settled by pioneers in the 1830s, it was named the capital of the Republic of Texas in 1839, a move that propelled its early growth. The anchoring of the University of Texas at Austin in 1883 further solidified its significance, both academically and economically, introducing a student population and fostering a climate of intellectual exchange. Throughout the 20th century, Austin underwent a transformation from a predominantly governmental and educational hub to becoming an epicenter for technology and innovation, earning the moniker "Silicon Hills" by the 1990s due to the influx of tech companies. This shift was predicated on deliberate urban planning decisions, such as the development of research parks, and was boosted by a synergy between academic research, from the University and the entrepreneurial spirit of its residents. Recent decades have seen Austin grapple with challenges like rapid population growth, housing affordability, and infrastructural stress. Nevertheless, its rich history, combined with a forward-looking economic strategy, positions Austin as a pivotal city in discussions of American urban development.

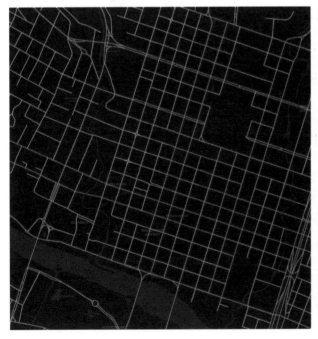

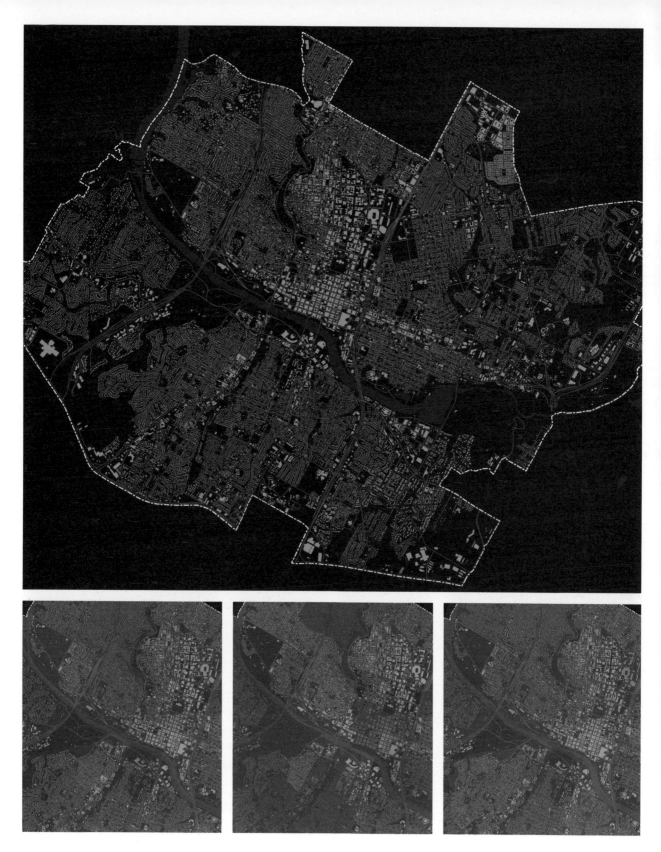

Bangkok

Central Thailand
Thailand

City Population
11,069,982

City Area
1,569 km²

City Density
7,056.92 /km²

Metropolitan Population
16,255,900

Metropolitan Area
7,762 km²

Metropolitan Density
2,094.29 /km²

City Form Typologies
Organic, Atomized, Random, Radial

The urban and economic development of Bangkok, the capital city of Thailand is intricately interwoven with its historical, political, and social transformations. Founded in the late 18th century, Bangkok rapidly emerged as the principal trade and political hub of the Siamese Kingdom, attracting migrants and foreign traders alike. By the early 20th century, Bangkok's economy had begun shifting towards modern industrialization, with the establishment of infrastructure projects such as railways and roads fostering greater urban concentration. The mid-20th century witnessed Bangkok's metamorphosis into a sprawling metropolis, exacerbated by rural-urban migration and global economic changes. The 1980s and 1990s were particularly transformative, as Thailand's economy was liberalized, leading to significant direct foreign investments. The city became a nexus for multinational corporations and the burgeoning tourism industry. Yet, this rapid growth also brought urban challenges, including environmental degradation and informal settlements. Recent decades have witnessed concerted urban planning efforts to remedy some of these issues, emphasizing sustainable development and public transportation. Nonetheless, Bangkok continues to grapple with its dynamic urban fabric, reflecting its multifaceted economic trajectory.

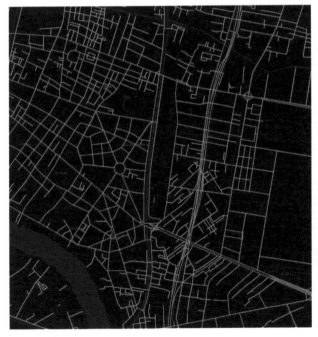

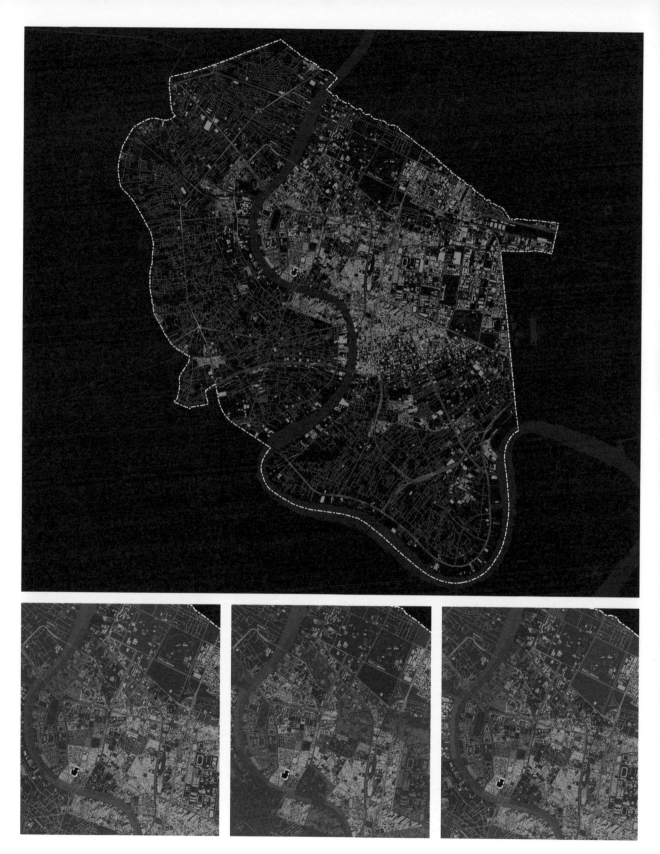

Barcelona

Catalonia
Spain

City Population
1,620,343

City Area
101 km²

City Density
15,979.71 /km²

Metropolitan Population
5,687,356

Metropolitan Area
4,268 km²

Metropolitan Density
1,332.56 /km²

City Form Typologies
Fractal, Organic, Small World, Monumental, Reticular, Linear, Random

The Roman colony of Barcino was founded by Emperor Augustus, following a military castrum pattern involving enclosing walls and a *cardo* and *decumanus* defining the reticular layout. Medieval Barcelona underwent substantial expansion, with the construction of monumental landmarks such as the Barcelona cathedral, and other singular buildings spread across the Gothic Quarter, characterized by its narrow and sinuous streets.

In the Renaissance and Baroque periods Barcelona experienced an architectural revival. However, the 18th century postwar restrictions imposed by the absolutist regime severely damaged the city's expansion potential, giving rise to one of the densest cities in Europe. The Eixample district envisioned by urban planner Ildefons Cerdà introduced a revolutionary fractal pattern, combining nested hierarchies of streets and buildings with egalitarian, octagonal blocks, following Hygienist principles, and inspiring iconic landmarks of Catalan Modernist architecture. The city's development suffered the consequences of severe malpractice during Franco's dictatorship, with the emergence of low-quality organic/random patterns, but it experienced a rebirth under the 1976 metropolitan plan, which aspired to seamlessly connect heterogeneous patterns by adopting design interventions aiming to regenerate the urban fabric while integrating the city's waterfront façade with the booming urban metropolis.

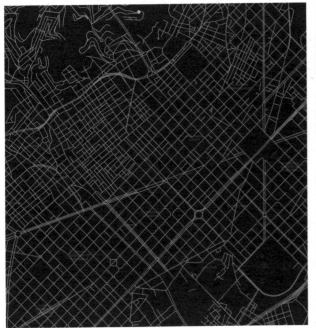
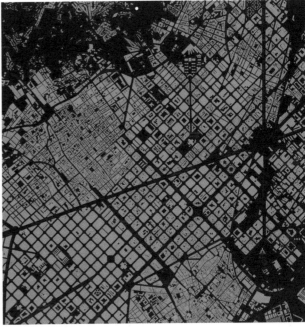

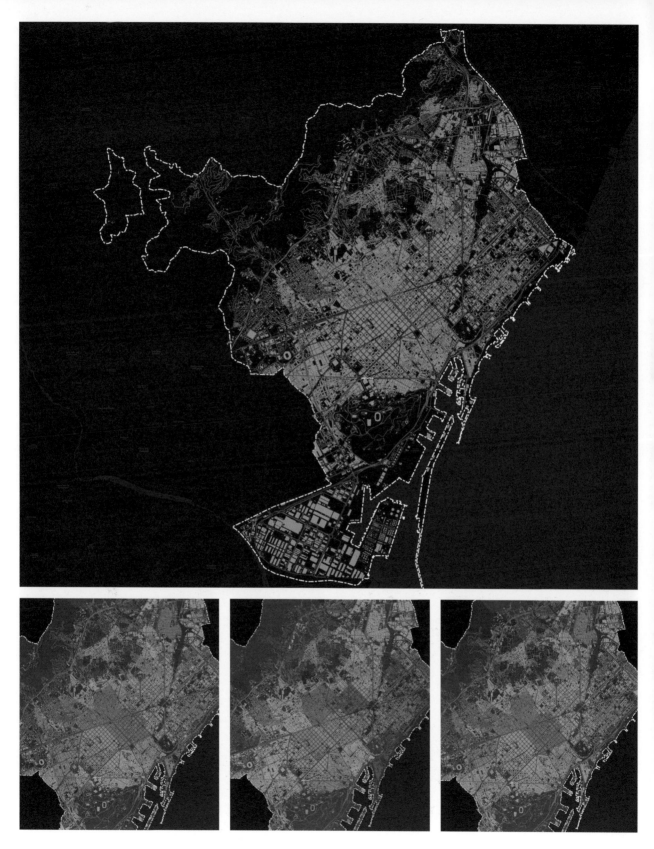

Beijing
Tongzhou
China

City Population
21,766,214

City Area
4,567 km²

City Density
4,765.98 /km²

Metropolitan Population
22,366,547

Metropolitan Area
16,808 km²

Metropolitan Density
1,330.72 /km²

City Form Typologies
**Monumental,
Reticular / Organic, Radial,
Random**

Beijing's Tongzhou District serves as an illuminating case study in urban economic evolution, reflecting China's broader trajectory of development. Historically, Tongzhou played a significant role in Beijing's water transportation due to its strategic location at the confluence of the Grand Canal and several other rivers, fostering trade and commerce for centuries. In the era of the Ming and Qing Dynasties, it became a grain transportation hub, connecting the southern and northern parts of the country. However, by the 20th century, as Beijing burgeoned, Tongzhou's prominence waned, overshadowed by the capital's rapid urban expansion. The district underwent significant transformation in the late 20th century, with the Chinese government initiating several infrastructure projects to decentralize Beijing's core functions. The unveiling of the "Beijing Sub-center" plan in the 2010s signaled the district's resurgence. This strategic vision sought to transform Tongzhou into an administrative, cultural, and ecological hub to alleviate Beijing's urban pressures, particularly its population density and traffic congestion. Recent urban developments, such as the establishment of new government offices, cultural centers, and the expansion of the Beijing subway to Tongzhou, have begun to shift economic and administrative functions from Beijing's core to this periphery, marking the district's latest phase of urban revitalization.

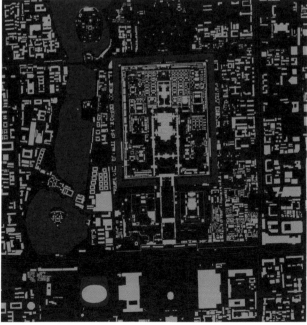

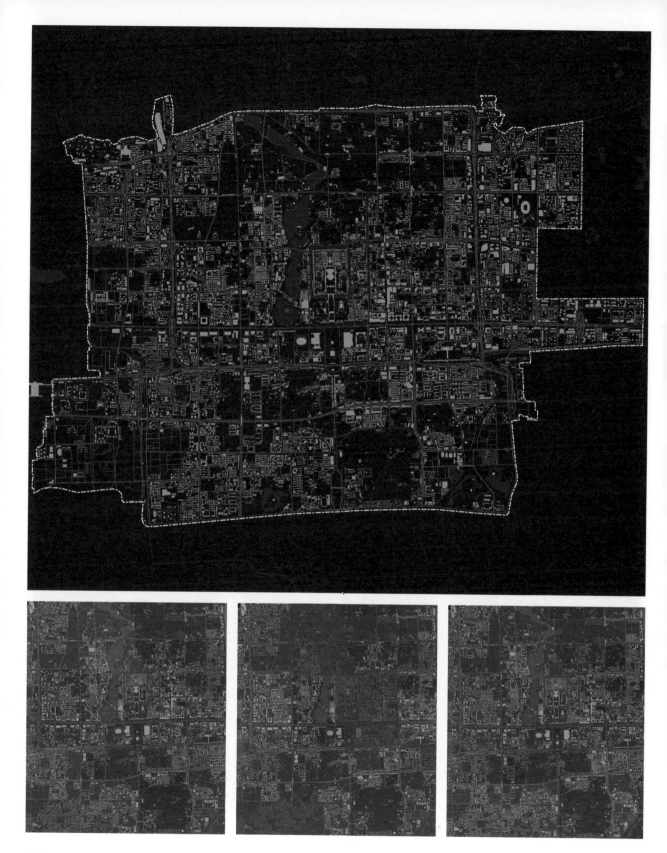

Beirut

Beirut
Lebanon

City Population
1,916,100

City Area
67 km²

City Density
28,598.51 /km²

Metropolitan Population
2,421,354

Metropolitan Area
200 km²

Metropolitan Density
12,106.77 /km²

City Form Typologies
Organic, Random, Small World

Beirut, the capital of Lebanon and its largest city, boasts a rich tapestry of economic and urban development that reflects its ancient and modern history. Originally a Phoenician city-state dating back more than 5,000 years, Beirut's strategic coastal location made it a valuable port and trading hub for empires such as the Romans, Byzantines, and Ottomans. This historical significance laid the foundations for Beirut's importance in the Levantine region. In the 20th century, following its independence from the French mandate in 1943, Beirut witnessed a rapid urbanization process, transforming it into a commercial and banking powerhouse in the Middle East. Notably, the 1950s and 1960s saw the city become the "Paris of the Middle East" due to its vibrant cultural, intellectual, and financial activities. The Lebanese Civil War (1975-1990), however, drastically altered its urban fabric, causing significant infrastructural damage and population displacement. Post-war reconstruction efforts in the 1990s under the Solidere project aimed to revitalize the city center but were met with criticisms of erasing historical authenticity in favor of commercial interests. In recent years, Beirut's urban and economic challenges have been compounded by political instability, the influx of Syrian refugees, and the tragic 2020 port explosion, while also underscoring the city's resilience and continual evolution in the face of adversity.

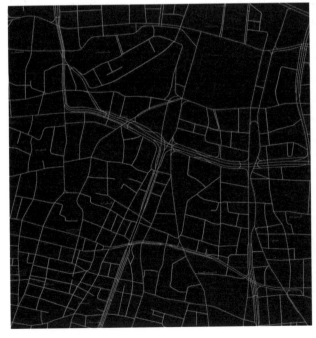

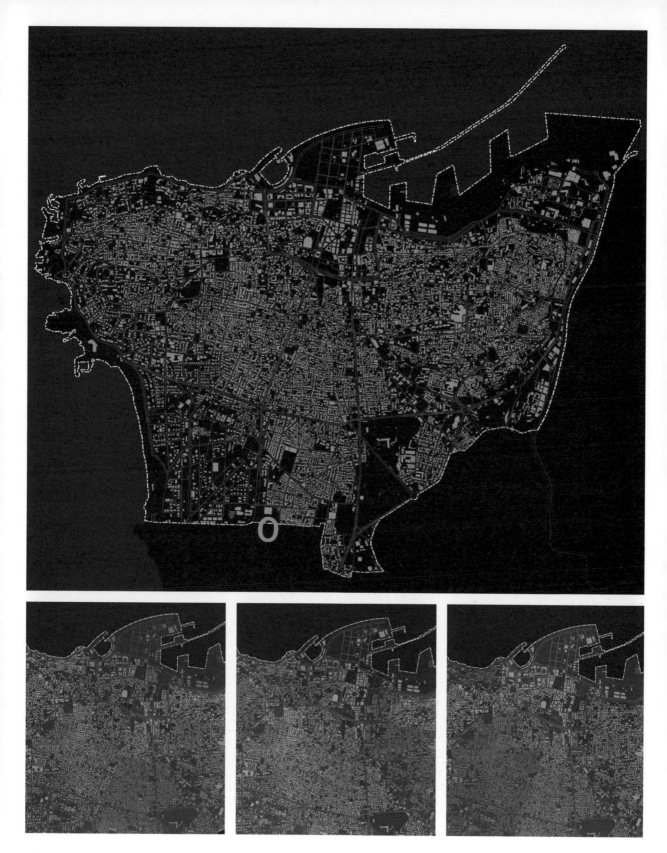

Berlin

Berlin
Germany

City Population
3,574,000

City Area
891 km²

City Density
4,009.87 /km²

Metropolitan Population
6,144,600

Metropolitan Area
30,546 km²

Metropolitan Density
201.16 /km²

City Form Typologies
Monumental, Atomized, Garden, Linear, Random

Medieval Berlin was founded as a small trading settlement, which progressively morphed into a fortified medieval town formed by narrow streets, city walls and strategic gates. Berlin's monumental heritage came into being primarily as a result of the potency of the Prussian Kingdom, whose monarchs promoted the construction of the Unter den Linden Boulevard. At the height of its imperial expansion, the city experienced a process of growth and modernization, following rapid industrialization patterns, and ultimately became the capital of the newly unified German Empire. The new city embraced the construction of grand boulevards, major national railway stations, and political landmarks. The collapse of the totalitarian Nazi regime as a result of its military defeat during World War II led to the dramatic division of the city between 1949-1989. The wall built in 1961 at the height of the Cold War divided Berlin and violently split the city into two confronted halves. East Berlin adopted Marxist-influenced urban planning (large-scale impersonal housing projects like Karl-Marx-Allee), whereas West Berlin saw unique developments characterized by Modernist architecture and became home to a vibrant counterculture scene. After the fall of the Berlin Wall and the reunification of Germany, Berlin began a broad integration, urban renewal and reconstruction process involving the revitalization of the Brandenburg Gate and the Berlin Hauptbahnhof.

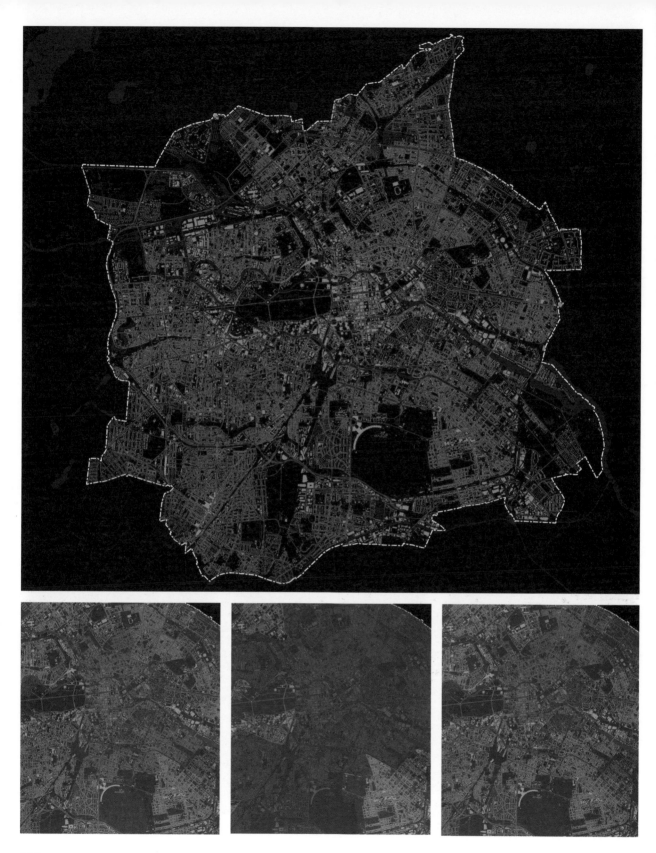

Bilbao

Basque Country
Spain

City Population
346,405

City Area
42 km²

City Density
8,347.11 /km²

Metropolitan Population
1,037,847

Metropolitan Area
500 km²

Metropolitan Density
2,074.86 /km²

City Form Typologies
Atomized, Linear, Small World, Organic, Garden

Bilbao began as a small medieval fishing village, structured around a modest urban layout formed by narrow streets leading to a local fluvial port along the Nervión River. The city evolved into a trading center under the Spanish crown from the 15th century. The Bourbon reforms implemented throughout the 18th century spurred urban and port developments driven by the efforts to shape a centralized infrastructure network. Bilbao embraced liberal reforms during the 19th century, becoming a pioneering Industrial Revolution town and stronghold. The city saw a significant shift due to rapid mechanization, a vibrant steel metal manufacturing industry, a financial hub, and a constellation of factories shaping its urban landscape. Atomized city form developments along the riverbed of the Nervión-Ibaizabal fluvial system were combined with a Small World structure, expanded by means of organic and garden city neighborhoods. Bilbao suffered from post-industrial decline in the latter 20th century, experiencing urban deterioration and the closing of industries. The ambitious urban renewal plan envisioned in the 1990s gave rise to distinctive landmarks such as Frank Gehry's Guggenheim Museum, aiming to transform neglected industrial areas into amiable public spaces (Abandoibarra), accompanied by a significant transportation upgrade (metro and airport), often referred to as the "Bilbao effect".

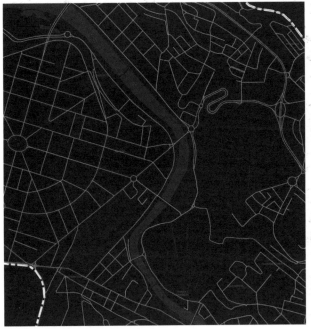

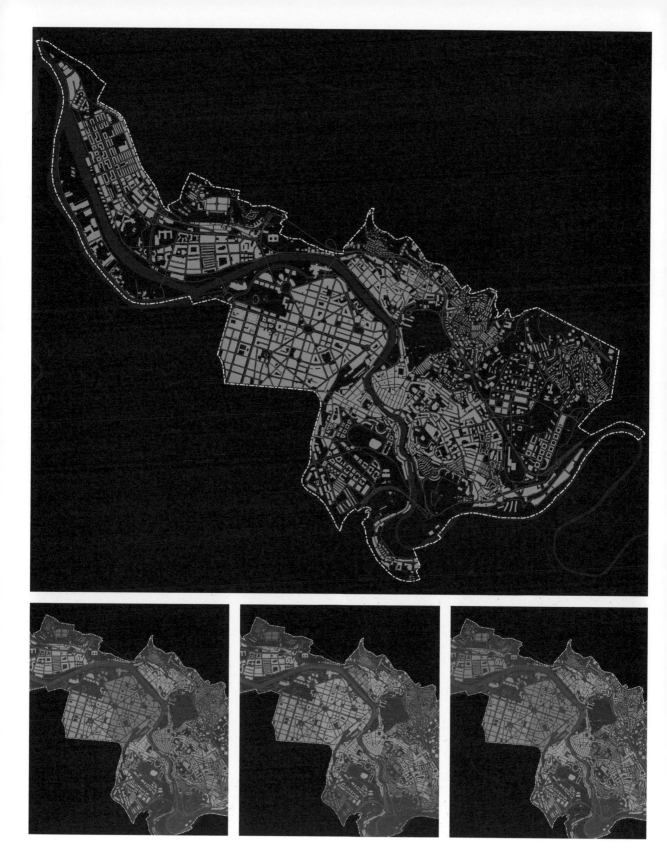

Birmingham

West Midlands England
United Kingdom

City Population
1,144,919

City Area
268 km²

City Density
4,275.28 /km²

Metropolitan Population
4,332,629

Metropolitan Area
598 km²

Metropolitan Density
7,245.20 /km²

City Form Typologies
Random, Organic, Garden, Small World

Once a modest Medieval market town, the city of Birmingham ultimately became the second largest metropolis in England and Great Britain.
The town's fantastic location at the intersection of important trade routes situated it as the regulator of major commercial flows. Birmingham's urban layout was originally a classical Small World network, with narrow streets and timber-framed buildings. However, the advent of the Industrial Revolution permitted its emergence as a true manufacturing hub, and the city became a leading center for innovation and sophisticated production. The development of metalworking, textile production, and jewelry manufacturing industries brought new life to the city and propelled major innovations (steam engine), while the construction of the Birmingham Canal Navigations facilitated the transportation of goods and raw materials. The city's layout adapted to the demand of the local manufacturing industry, experiencing vast transformations during the Victorian expansion era (Council House, Victoria Law Courts, Cannon Hill Park, Victoria Square). Extensive reconstruction was required after World War II, involving the development of new neighborhoods and housing complexes, modern architecture (Alpha Tower, Rotunda), and the redevelopment of Brindleyplace.

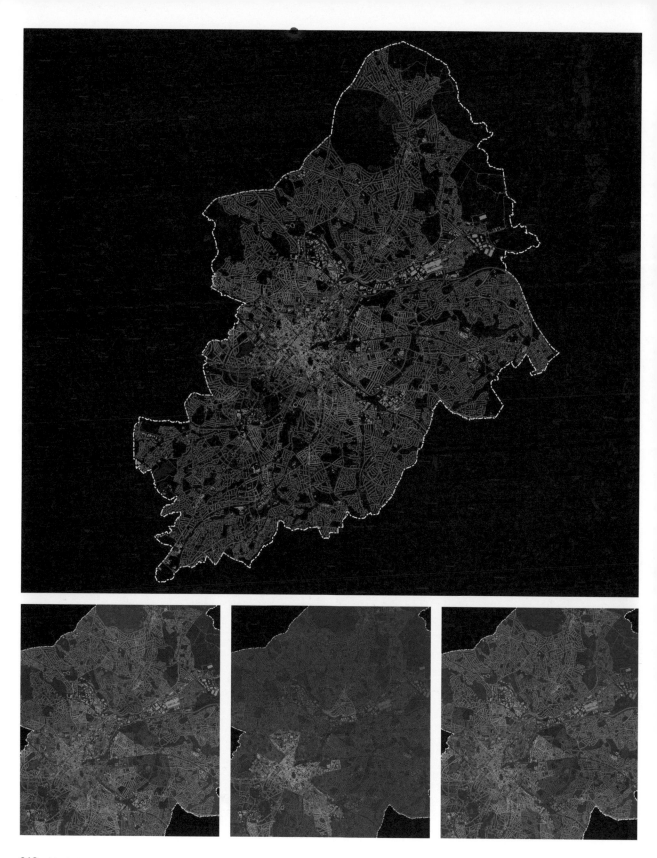

Bogotá
Cundinamarca
Colombia

City Population
8,034,649

City Area
307 km²

City Density
26,140.84 /km²

Metropolitan Population
12,772,828

Metropolitan Area
1,587 km²

Metropolitan Density
8,048.41 /km²

City Form Typologies
Organic

Bogotá, the capital city of Colombia, has undergone significant transformations over the course of its economic and urban development. Founded in 1538 by the Spanish conquistador Gonzalo Jiménez de Quesada, Bogotá initially served as the capital of the New Kingdom of Granada and later the Viceroyalty of New Granada. Its advantageous location on the Andean plateau endowed it with a strategic importance that would later become instrumental for trade and governance. By the 20th century, rapid urbanization propelled by rural-urban migration resulted in the expansion of Bogotá. The city underwent a series of planning and infrastructural developments, the most notable being the Karl Brunner plan in the 1950s that aimed at modernizing the city's urban infrastructure. Migration also led to the emergence of informal settlements, challenging urban planners and policymakers. In recent decades, the city has witnessed innovative urban initiatives such as the TransMilenio, a Bus Rapid Transit system introduced in 2000, which became a model for many cities around the world. While the city is still grappling with challenges like traffic congestion and housing, Bogotá's journey reflects a blend of colonial heritage, rapid urbanization, and progressive urban planning.

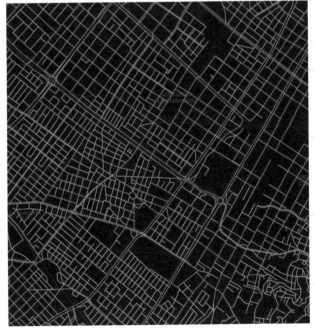

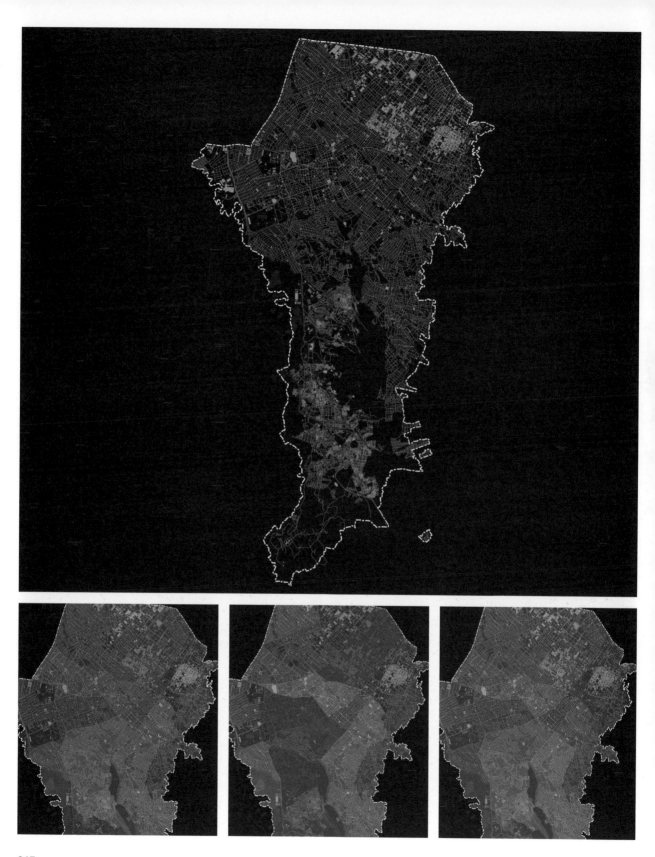

Boston

Massachusetts
United States of America

City Population
617,459

City Area
125

City Density
4,931.78 /km²

Metropolitan Population
4,941,632

Metropolitan Area
11,700 km²

Metropolitan Density
422.36 /km²

City Form Typologies
Fractal, Organic, Small World, Reticular, Linear, Garden

The economic and urban development of Boston has been a dynamic interplay of geography, commerce, and innovation spanning over four centuries. Founded in 1630, Boston rapidly flourished as a port town, benefitting from its strategic location along the Atlantic seaboard. Throughout the 18th century, its maritime commerce and mercantile activities were integral to the Atlantic trade network, positioning it as one of the foremost colonial ports. The 19th century ushered in transformative changes: the Industrial Revolution witnessed Boston evolving into a manufacturing hub, with sectors like textiles and machinery dominating. This era also saw an influx of immigrants, leading to urbanization trends that reshaped its physical landscape. The city's economic complexion further evolved in the 20th century as it transitioned from manufacturing to a knowledge-based economy. Its institutions of higher education, notably Harvard and MIT, played pivotal roles in this shift, making the city a nexus of intellectual and technological innovation. By the 21st century, Boston's urban fabric had expanded considerably, embracing urban renewal projects, waterfront development, and infrastructural investments. Today, the city stands as a testament to its adaptive resilience, integrating its rich heritage with its role as a modern global city.

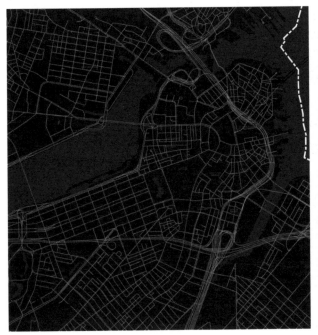

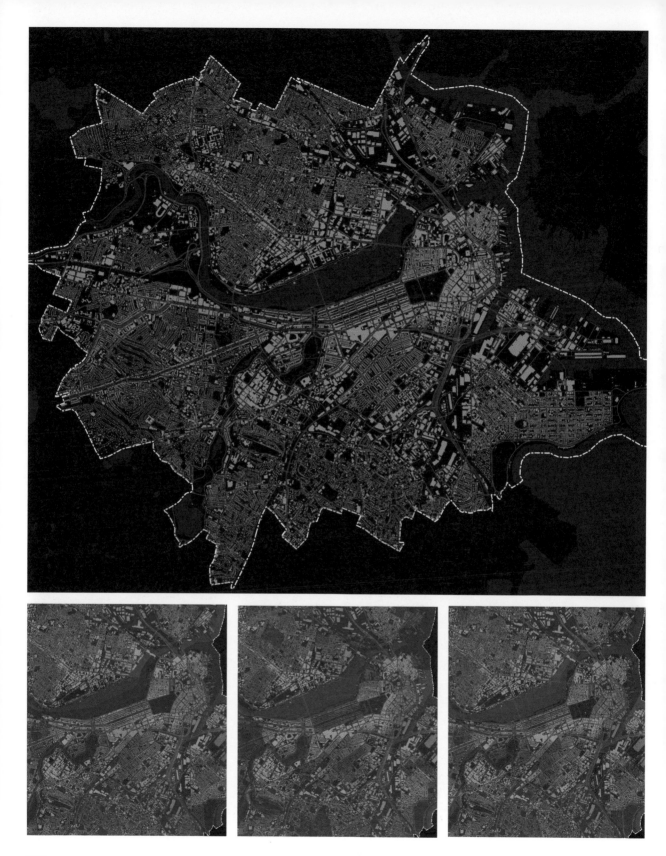

Brisbane

Queensland
Australia

City Population
2,287,896

City Area
2,027 km²

City Density
1,128.71 /km²

Metropolitan Population
2,628,083

Metropolitan Area
15,842 km²

Metropolitan Density
165.89 /km²

City Form Typologies
Atomized, Reticular, Organic, Garden

Brisbane was originally established as a British penal colony in 1824, placed in a strategic location along the Brisbane River. The original composition of the city pursued a reticular grid pattern structured around a series of wide corridors along the riverfront, populated by freight logistics warehouses supplying a solid foundation for trade infrastructure. The construction of St. John's Cathedral in the mid-19th century preceded the accelerated economic growth and population influx derived from the Gold Rush. Brisbane expanded, articulating its growth around a constellation of commercial markets and government buildings (Customs House, Old Treasury Buildings) connected by means of tramway systems. The post-war modernization impulse attracted significant growth, allowing for its profound transformation from a colonial town into a modern city. Suburban areas (Toowong, New Farm) and critical infrastructure projects (Story Bridge, Riverside Expressway) enabled its transition into a cultural and economic hub. Certain architectural landmarks (Queensland Cultural Centre) and South Bank Parklands (site of Expo '88) laid the foundations for a recreational and cultural center. The current Brisbane Riverfront Redevelopment and Urban Renewal process is attracting modern apartment complexes, technology-led office buildings and entertainment venues along the riverbanks, connected by ferry and bus services.

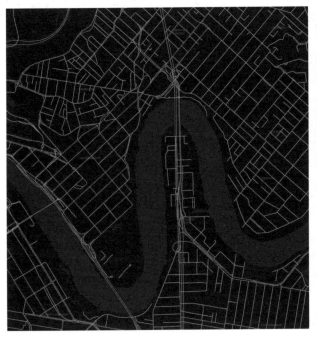

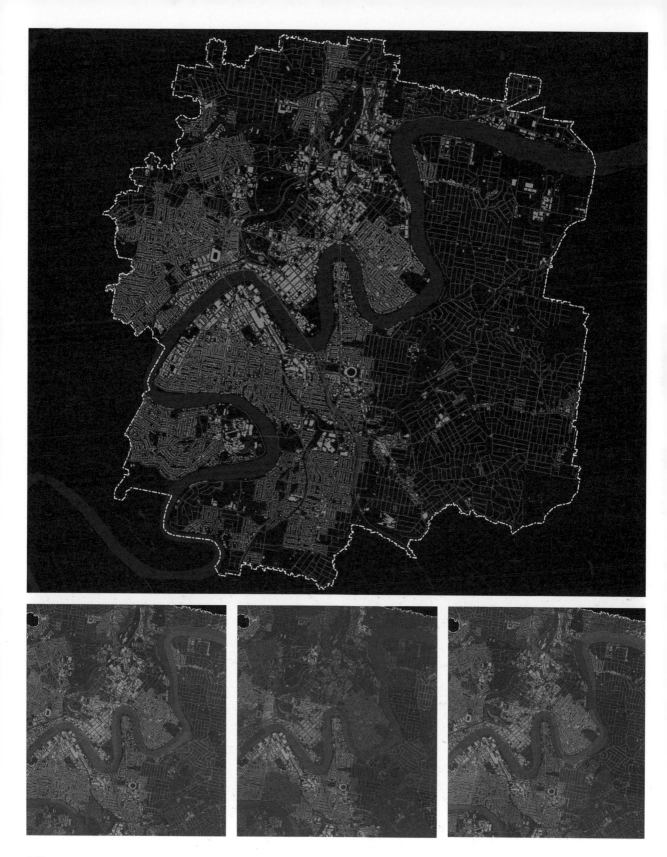

Brussels

City of Brussels
Belgium

City Population
188,737

City Area
33 km²

City Density
5,719.30 /km²

Metropolitan Population
1,219,970

Metropolitan Area
162 km²

Metropolitan Density
7,530.68 /km²

City Form Typologies
Small World, Garden, Random

Brussels constitutes one of the foremost examples of Small World city development patterns. Founded in the 10th century, Brussels origins date back to an originally modest village, which naturally evolved into a market town at the heart of Carolingian Europe. Medieval Brussels featured human-scale, highly walkable streets, market squares, and military defense fortifications, where Grote Markt (Grand-Place), became the social heart of the city. Throughout the Burgundian and Habsburg rule, Brussels remained a prominent city. It served as the de facto capital of the Spanish-Austrian Netherlands. The city's architectural landscape was subsequently enriched with Gothic, Renaissance and Baroque buildings (Palais Royal and Cathédrale des Saints-Michel-et-Gudule). Shortly after Belgium attained its independence, Brussels became its official capital. It experienced substantial population growth, and the city's walls were demolished to accommodate the construction of monumental style boulevards and public parks. Strategically located at the intersection of Latin and Germanic Europe, Brussels became the de facto capital of the European Union as the host of its headquarters. The construction of the Atomium became an aesthetic symbol of its modernization . Today's Brussels aspires to champion sustainable urban development, while combining its role as a national capital with European political leadership.

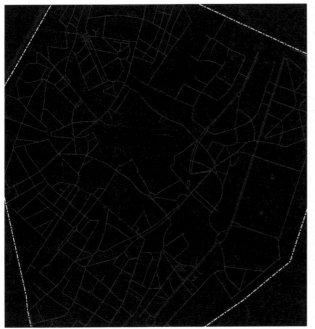
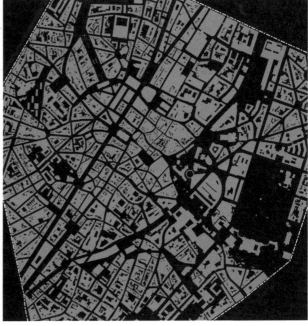

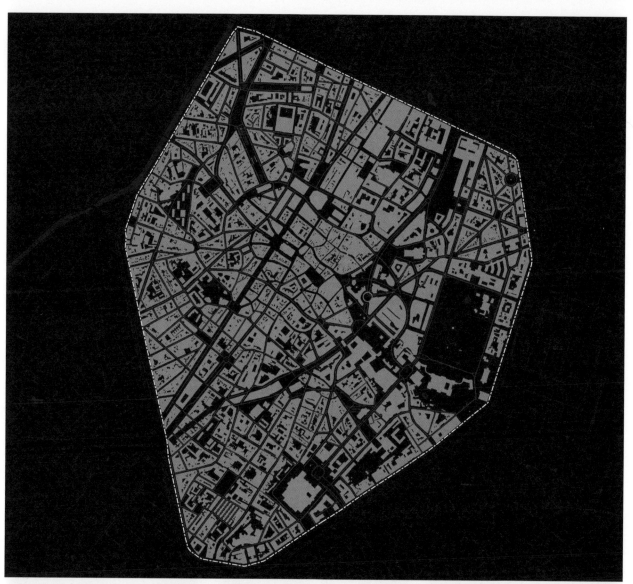

Budapest

Central Hungary
Hungary

City Population
1,778,052

City Area
525 km²

City Density
3,385.48 /km²

Metropolitan Population
3,011,598

Metropolitan Area
7,626 km²

Metropolitan Density
394.91 /km²

City Form Typologies
Monumental, Small World, Atomized, Organic, Reticular, Garden

The predecessor of present-day Budapest, the ancient Roman settlement of Aquincum, was established in the 1st century AD as a military camp along the Danube River. Aquincum featured typical Roman city traits involving reticular patterns, temples, amphitheaters, baths and major road connections leading to the Empire's capital. Medieval Buda and Pest evolved as two distinct cities on either side of the Danube River. Buda was a west bank medieval fortress and royal residence during King Matthias' rule. Pest was an east bank trading and commercial center. Both cities were connected by bridges (Chain Bridge), narrow streets, fortifications and Buda Castle. Under Ottoman rule and occupation, Budapest saw the emergence of mosques and Turkish baths. In the late 17th century, the Habsburgs reclaimed Buda and Pest, and a period of reconstruction started for the city, inspired by Baroque influence (grand palaces, churches, public squares). In 1873 Buda, Pest and Óbuda were merged to form Budapest. The new Hungarian capital underwent rapid urban expansion and modernization, involving the construction of the Hungarian Parliament, the Budapest Opera House, and grand boulevards such as Andrássy Avenue. Contemporary Budapest stands like a beacon of popular resistance to oppression after two World Wars, resiliently overcoming the scars of the Nazi and Soviet occupations.

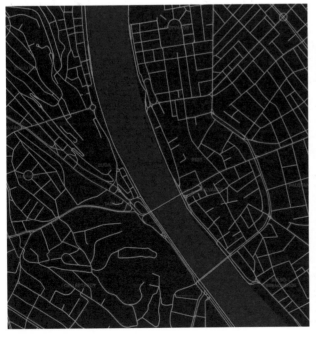

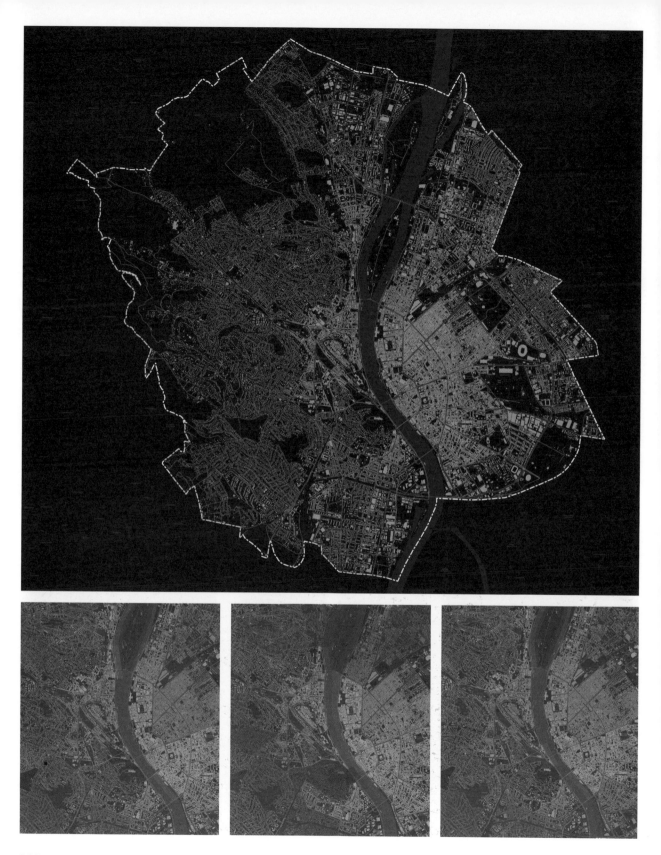

Buenos Aires

Buenos Aires
Argentina

City Population
3,120,612

City Area
200 km²

City Density
15,603.06 /km²

Metropolitan Population
15,490,415

Metropolitan Area
3,833 km²

Metropolitan Density
4,041.33 /km²

City Form Typologies
Reticular, Organic, Radial, Garden

Buenos Aires, Argentina's vibrant capital, has undergone significant economic and urban transformation since its founding in the 16th century. Initially a Spanish colonial port, its economic role was shaped by the mercantilist policies of the Spanish Crown, which limited its trade activities. It wasn't until the early 19th century, following Argentina's independence from Spain, that Buenos Aires began to assert itself as a major trade hub, taking advantage of its natural port and the expansion of global commerce. The late 19th and early 20th centuries marked an era of rapid urbanization, driven by European immigration and the booming agricultural export sector, particularly beef and grain. This period, known as the Conquest of the Desert, witnessed the consolidation of national territories, directly influencing Buenos Aires' role as the primary urban and economic center. The 20th century saw Buenos Aires evolving into a cosmopolitan city with Haussmann-inspired urban planning. However, it also experienced economic challenges, particularly during the late '90s when Argentina faced hyperinflation and fiscal crises. Despite these setbacks, Buenos Aires has remained resilient, harnessing its cultural, architectural, and economic assets to remain one of South America's paramount cities.

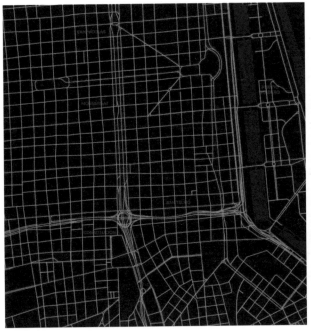

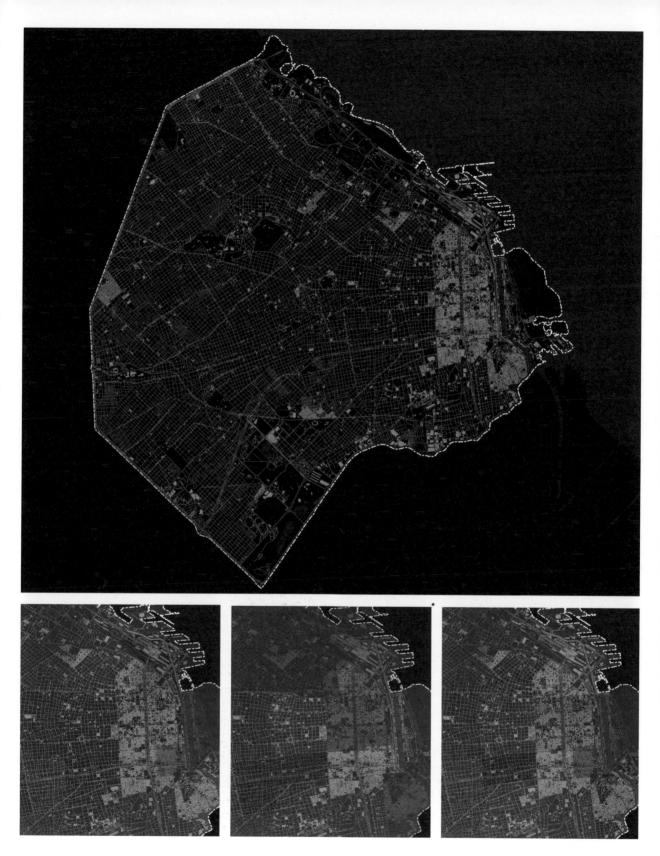

Cairo

Cairo
Egypt

City Population
7,734,614

City Area
606 km²

City Density
12,763.39 /km²

Metropolitan Population
22,183,000

Metropolitan Area
2,734 km²

Metropolitan Density
8,113.75 /km²

City Form Typologies
**Atomized, Reticular,
Monumental, Organic, Random**

Cairo, established in the 10th century as Al-Qahira, has a storied history rooted in its strategic location on the Nile and its early role as an Islamic metropolis. The Fatimid dynasty founded the city and positioned it as both a political and economic center. Over the centuries, Cairo became an intricate tapestry of religious, commercial, and residential spaces. During the Ottoman period (1517–1798), the city's economy thrived on trade, facilitated by the Nile and its extensive canal system, linking Cairo to the Red Sea and the Mediterranean. As European powers grew more influential in the 19th century, the city's architecture and infrastructure were reshaped. Baron Haussmann's Parisian urban concepts were adopted by Khedive Ismail, with the aim of modernizing Cairo. The 20th century brought substantial growth, leading to urban sprawl. The relocation of the rural population to the city spurred unplanned expansions and informal settlements. Neoliberal policies in the late 20th century and ambitious mega-projects have continued to shape its urban and economic landscapes. Today, amidst historical layers, Cairo continues to evolve, confronting challenges of urban density, heritage conservation, and sustainable development.

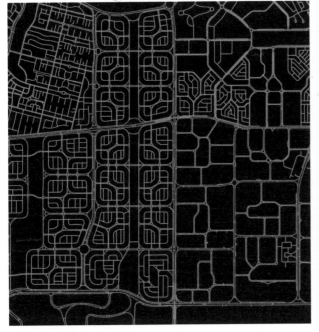
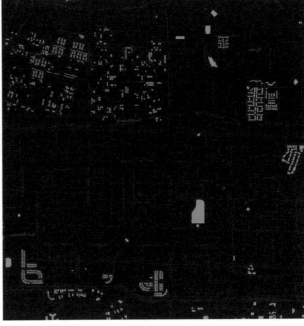

Canberra
Australian Capital Territory
Australia

City Population
472,000

City Area
814 km²

City Density
579.71 /km²

Metropolitan Population
455,869

Metropolitan Area
2,358 km²

Metropolitan Density
193.33 /km²

City Form Typologies
Garden / Radial, Monumental

Canberra was established as Australia's capital city in 1913. Its development adopted a hybrid pattern composed of Garden City and Monumental City design features, planned by the American architect Walter Burley Griffin and his wife Marion Mahony Griffin. Influenced by the principles of the Garden City movement, they combined geometric shapes, radial boulevards, and a network of artificial lakes (Lake Burley Griffin). From the 1930s to the 1950s, Canberra embraced the construction of nationwide government institutions and consolidated its garden-monumental essence by adopting grand boulevards and avenues connecting government buildings. The low-density suburbs (Barton & Yarralumla) provided housing for public servants and diplomats. The city experienced rapid population growth and modernization in the mid-20th century. The adoption of modern architecture styles and the construction of the new Parliament House on Capital Hill in 1988 cemented Canberra's aesthetic vibe, characterized by its generous green spaces and pleasant natural landscapes. Canberra is a comfortable multicultural capital that has combined its bureaucratic economic base with noteworthy commercial districts and cultural institutions. Canberra's emphasis on sustainable urban planning and environmental conservation has earned it the nickname of the "Bush Capital" because of the valiant effort to preserve its natural surroundings.

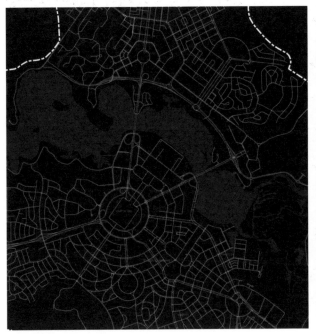

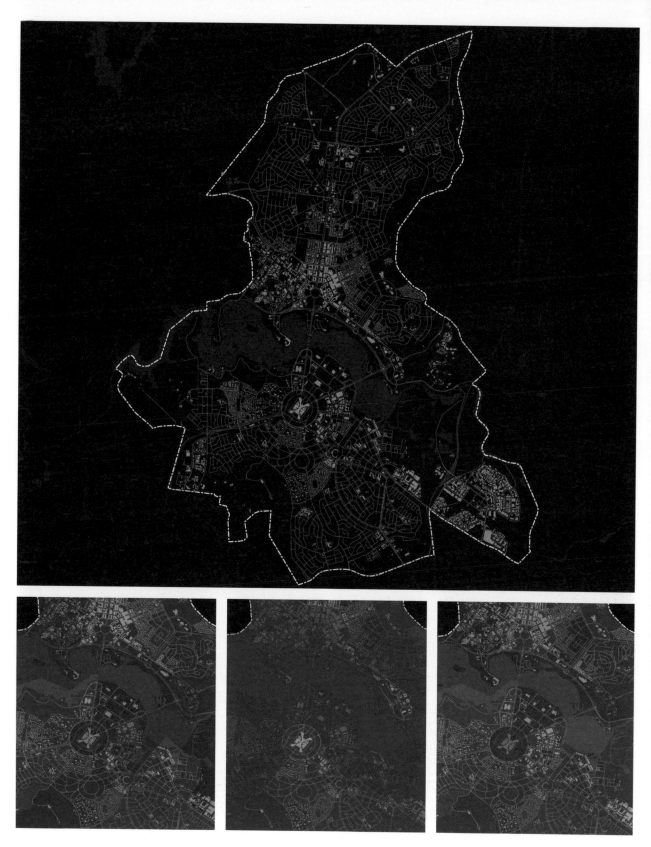

Cape Town

Western Cape
South Africa

City Population
4,890,280

City Area
2,461 km²

City Density
1,987.11 /km²

Metropolitan Population
7,212,142

Metropolitan Area
129,462 km²

Metropolitan Density
55.71 /km²

City Form Typologies
Atomized, Organic, Random, Garden

Cape Town, nestled at the tip of the African continent, has a rich urban and economic history shaped by both indigenous cultures and colonial powers. Established in 1652 by the Dutch East India Company as a refueling point for ships en route to Asia, it became a nexus of trade, serving European and global markets. The initial economic growth was sustained by the farming sector, largely built on the backs of slave labor, with slaves imported from East Africa, Madagascar, and the East Indies. During the 19th century, British colonization intensified urban development, further integrating Cape Town into the global economy. The discovery of diamonds and gold in the hinterland of South Africa in the latter half of the 19th century positioned Cape Town as a significant port city facilitating export. The 20th century brought apartheid, which drastically affected urban development. Racially discriminatory policies marginalized non-White populations, pushing them into townships with limited services and infrastructural support. Post-apartheid, from 1994 onwards, there has been a concerted effort to redress these spatial and economic inequalities. Cape Town has since grown as a major tourist hub, driven by its natural beauty and cultural heritage, while also becoming a hotspot for tech startups in Africa.

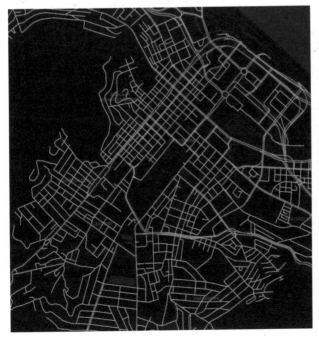

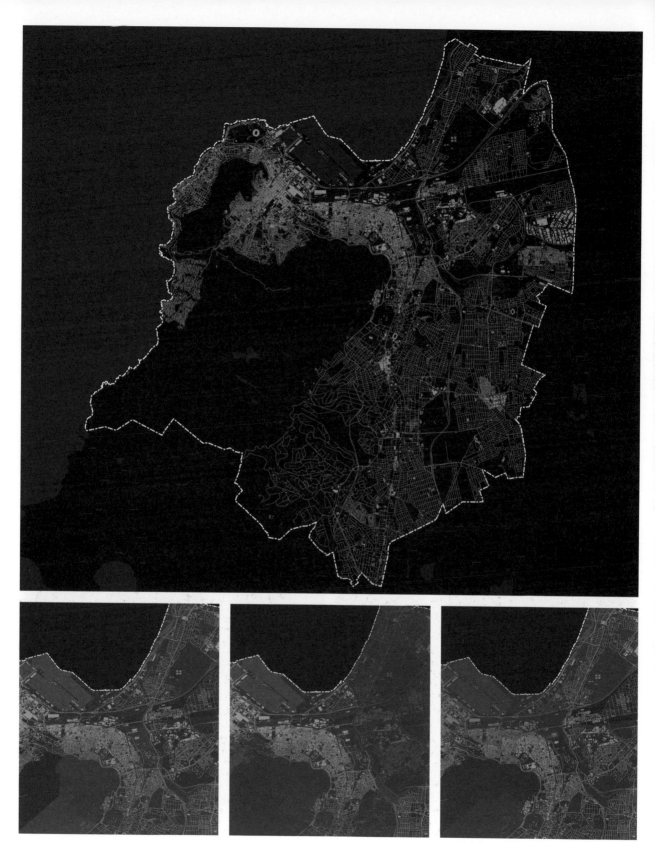

Casablanca

Casablanca-Settat
Morocco

City Population
3,893,000

City Area
220 km²

City Density
17,695.45 /km²

Metropolitan Population
6,000,000

Metropolitan Area
1,117 km²

Metropolitan Density
5,371.53 /km²

City Form Typologies
Organic, Small World, Random

The economic and urban development of Casablanca has historically been contingent on its strategic location along the Atlantic coast. Casablanca's evolution from a modest port town to Morocco's urban and economic nerve center is emblematic of its complex intertwining of indigenous, colonial, and post-colonial influences. During the early 20th century, the city underwent rapid transformation under the French Protectorate. The architectural ethos during this period, showcased by the Ville Nouvelle, embodied a fusion of French colonial and Moroccan elements, highlighting Casablanca as a laboratory for urban experimentation. As the hub of Morocco's colonial economy, the city attracted a diverse workforce, enriching its cultural milieu. Following Moroccan independence in 1956, Casablanca emerged as the country's primary industrial and financial center, experiencing significant rural-to-urban migration. This period was characterized by an expansive urban sprawl, with informal settlements cropping up against the backdrop of modern skyscrapers. Today, with initiatives like the Casablanca Finance City, the city is seeking to position itself as a pivotal economic locus in Africa and the MENA region.

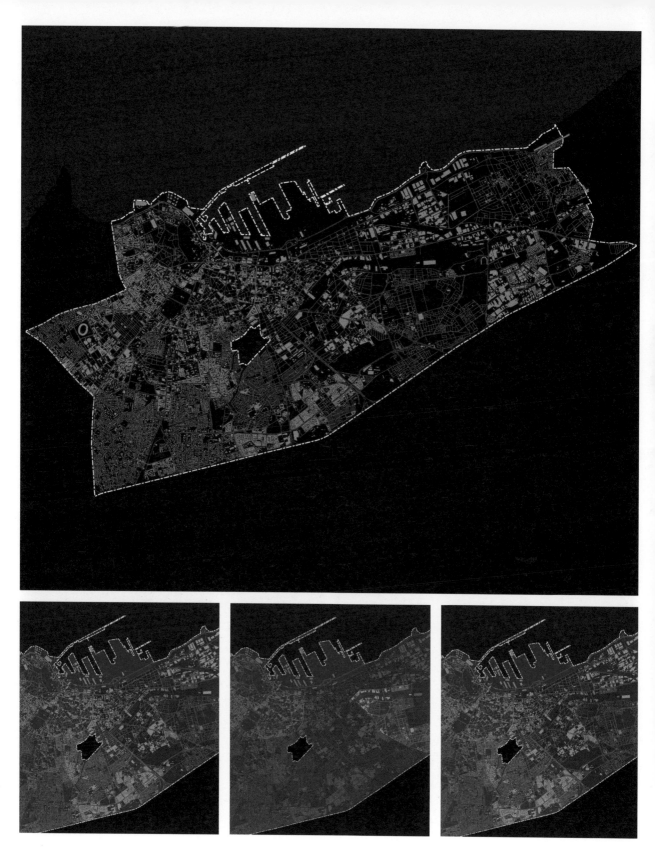

Charlotte

North Carolina
United States of America

City Population
885,663

City Area
803 km²

City Density
1,103.03 /km²

Metropolitan Population
2,756,069

Metropolitan Area
14,502 km²

Metropolitan Density
190.04 /km²

City Form Typologies
Reticular, Organic, Garden

The urban and economic trajectory of Charlotte, North Carolina, is emblematic of the shifts experienced by many Southern U.S. cities over the past two centuries. Founded in 1768, Charlotte initially prospered as a cotton processing center and later as a railroad hub in the 19th century. The convergence of several rail lines boosted the city's economic potential, attracting merchants and investors, making it a significant commercial nucleus for the Piedmont region. The 20th century saw Charlotte transition from a textile-based economy to one significantly influenced by banking and finance. The establishment of Federal Reserve banks and progressive state banking legislation in the 1980s and 1990s expedited Charlotte's emergence as the second-largest banking center in the U.S., only behind New York City. This banking boom dramatically reshaped the city's urban landscape, with high-rise office towers altering the skyline and an influx of professionals diversifying the population. Recent decades have seen further diversification, with energy, technology, and healthcare sectors blossoming, augmenting Charlotte's economic base. Urban development initiatives have concurrently focused on revitalizing historic neighborhoods and enhancing public infrastructure, ensuring that Charlotte remains a dynamic and evolving urban entity.

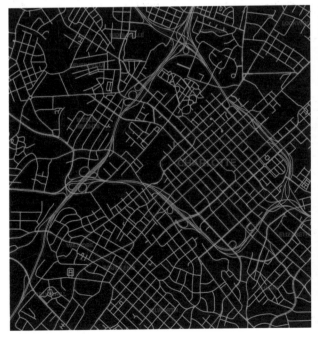
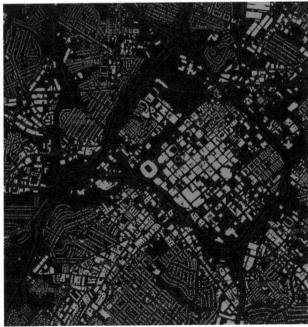

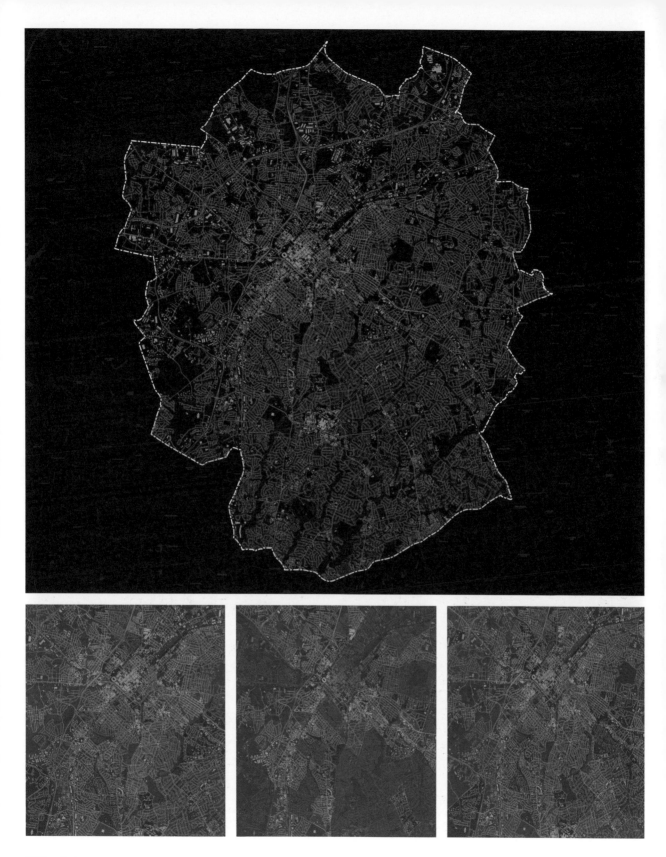

Chicago

Illinois
United States of America

City Population
2,608,425

City Area
590 km²

City Density
4,421.06 /km²

Metropolitan Population
9,441,957

Metropolitan Area
28,120 km²

Metropolitan Density
335.77 /km²

City Form Typologies
Reticular, Linear, Atomized

The history of Chicago's urban and economic development is a chronicle of its evolution from a modest fur trading post in the early 19th century to a global metropolis by the 20th century. The city's strategic location at the crossroads of the Great Lakes and the Mississippi River Basin facilitated its rapid growth, underscored by the completion of the Illinois and Michigan Canal in 1848, which linked the Great Lakes to the Mississippi River, fueling commerce and attracting an influx of immigrants. The Great Chicago Fire of 1871, though devastating, paradoxically catalyzed the city's redevelopment, paving the way for a surge in architectural innovation and the birth of the skyscraper. Chicago's industrial ascent in the late 19th and early 20th centuries, epitomized by its meatpacking, steel, and railway sectors, solidified its status as the Midwest's economic hub. The post-WWII era witnessed deindustrialization and racial tensions, but also saw the city strategically reinvent itself as a nexus of finance, services, and culture. Chicago's commitment to urban revitalization in recent decades, such as the revitalization of Navy Pier and Millennium Park, underlines its continuous adaptation to the shifting paradigms of urban and economic landscapes.

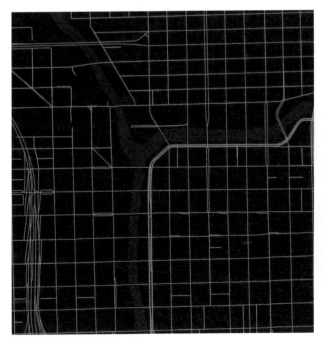

Cincinnati

Ohio
United States of America

City Population
306,592

City Area
202 km²

City Density
1,519.29 /km²

Metropolitan Population
2,265,051

Metropolitan Area
12,450 km²

Metropolitan Density
181.93 /km²

City Form Typologies
**Atomized, Random, Organic,
Reticular, Garden**

The economic and urban development of Cincinnati has been historically intertwined with its geographical position along the Ohio River. Founded in 1788, Cincinnati rapidly became a pivotal inland port, facilitating the movement of goods and people to the American West. By the mid-19th century, the city's location augmented its role as a nexus for both canal and railroad transportation, propelling it into an industrial powerhouse with strong sectors in meatpacking, woodworking, and especially in the brewing industry due to the influx of German immigrants. The post-World War II era, however, saw a decline in manufacturing paralleling the trend in many U.S. cities. Cincinnati faced deindustrialization, which triggered urban flight and left economic and social scars on the urban fabric. Nevertheless, starting from the late 20th century, the city has sought to reinvent itself. Urban revitalization projects, such as the development of the Over-the-Rhine district and the construction of sports stadiums, underscored a commitment to downtown redevelopment. Additionally, the city's investment in medical research and services, education, and tech startups signals a shifting economic landscape, positioning Cincinnati for a diversified 21st-century economy.

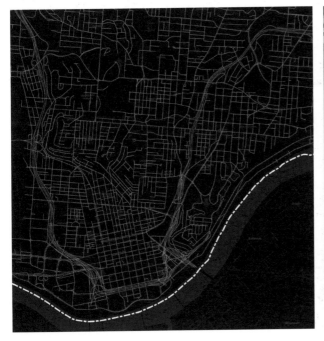

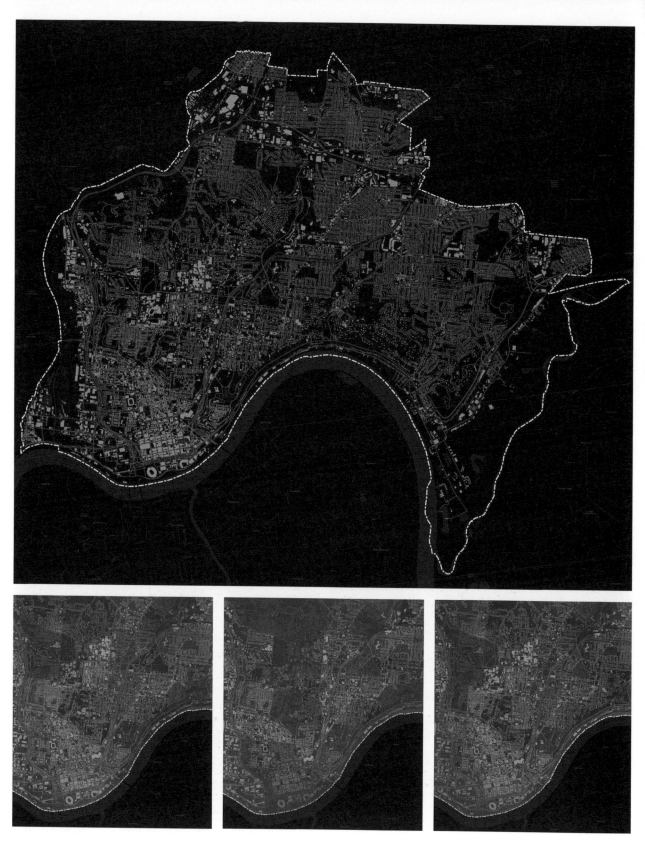

Copenhagen

Copenhagen
Denmark

City Population
656,787

City Area
179 km²

City Density
3,680.30 /km²

Metropolitan Population
1,381,005

Metropolitan Area
1,768 km²

Metropolitan Density
781.32 /km²

City Form Typologies
**Small World, Atomized, Radial,
Organic, Garden**

Copenhagen began as a small fishing village, strategically located on the island of Zealand. The city grew as a center for trade and commerce due to its coveted location on the Baltic Sea. Copenhagen's medieval urban layout adhered to traditional Small World network patterns, combining narrow streets, military fortifications, and a relevant Scandinavian harbor. Copenhagen became the Royal Capital of Denmark and Norway in the 15th century and played a singular role in the expansion led by King Christian IV. During that period, the city was embellished by grand architectural projects (Rosenborg Castle, district of Frederiksstaden), scattered throughout a grid-like street plan (Rundertån). The need to expand the ancient medieval city beyond its historic boundaries let to the dismantling of fortifications, making space for green areas, new industrial corridors, and significant urban expansion (Tivoli Gardens, one of the world's first amusement parks, opened in 1843). The development of residential suburbs and peripheral neighborhoods expanded the city's boundaries, eventually forming a globally admired combination of high-quality public transit and generalized cycling infrastructure (Finger Plan). Contemporary Copenhagen is consolidating its prestige as a champion of urban sustainability, leading initiatives such as the Strøget pedestrian area, extensive parks and waterfront developments, and innovative urban spaces like Superkilen.

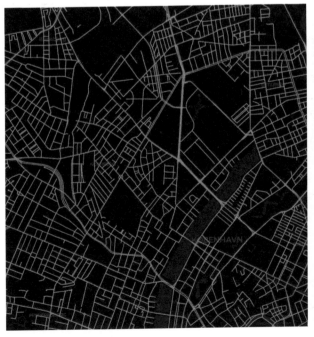

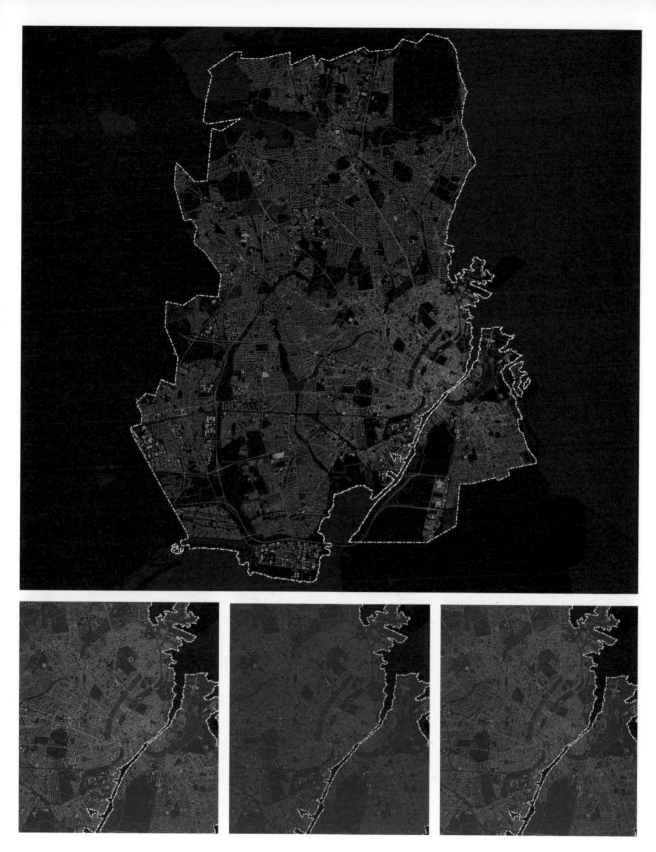

Dakar

Dakar
Senegal

City Population
1,300,000

City Area
83 km²

City Density
15,662.65 /km²

Metropolitan Population
3,429,536

Metropolitan Area
550 km²

Metropolitan Density
6,235.52 /km²

City Form Typologies
Organic, Random, Atomized, Reticular

Dakar, the capital of Senegal, boasts a complex tapestry of urban and economic evolution derived from its pre-colonial, colonial, and post-colonial history. In the 15th century, Dakar's strategic location on the Cape Verde Peninsula made it an attractive focal point for European explorers and traders. With the establishment of the French in the 19th century, the city emerged as a major port and administrative center, cementing its urban infrastructure and layout based on European urban ideals. Post World War II, the urban morphology underwent significant transformations, accommodating migrants and responding to socio-economic pressures. Dakar's transition to independence in 1960 was pivotal, ushering in endeavors to decolonize its urban fabric and reclaim its indigenous identity. The latter half of the 20th century was characterized by rapid urban sprawl, with informal settlements proliferating due to rural-urban migration patterns and economic challenges. Recent decades have seen concerted efforts toward urban renewal and infrastructure projects. The Special Economic Zone near Blaise Diagne International Airport exemplifies initiatives to bolster economic prospects and position Dakar as a key African metropolis. Despite strides in urban development, Dakar grapples with challenges including infrastructure deficits and environmental concerns.

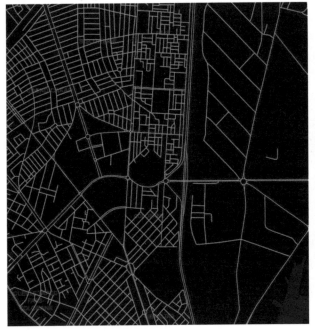

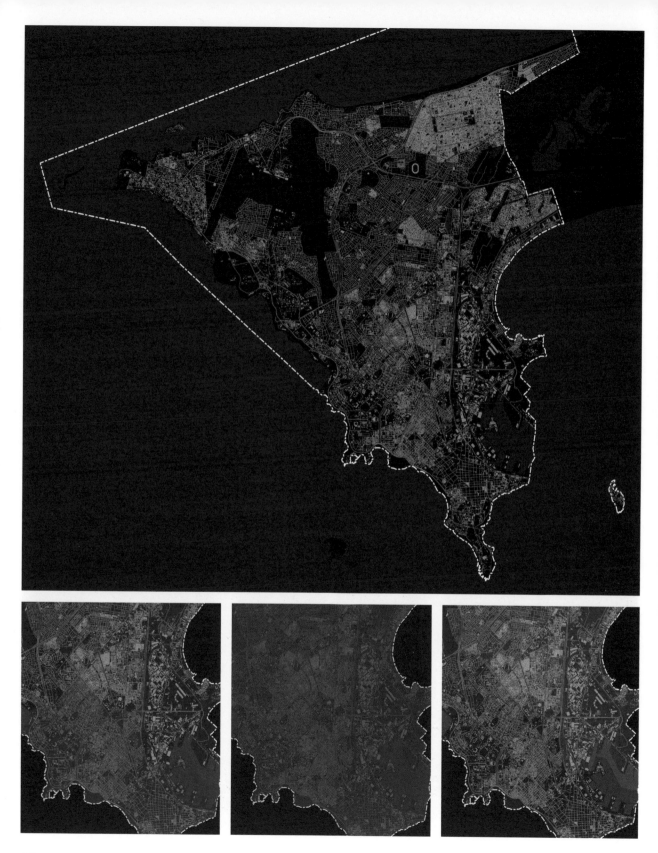

Delhi

North India
India

City Population
212,912

City Area
43 km²

City Density
4,986.23 /km²

Metropolitan Population
32,941,309

Metropolitan Area
1,484 km²

Metropolitan Density
22,197.65 /km²

City Form Typologies
Random, Organic, Monumental,
Atomized

Delhi, the capital city of India, boasts a complex and dynamic history of economic and urban development that spans millennia. Historically a strategic epicenter, Delhi has been the seat of various empires and kingdoms, including the Delhi Sultanate and the Mughal Empire, which considerably influenced its architectural and urban fabric. The city's landscape is replete with a myriad of historical constructions, such as the Red Fort and Jama Masjid, which are testament to its rich Mughal legacy. The colonial period brought significant transformations, with the British designating Delhi as the capital in 1911 and subsequently commissioning Sir Edwin Lutyens and Sir Herbert Baker to design the central administrative area, now referred to as Lutyens' Delhi. Following India's independence in 1947, Delhi grappled with a surge in population due to the Partition-led migrations, spurring extensive urban development initiatives. In recent decades, Delhi has metamorphosed into a global city, with rapid urbanization and burgeoning sectors like IT, telecommunications, and services contributing significantly to its economic growth. However, this development has been dual-edged, bringing with it challenges such as pollution, traffic congestion, and inequality.

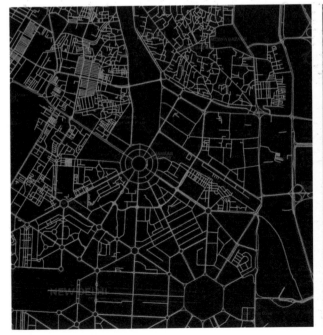

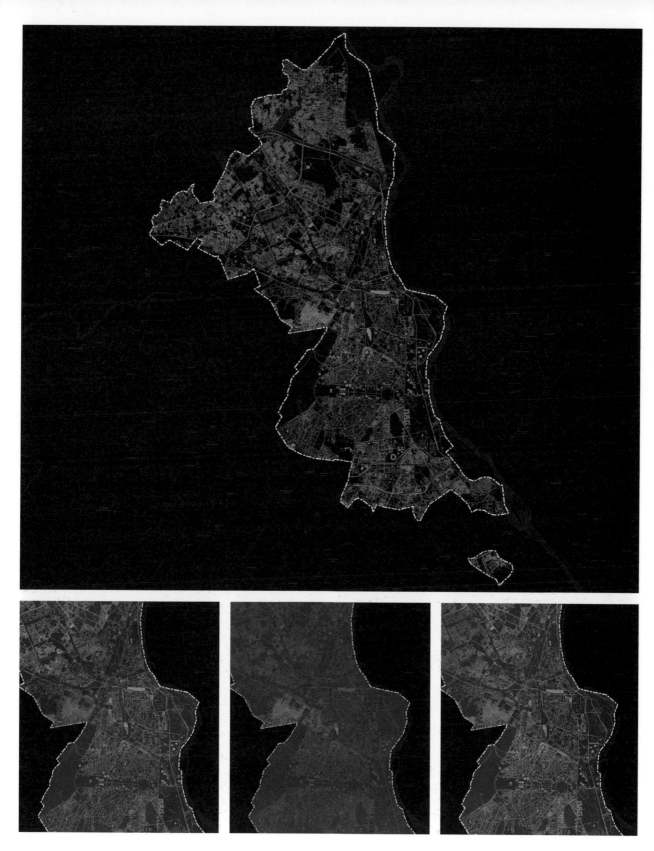

Denver

Colorado
United States of America

City Population
699,288

City Area
396 km²

City Density
1,763.82 /km²

Metropolitan Population
2,963,821

Metropolitan Area
21,764 km²

Metropolitan Density
136.18 /km²

City Form Typologies
**Reticular / Organic,
Random, Garden**

The economic and urban development of Denver can be traced back to its establishment during the Pike's Peak Gold Rush of 1858. Originally a mining town named Denver City, the city became a pivotal point for miners seeking fortune in the Rocky Mountains. The influx of miners and settlers facilitated Denver's rapid urbanization, establishing it as a trading and supply hub. The arrival of the railroad in the 1870s further accelerated Denver's growth, cementing its role as the gateway to the American West. By the 20th century, Denver diversified its economy, reducing its dependence on mining. The city strategically developed transportation infrastructure, including Stapleton Airport in the 1920s, which eventually transformed into Denver International Airport, one of the largest in the U.S. The federal government's presence, notably the establishment of the Denver Federal Center in the 1940s, added stability to the local economy. In the latter half of the century, Denver experienced a boom in the energy sector and a rise in its technology industries, further diversifying its economic base. Despite facing economic downturns, like the 1980s energy bust, Denver's urban strategy, underpinned by investments in infrastructure and diversification, has consistently facilitated its economic resilience and growth.

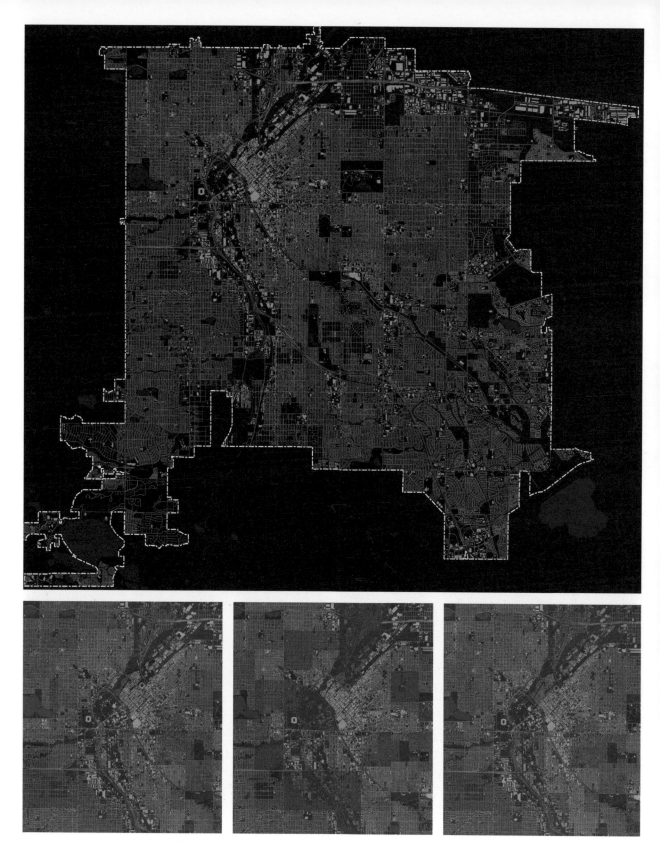

Detroit

Michigan
United States of America

City Population
621,193

City Area
359 km²

City Density
1,728.85 /km²

Metropolitan Population
4,365,205

Metropolitan Area
10,071 km²

Metropolitan Density
433.44 /km²

City Form Typologies
Reticular

The economic and urban development of Detroit is emblematic of the broader narrative of American industrialization, subsequent deindustrialization, and the quest for renewal. At the dawn of the 20th century, Detroit emerged as the epicenter of the automotive industry, with Henry Ford's 1913 introduction of the assembly line at the Highland Park Plant, catalyzing its position. As automakers like Ford, General Motors, and Chrysler flourished, so did the city, attracting waves of migrants and experiencing expansive urban development. However, the post-war period marked a turning point. External pressures, including competition from foreign automakers and the 1973 oil crisis, combined with internal challenges such as racial tensions — exemplified by the 1967 Detroit riots — and a declining tax base, contributed to Detroit's economic downturn. The subsequent decades were characterized by significant population loss and urban decay. The culmination of these factors led to Detroit's bankruptcy in 2013, the largest by any U.S. city to date. Nevertheless, recent years have witnessed initiatives aimed at revitalizing Detroit's economy and urban landscape, from public-private partnerships to grassroots movements, attempting to reforge Detroit's storied legacy in a modern context.

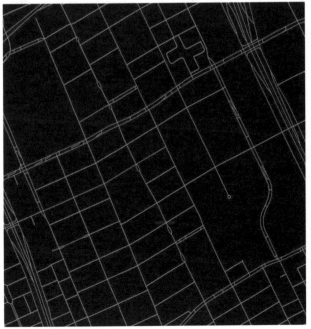

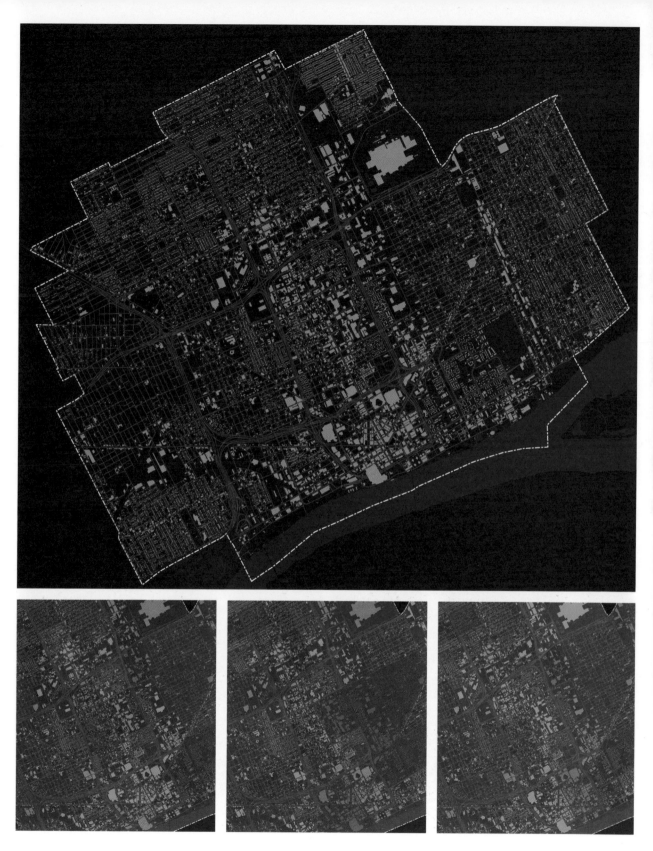

Dhaka

Dhaka
Bangladesh

City Population
10,278,882

City Area
305 km²

City Density
33,649.40 /km²

Metropolitan Population
22,478,116

Metropolitan Area
2,161 km²

Metropolitan Density
10,400.90 /km²

City Form Typologies
Atomized, Random, Organic

The economic and urban trajectory of Dhaka, the capital of Bangladesh, presents a compelling narrative of transformation from a Mughal-era trading hub to a rapidly expanding megacity. Dhaka's historical significance began as early as the 17th century when the Mughals recognized it as an advantageous administrative center due to its strategic location. The Mughal influence culminated in architectural marvels, including the Lalbagh Fort, emblematic of the city's rich past. The more modern underpinnings of Dhaka's urban growth can be traced back to the aftermath of the Partition in 1947. With the creation of East Pakistan, Dhaka's importance surged both politically and economically. After the tumultuous Liberation War in 1971, with Bangladesh emerging as an independent nation, Dhaka took center stage as the capital. The subsequent decades were characterized by a concentrated urban influx, largely attributed to rural-to-urban migration induced by economic opportunities and environmental vulnerabilities in the periphery. In the 21st century, Dhaka has been grappling with challenges emblematic of rapid urbanization: traffic congestion, inadequate infrastructure, and environmental degradation. Despite these issues, its economic role remains formidable, with the garment industry as a noteworthy contributor, making Bangladesh to one of the world's top clothing exporters.

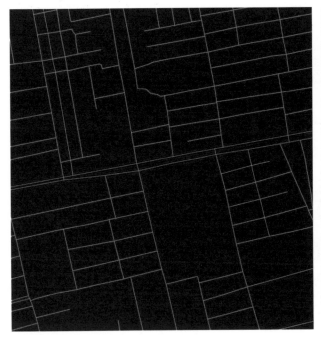

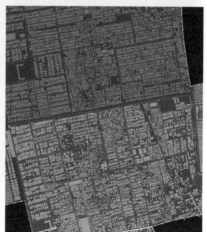

Dubai

Dubai
United Arab Emirates

City Population
3,007,583

City Area
1,610 km²

City Density
1,868.06 /km²

Metropolitan Population
3,478,300

Metropolitan Area
4,114 km²

Metropolitan Density
845.48 /km²

City Form Typologies
**Linear, Organic, Random,
Reticular, Monumental, Radial**

The urban metamorphosis of Dubai, from a tranquil fishing village to a global metropolis remains one of the most striking transformations in recent history. Established in the early 19th century, Dubai initially thrived as a strategic port and center for pearl diving. However, the trajectory of its economic and urban development shifted dramatically post-1966, following the discovery of oil. The subsequent oil revenues accelerated infrastructural development, paving the way for the city's modern urban morphology. Under the leadership of the ruling Al Maktoum family, Dubai invested its oil revenues, aspiring to rely not only on finite petroleum resources. By the late 20th century, the emirate had embarked on a strategic shift towards sectors like tourism, aviation, and real estate, epitomized by landmarks such as the Burj Khalifa and Palm Jumeirah. The establishment of free zones like the Dubai International Financial Centre further endorsed Dubai's role as a hub for business and finance in the region. This multi-pronged development strategy has seen Dubai evolve into a nexus of international trade, tourism, and innovation, reflecting a resilience and adaptability that distinguishes the city within the global urban hierarchy.

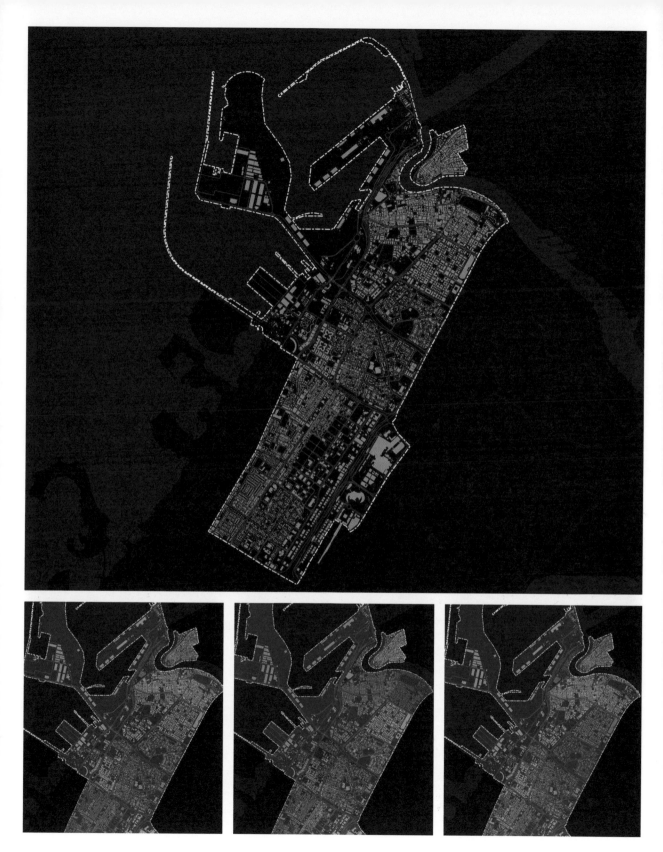

Frankfurt

Hesse
Germany

City Population
796,437

City Area
248 km²

City Density
3,207.43 /km²

Metropolitan Population
5,808,518

Metropolitan Area
14,800 km²

Metropolitan Density
392.47 /km²

City Form Typologies
Small World, Radial / Organic, Garden

Housing a Carolingian royal court was the original purpose and the impulse behind the urban composition of medieval Frankfurt, from the 8th to the 16th centuries, during which it emerged as a quintessential European Small World city, shaped by vernacular architecture, narrow streets, and timber-framed buildings. Frankfurt expanded beyond its ancient walls by means of radial-organic patterns, a common trait of Germanic cities during the Renaissance and Baroque eras. A major push toward urbanization conformed a culturally dynamic city, driven by the development of monumental architectural, including singular buildings such as St Bartholomew's Cathedral and the city hall (Römer). The accelerated industrialization espoused during the 19th-century modernization involved replacing the antique city walls with wide boulevards and open squares. The construction of the Frankfurt Hauptbahnhof enabled the consolidation of Frankfurt as a transportation and financial hub in Central Europe. The bombing raids suffered during World War II destroyed a major part of the historic city center, hence requiring a massive reconstruction effort throughout the late 1940s and 1950s, involving the restoration of historic sites and modern architecture (old town, Dom- Römer Quarter). Contemporary Frankfurt embraced a high-rise financial district, making it the most "American" of German cities. The city's skyline is currently home to a myriad of sleek skyscrapers .

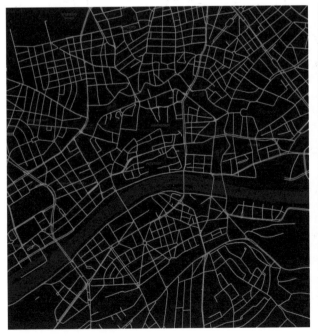

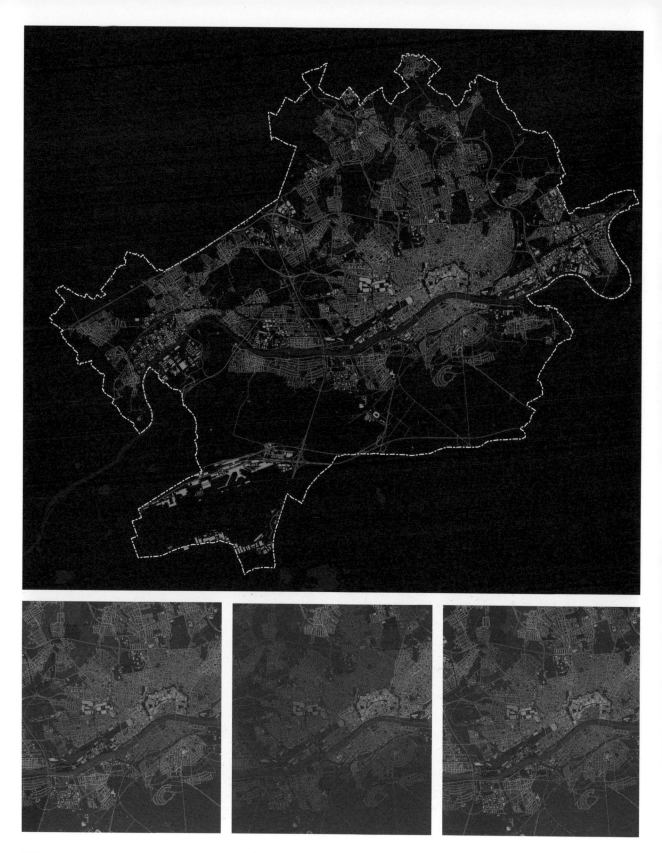

Geneva

Geneva
Switzerland

City Population
203,757

City Area
16 km²

City Density
12,798.81 /km²

Metropolitan Population
632,830

Metropolitan Area
282 km²

Metropolitan Density
2,244.08 /km²

City Form Typologies
Small World, Atomized, Garden

Geneva was founded in the 1st century BC as the evolution of a fortified settlement built by Celts, strategically placed on an easily defended hill dominating the outlet of the lake. Originally established as a Roman town, the urban form features adhered to the reticular model, with an orthogonal topology, imperial style public buildings, and a bridge over the Rhône River. Geneva slowly evolved into a medieval city, known for its trade centrality and cultural appeal. By the 12th century, Geneva had adopted Small World development patterns, with sinuous streets, fortifications, and a cathedral. During the Reformation, Geneva played a major role as a religious and political center under John Calvin. The Helvetic city acquired centrality as a commerce hub under the rule of the House of Savoy, subsequently becoming part of the French Republic. The city's fortifications were dismantled and the urban layout revamped to adapt to the needs of the Industrial Revolution, and after the Congress of Vienna the city joined the Swiss Confederation. Geneva underwent remarkable urban expansion with the development of new neighborhoods and public parks (Parc des Bastions). Today, Geneva is a global diplomatic hub, and is internationally recognized for its ability to attract talent from overseas and its sustainable development initiatives.

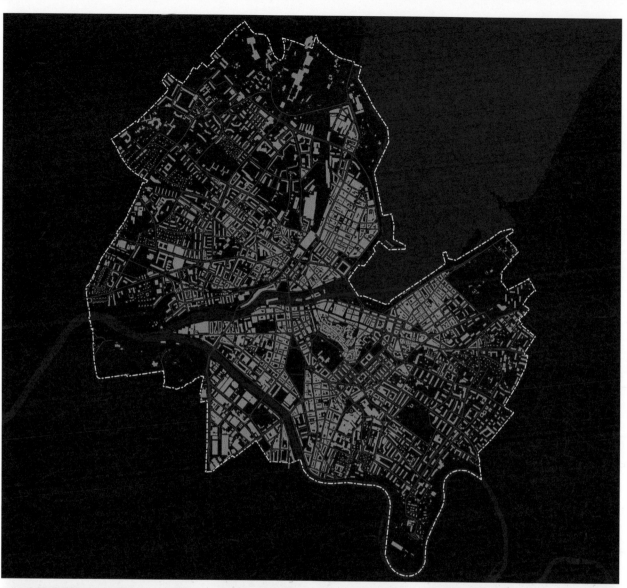

Hamburg

Hamburg
Germany

City Population
1,787,520

City Area
755 km²

City Density
2,366.89 /km²

Metropolitan Population
5,425,628

Metropolitan Area
28,529 km²

Metropolitan Density
190.18 /km²

City Form Typologies
Atomized, Small World, Organic

The Free and Hanseatic City of Hamburg has shared a common trait through the ages: its privileged position as a trading settlement and international commerce hub. Medieval Hamburg emerged in the 9th century as a regional port and a market for the exchange of goods. With its Hanseatic roots in maritime and freight trading, the widespread construction of warehouses, fortifications and the church of St. Nicholas are the hallmarks of a cosmopolitan urban center on a major river. The city also benefited from cultural sophistication, becoming home to theaters, libraries and scientific societies during the Swedish Occupation and the Enlightenment, while seamlessly integrating a mixture of Scandinavian and Central Germanic architectural features. The port of Hamburg became one of Europe's busiest trade centers, adopting the mass construction of docks, piers and the Speicherstadt – its historic warehouse district, while integrating maritime commercial routes with a modern railway network. Hamburg's urban fabric was severely damaged by the bombing raids during World War II, requiring massive reconstruction efforts that resulted in a notable modernization of port facilities and the emergence of new neighborhoods. Contemporary Hamburg is a major European port city characterized by its modern urban planning and sustainability initiatives, such as HafenCity, one of Europe's largest development projects.

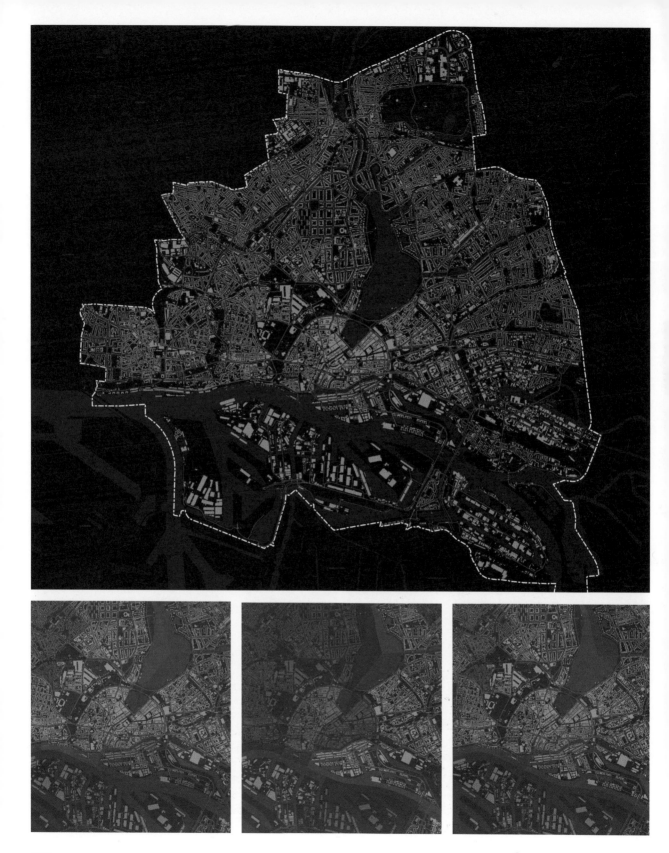

Havana

Havana
Cuba

City Population
2,130,517

City Area
728 km²

City Density
2,925.49 /km²

Metropolitan Population
3,015,255

Metropolitan Area
8,476 km²

Metropolitan Density
355.76 /km²

City Form Typologies
Reticular, Organic, Random

The urban and economic history of Havana is deeply intertwined with its colonial legacy, its strategic position in the Caribbean, and the political changes of the 20th century. Founded in 1519 by the Spanish as San Cristóbal de la Habana, the city quickly became a pivotal port due to its location, facilitating trade between the New World and Europe. By the 18th century, its baroque and neoclassical monuments bore testimony to its prosperity. However, Havana's urban morphology evolved significantly in the 19th and early 20th centuries, heavily influenced by the burgeoning sugar and tobacco industries, which drew foreign investment, especially from the United States. The city's waterfront and the Vedado neighborhood experienced infrastructural advancements, reflecting an international influence and cosmopolitan aspirations. After 1959 and Fidel Castro's revolution, Havana saw economic nationalization and a reorientation towards socialist principles. While the initial years were characterized by significant investment in public services and housing, the economic downturn of the 1990s, after the collapse of the Soviet Union, led to infrastructural stagnation. Nevertheless, with the onset of the 21st century, tourism emerged as a dominant sector, leading to urban regeneration projects, particularly in Old Havana, although challenges persist due to economic embargoes and political constraints.

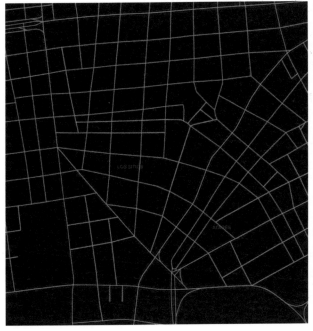

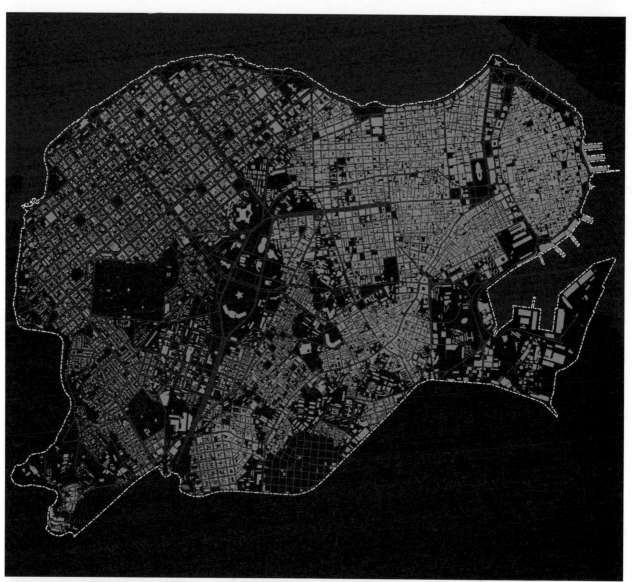

Hong Kong

Special Administrative Region of China
Hong Kong

City Population
7,684,801

City Area
1,114 km²

City Density
6,896.22 /km²

Metropolitan Population
86,620,000

Metropolitan Area
56,000 km²

Metropolitan Density
1,546.79 /km²

City Form Typologies
Atomized, Linear, Organic, Garden

Hong Kong has a distinctive history marked by its unique blend of Eastern and Western influences. Beginning as a modest fishing village, the region's urban and economic trajectory shifted drastically following the Treaty of Nanking in 1842, which ceded Hong Kong Island to the British Empire. As a British colony, Hong Kong soon developed into a major port, with its deep harbor facilitating a burgeoning trade network. The 20th century saw rapid industrialization and urbanization in response to both external and internal stimuli. Post-World War II, Hong Kong transitioned from a trading post to an industrial powerhouse. Political instability in mainland China during the 1950s-60s, led to an influx of refugees and skilled laborers, further bolstering its manufacturing sector. In 1997, Hong Kong's sovereignty was transferred to China under the principle of "one country, two systems." While Hong Kong maintained its distinct economic and legal systems, its urban fabric continued to densify and modernize. The city's transition from a manufacturing to a service-based economy, solidified its status as a global city. As it moves forward in the 21st century, Hong Kong grapples with complex socio-economic challenges, including high property prices and socio-political tensions, while its significance in the international economic landscape remains undisputed.

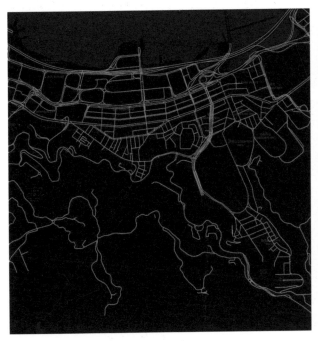
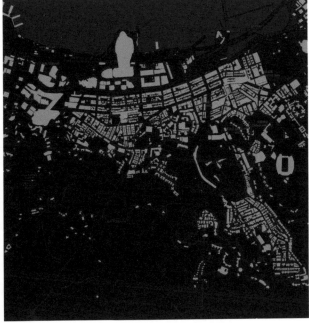

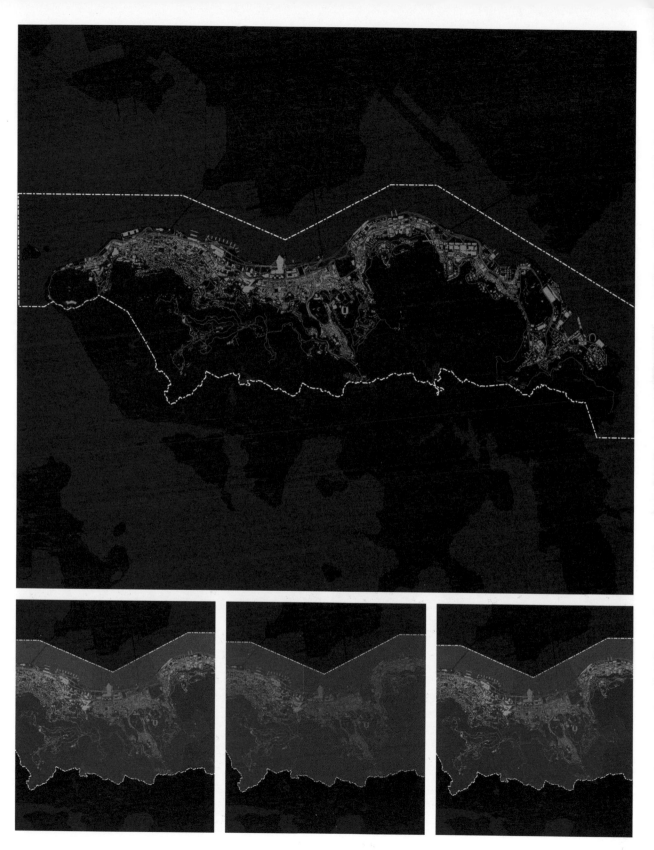

Houston

Texas
United States of America

City Population
2,264,876

City Area
1,659 km²

City Density
1,365.43 /km²

Metropolitan Population
7,340,118

Metropolitan Area
21,415 km²

Metropolitan Density
342.75 /km²

City Form Typologies
Random, Reticular / Organic, Garden

Houston stands as a testament to the intertwining of economic progress and urban development in the United States. Originating as a speculative venture in the 1830s by the Allen brothers, the city's early growth was propelled by its port and rail connections, notably after the completion of the Houston Ship Channel in 1914, enabling maritime access to the Gulf of Mexico. The discovery of oil in the Spindletop field near Beaumont in 1901 catalyzed Houston's transition into an energy hub. The subsequent establishment of major energy corporations, such as Shell and Exxon, not only drove the city's economy but also steered its urban form, with the establishment of sprawling suburban developments. Post World War II, the Space Race further diversified Houston's economic base, leading to the creation of the Manned Spacecraft Center, now known as NASA's Johnson Space Center, in 1961. This cemented the city's role in aerospace industries. The city's lack of zoning laws, a unique characteristic, facilitated its rapid and often unplanned expansion, leading to extensive suburban sprawl and car dependency, often at the expense of cohesive urban form. Despite challenges, Houston's adaptability to shifting economic winds — from transport to energy and space — highlights its resilience as an evolving urban entity.

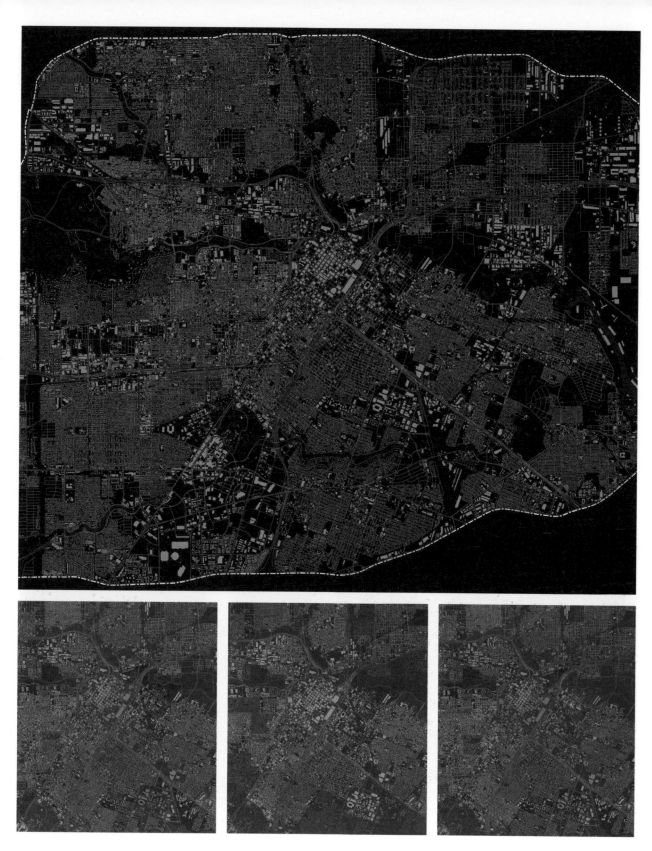

Istanbul

Marmara
Turkey

City Population
15,244,936

City Area
2,577 km²

City Density
5,916.11 /km²

Metropolitan Population
15,907,951

Metropolitan Area
5,343 km²

Metropolitan Density
2,977.22 /km²

City Form Typologies
Atomized, Organic,
Monumental

The Ancient Greek city of Byzantium was originally founded in the 7th century BC and later renamed Constantinople by the Roman emperor Constantine the Great. As the capital of the Byzantine Empire, it shone as a foremost center of culture, religion and trade. The city's monumental layout was crowded with impressive architecture (Hagia Sophia, Great Palace of Constantinople, Theodosian Walls). After the fall of Constantinople in 1453, Istanbul became the capital of the emerging Ottoman Empire under Sultan Mehmed the Conqueror. Its urban landscape was transformed with monumental landmarks (Topkapi Palace, Blue Mosque, Grand Bazaar), consolidating its presence as a cultural and commercial bridge between Europe and Asia. After WWI, the Ottoman Empire collapsed, and Istanbul became the most prominent city of the newly formed Republic of Turkey. The city underwent notable modernization processes involving the redesign of its urban infrastructure and the creation of new neighborhoods, as well as the widespread introduction of Western style architecture. Today's Istanbul is populated by modern skyscrapers, and recent transportation improvements (Bosphorus Bridge, Marmaray Tunnel) have increased the connectivity between the European and Asian halves of the city. The expansion of the city's metropolitan area and neighborhood revitalization efforts (Karaköy, Galata) are propelling the city into the future.

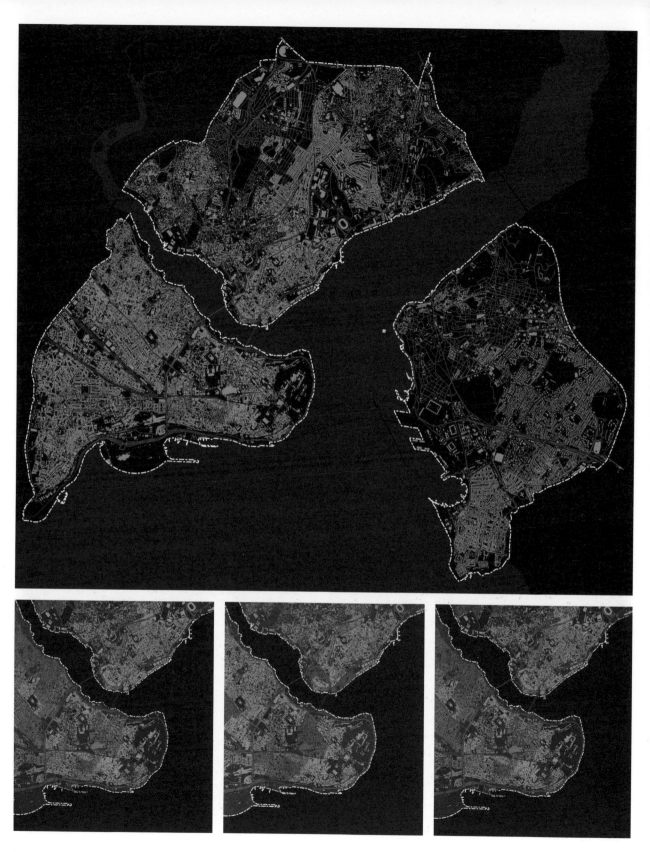

Jakarta

Jakarta
Indonesia

City Population
11,248,839

City Area
661 km²

City Density
17,011.99 /km²

Metropolitan Population
33,430,285

Metropolitan Area
7,063 km²

Metropolitan Density
4,733.49 /km²

City Form Typologies
Random, Monumental, Organic

The history of Jakarta, formerly known as Batavia under Dutch colonial rule, is deeply intertwined with its economic and urban evolution. Originally a thriving trading port of the Hindu Kingdom of Sunda, its strategic location attracted the attention of the Portuguese and subsequently the Dutch East India Company (VOC) in the 16th century. Under the VOC, Batavia was transformed into a significant trading hub, facilitating the spice trade from the archipelago. The colonial imprint is evident in the city's early urban infrastructure, with the construction of canals, forts, and European-style architecture. Following Indonesian independence in 1945, Jakarta experienced dramatic population growth and urban sprawl as the nation's capital. Economic policies of the Sukarno and Suharto eras, such as the establishment of the National Logistics Agency (Bulog) and deregulation initiatives from the late 20th century, underscored the city's economic importance. Jakarta's development, however, was not without challenges. The rapid urbanization exacerbated issues like traffic congestion, informal settlements, and environmental degradation. Notably, the city faces critical challenges from land subsidence and flooding, demanding innovative urban planning solutions. The confluence of historical trade importance, colonial infrastructure legacy, and post-independence urban and economic growth forms Jakarta's distinctive urban-economic tapestry.

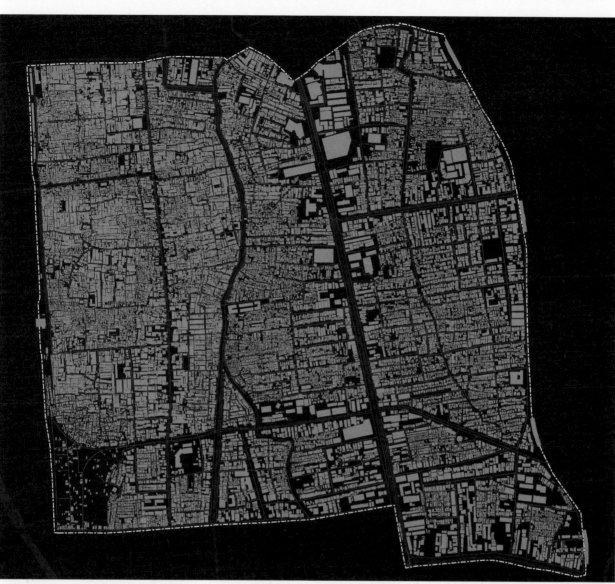

Jerusalem

Jerusalem / Quds
Israel / Palestine

City Population
971,800

City Area
125 km²

City Density
7,764.71 /km²

Metropolitan Population
1,253,900

Metropolitan Area
652 km²

Metropolitan Density
1,923.16 /km²

City Form Typologies
Monumental

Jerusalem, with a history spanning over three millennia, reveals a rich tapestry of economic and urban development shaped by religious, political, and social forces. Originally settled by ancient Canaanites, Jerusalem's urban significance burgeoned under King David, who designated it the capital of the United Kingdom of Israel around 1000 BCE. Subsequent rulers expanded the city's walls and infrastructure, most notably King Herod's monumental constructions, including the Second Temple dating from the 1st century BCE. Throughout its existence, Jerusalem's economic dynamics largely oscillated with its political status. Conquests by the Romans, Muslims, Christian Crusaders, and Ottomans influenced the city's trade networks, infrastructure, and urban morphology. The Ottoman period (1517–1917) saw modest urban developments and the commencement of European missionary and consular activities, which introduced Western-style buildings into the cityscape. The British Mandate (1917–1948) spurred significant urban growth, but the city's division in 1948, with Israel controlling West Jerusalem and Jordan the East, hampered comprehensive urban planning. Post-1967, following its reunification, Jerusalem witnessed rapid expansion, but also significant socio-political challenges tied to its diverse population and contentious status.

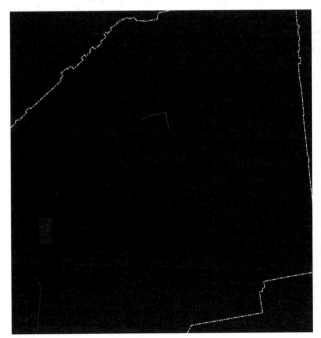

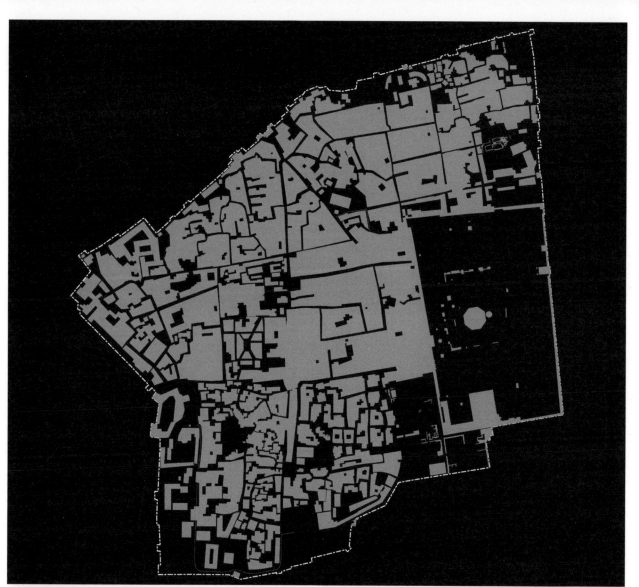

Johannesburg

Gauteng
South Africa

City Population
6,766,278

City Area
1,645 km²

City Density
4,113.29 /km²

Metropolitan Population
11,000,000

Metropolitan Area
3,357 km²

Metropolitan Density
3,276.74 /km²

City Form Typologies
Random, Organic, Garden

Johannesburg, often called the "City of Gold", owes its economic genesis to the 1886 discovery of gold on the Witwatersrand, a geological formation spanning the province of Gauteng. This discovery resulted in a rapid influx of fortune-seekers, propelling Johannesburg's metamorphosis from a modest mining camp to the economic hub of South Africa within mere decades. Unlike other mining towns, the city's economic prowess did not wane even after the gold reserves showed signs of depletion. Instead, its strategic location and developing infrastructure fortified its role as a commercial, financial, and industrial nerve center. Apartheid-era urban policies, driven by racial segregation, left an indelible imprint on Johannesburg's spatial development. The forced removals and the creation of peripheral townships, such as Soweto, relegated the non-White population to marginalized areas, exacerbating socio-economic disparities. Post-apartheid, the city faced deindustrialization and inner-city decay, prompting initiatives to rejuvenate the urban core and combat sprawl. Recent decades have seen Johannesburg evolve into a more inclusive, though still complex, metropolis, grappling with issues of spatial justice, infrastructure development, and economic inclusivity as it carves out its unique trajectory in the Global South.

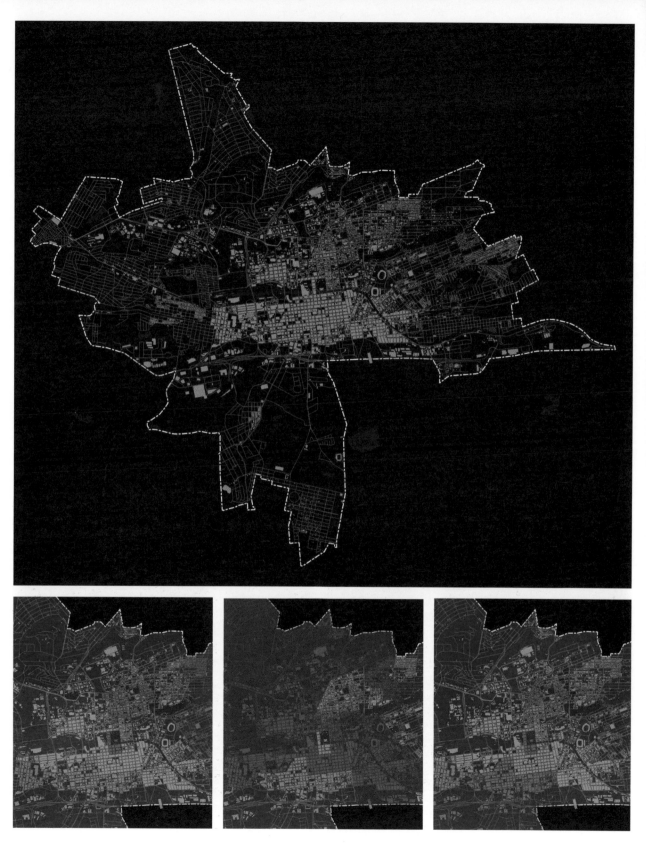

Kansas City

Missouri
United States of America

City Population
509,247

City Area
815 km²

City Density
624.74 /km²

Metropolitan Population
2,209,152

Metropolitan Area
18,787 km²

Metropolitan Density
117.59 /km²

City Form Typologies
Atomized, Random, Organic, Reticular, Garden

Kansas City, situated at the confluence of the Kansas and Missouri rivers, has been an epicenter for economic and urban development in the American Midwest since the 19th century. Its early growth can be attributed to its strategic position as a rail hub and gateway to the West. By the early 20th century, it was known for its stockyards, rivaling Chicago in terms of cattle trade volume. The city's economy was further buoyed by the Pendergast era in the 1920s and 1930s, during which there was a massive expansion in public works projects, despite national economic downturns. Post World War II, Kansas City, like many U.S. cities, saw significant suburbanization. The construction of the interstate highway system in the 1950s and 1960s, particularly I-70, played a pivotal role in shaping the city's spatial and economic development. However, this also exacerbated patterns of urban sprawl, economic disparities, and racial segregation. By the late 20th and early 21st centuries, there was a concerted effort to rejuvenate the urban core, epitomized by projects like the Power & Light District, which aimed to spur economic development and create vibrant urban spaces.

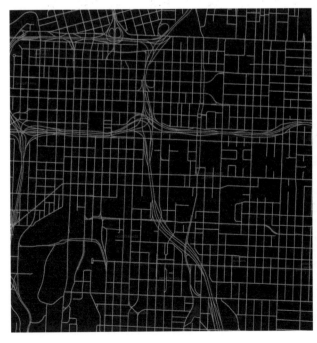

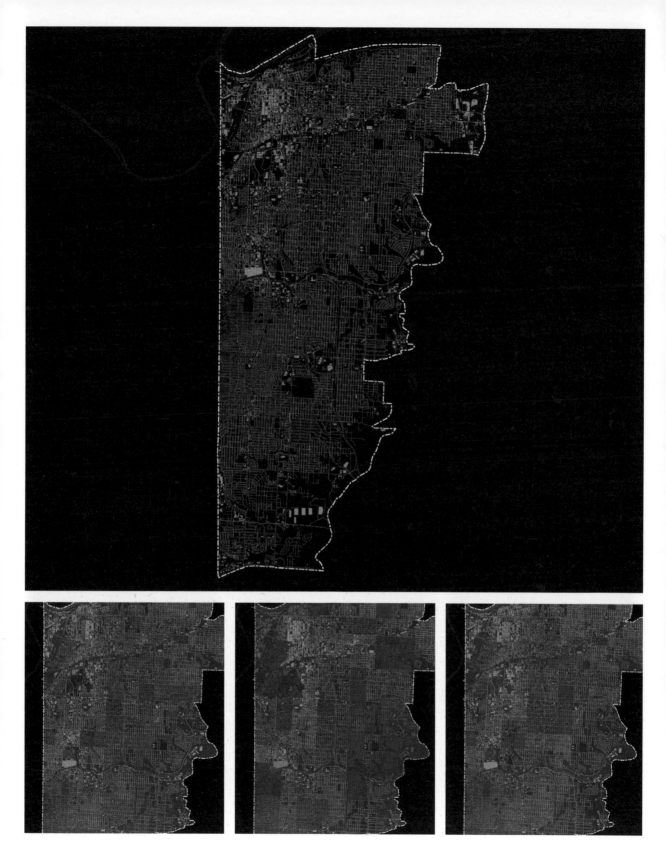

Kinshasa

Kinshasa
Congo

City Population
16,315,534

City Area
600 km²

City Density
27,192.56 /km²

Metropolitan Population
17,071,000

Metropolitan Area
9,965 km²

Metropolitan Density
1,713.10 /km²

City Form Typologies
Random, Organic, Reticular

The development of Kinshasa, the capital of the Democratic Republic of the Congo (DRC), stands as a testament to its dynamic historical and geopolitical influences. Initially established in 1881 as a trading post, named Léopoldville by the explorer Henry Morton Stanley in honor of King Leopold II of Belgium, the city experienced rapid growth, driven primarily by its role as a key node in the colonial administration and extractive industries of the Congo Free State. In the early 20th century, as transportation infrastructures developed – particularly the railway connecting the coast to the interior – Kinshasa cemented its role as an economic hub. Post-independence in 1960, the city grappled with the challenges of political instability, shifting from the relative growth of the Mobutu era to the subsequent period of decline in the late 1990s, which was intensified by the Congo Wars. Today, Kinshasa is one of Africa's megacities, exhibiting stark contrasts between informal settlements and modern urban developments. Its rapid urban expansion reflects broader socio-economic transformations, yet has been marred by the challenges of inadequate infrastructure and services, a consequence of its tumultuous historical and political legacies.

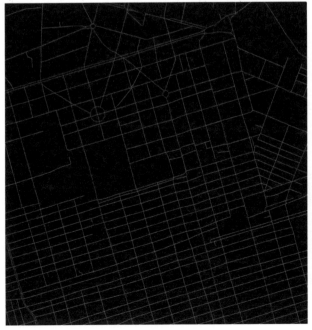

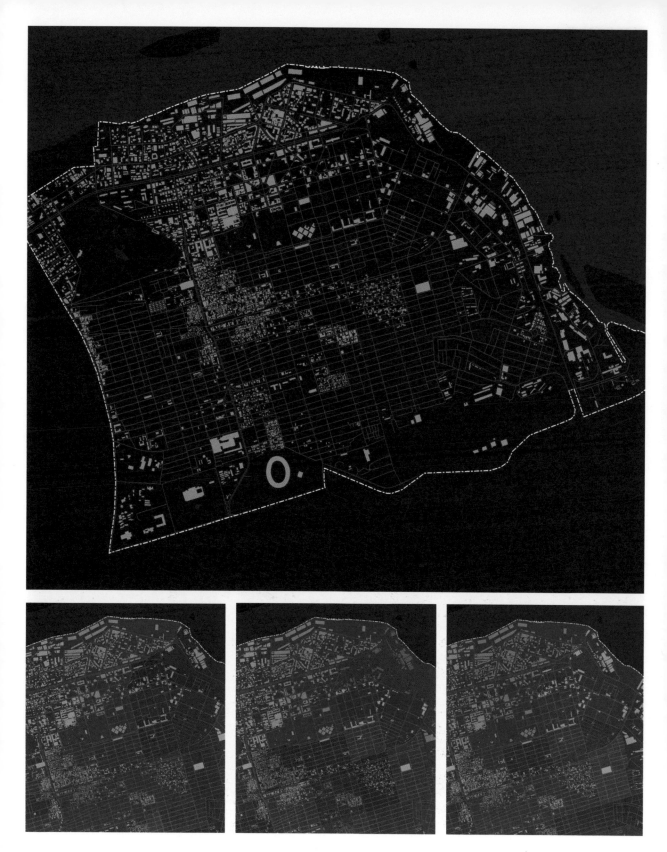

Kyoto

Kansai
Japan

City Population
1,463,723

City Area
828 km²

City Density
1,768.14 /km²

Metropolitan Population
3,783,014

Metropolitan Area
5,189 km²

Metropolitan Density
728.99 /km²

City Form Typologies
Monumental, Linear, Reticular, Organic, Garden

Kyoto has a rich history of urban and economic development rooted in its ancient history. As the imperial capital for over a millennium (794-1868), Kyoto cultivated a distinctive cultural and architectural heritage, which subsequently influenced its urban fabric. The Heian Period (794-1185) marked the establishment of the city grid, emulating the Tang capital of Chang'an (now Xi'an). This grid system, combined with a unique geomantic configuration between the Kamo River and the surrounding mountains, created a harmonious urban environment. During the Edo Period (1603-1868), despite Tokyo's emerging political significance, Kyoto retained its economic vigor through the proliferation of traditional crafts, such as textile manufacturing and sake brewing, which became cornerstones of the local economy. The modern era heralded substantial transformation, with the city embracing industrialization, particularly post World War II, without compromising its cultural integrity. Today, while Kyoto is an exemplar of historical preservation, it balances the contemporary demands of tourism, technology, and higher education, thereby ensuring a unique juxtaposition of antiquity and modernity in its urban development narrative.

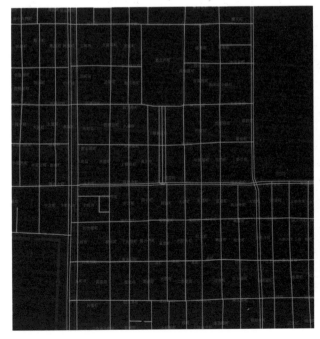 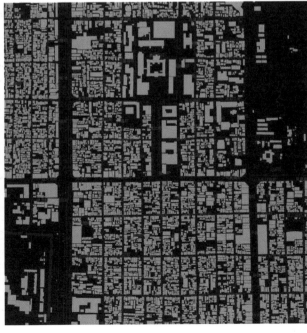

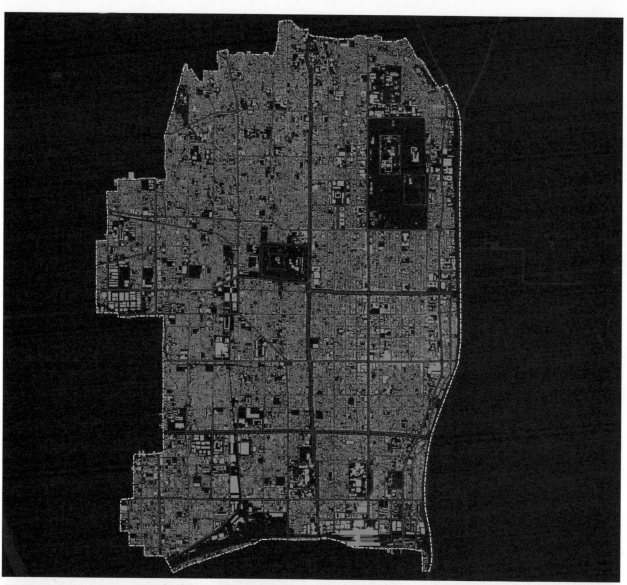

La Plata

Buenos Aires
Argentina

City Population
772,618

City Area
203 km²

City Density
3,806.00 /km²

Metropolitan Population
914,000

Metropolitan Area
893 km²

Metropolitan Density
1,023.52 /km²

City Form Typologies
Fractal

La Plata, the capital city of the province of Buenos Aires in Argentina, was purposefully designed in the late 19th century as an embodiment of modern urban planning. Founded in 1882, La Plata was intended to alleviate the administrative burdens on Buenos Aires and serve as a model city. Planned by Pedro Benoit, its unique design comprised a grid pattern intersected by diagonals, resulting in a city with well-defined squares and parks at regular intervals. From an economic perspective, La Plata's growth was undergirded by the agricultural wealth of the Buenos Aires province, facilitating its role as an administrative and commercial hub. The construction of the port in the early 20th century further catalyzed the city's trade activities and its connection to global markets. La Plata University, founded in 1897 and nationalized in 1905, has also played a significant role in the city's cultural and socio-economic development, attracting scholars and students, and reinforcing La Plata's reputation as a center of learning and intellectual pursuits. However, like many Latin American cities, La Plata faced challenges in the 20th century. Economic fluctuations and political turmoil influenced its urban fabric. Nonetheless, the city's design legacy and its strategic economic role continue to shape its trajectory in the 21st century.

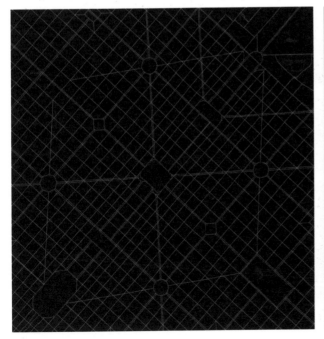
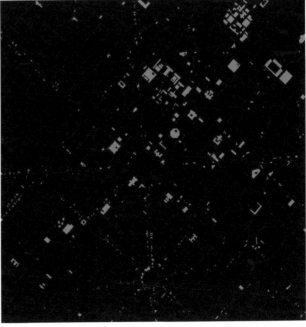

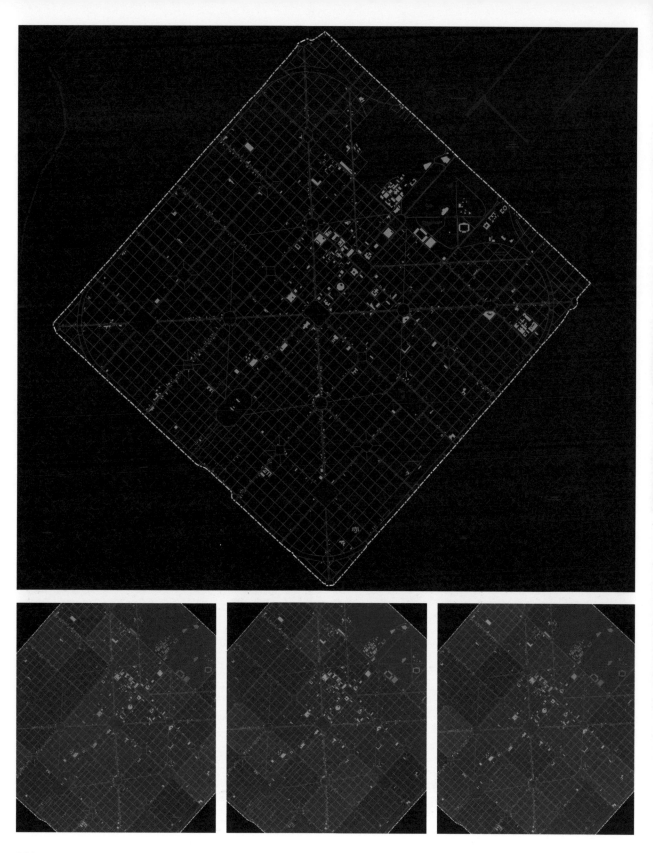

Lagos

Lagos
Nigeria

City Population
15,946,000

City Area
1,171 km²

City Density
13,614.17 /km²

Metropolitan Population
21,000,000

Metropolitan Area
2,707 km²

Metropolitan Density
7,758.53 /km²

City Form Typologies
Random, Organic, Atomized, Garden

Lagos, Nigeria's commercial nerve center, exemplifies a microcosm of Africa's urbanization challenges and potentials. Historically, the city's roots trace back to the Yoruba kingdom of Eko. British colonial intervention in the late 19th century transformed Lagos into a major port city, ushering in an era of trade and commerce that set it on a trajectory to become West Africa's economic hub. Post-independence, Lagos experienced unprecedented urbanization rates, buoyed by oil booms in the 1970s that drove rural-urban migration. This rapid growth, however, was not without its urban challenges.

The 1980s and 1990s witnessed infrastructural deficits and an informal settlement burgeon. The state's response was multifaceted; notable was the establishment of the New Lagos State Urban Development Policy in 1997 focusing on controlled urbanization and infrastructure renewal. By the 21st century, amidst the chaos, a burgeoning entrepreneurial spirit had emerged. Lagos became Africa's startup epicenter, with technology hubs like the Yabacon Valley gaining international acclaim. Urban regeneration projects, like the Eko Atlantic City, symbolize efforts to rebrand Lagos as a global metropolis, albeit with underlying socio-economic inequalities that have yet to be fully addressed.

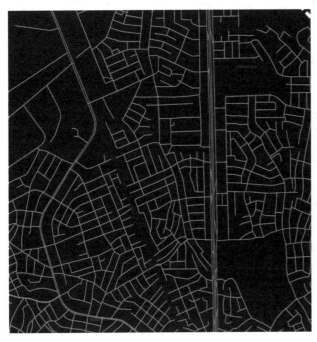

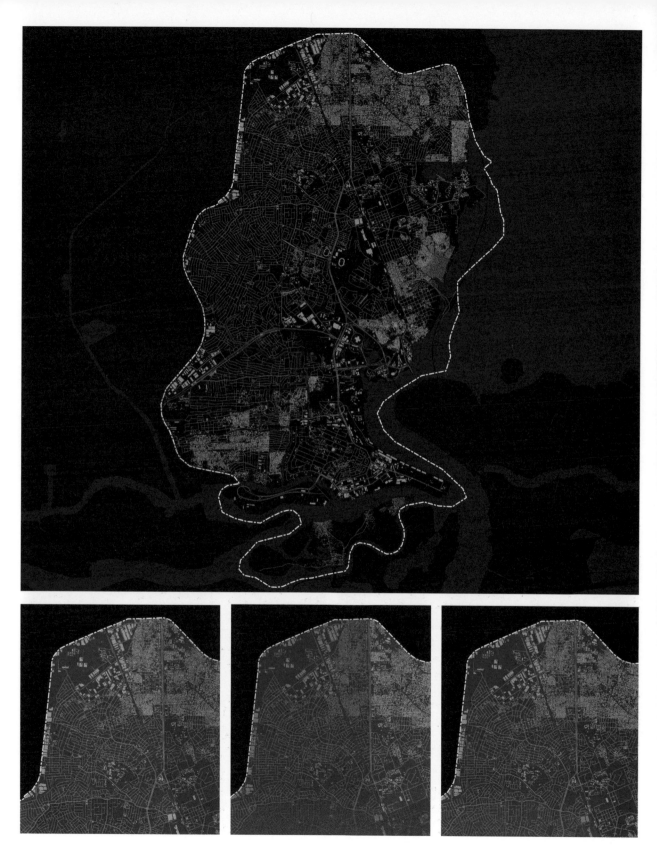

Las Vegas

Nevada
United States of America

City Population
653,843

City Area
367 km²

City Density
1779.65 /km²

Metropolitan Population
2,322,985

Metropolitan Area
20,441 km²

Metropolitan Density
113.64 /km²

City Form Typologies
Linear, Reticular, Organic, Random

The economic and urban development of Las Vegas is a striking tale of transformation. Situated in the Mojave Desert, Las Vegas was initially established as a railroad town in the early 1900s, serving as a key stopover between Los Angeles and Salt Lake City. By the 1930s, however, two major developments began to redefine its economic landscape. Firstly, the construction of the Boulder (later renamed Hoover) Dam between 1931 and 1936 brought thousands of workers to the area, providing an economic boost. Simultaneously, the state's liberal stance on gambling led to the legalization of casinos in 1931, setting the stage for Las Vegas's transformation into "The Entertainment Capital of the World." Post-World War II, Las Vegas capitalized on its gaming industry, with the development of iconic casinos on what would become the Las Vegas Strip. Notable figures such as Howard Hughes invested heavily in the city during the 1960s, signaling its maturation as a major urban and tourist center. Over the decades, the city diversified its offerings with entertainment shows, conventions, and even residential expansions. The Linear city growth of the city has been meteoric, but not without challenges, such as water scarcity. However, innovative urban planning measures have been taken to address these issues, making Las Vegas an exemplar of urban resilience in arid environments.

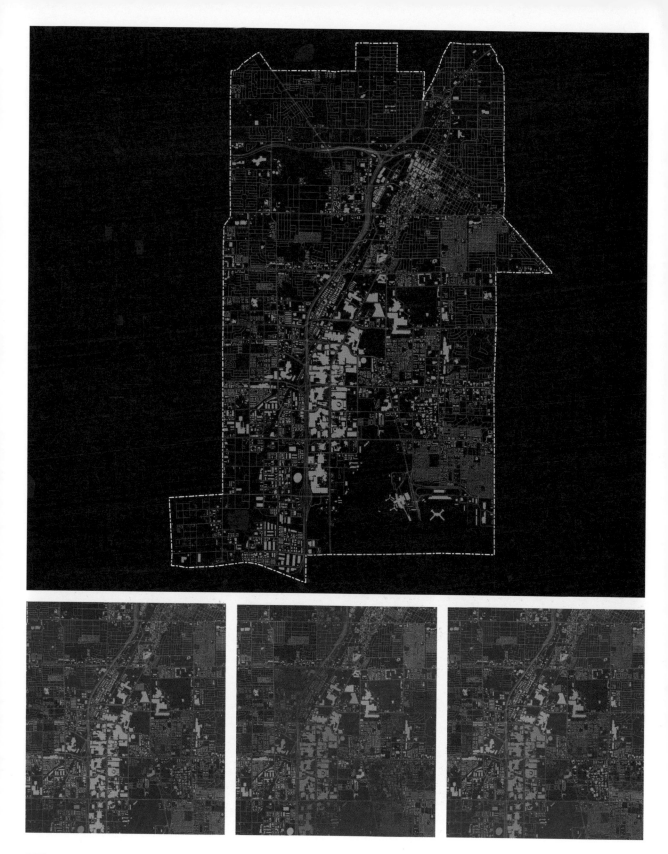

Lisbon

Lisbon
Portugal

City Population
548,703

City Area
100 km²

City Density
5,484.29 /km²

Metropolitan Population
2,899,670

Metropolitan Area
3,015 km²

Metropolitan Density
961.67 /km²

City Form Typologies
Small World, Organic, Monumental, Garden

Soon after its founding, the city of Olisipo became a major port and trading center in the Roman era. Traditional Roman urban planning principles were adopted, combining reticular layouts with public baths, an amphitheater, and a large forum. Known as Al-Ushbuna under Moorish rule, the city's layout and architecture were influenced by Islamic design and culture. The Reconquista by Christians in the 12th century was epitomized by the construction of numerous Catholic churches. Lisbon constituted a beacon during the Age of Exploration, leading to an era of continental maritime glory, during which Lisbon became a major maritime power and influential port city. The city's skyline was dominated by grand buildings and monuments as the Portuguese capital played a key role in the voyages of discovery (Vasco da Gama & Magellan). The Great Lisbon Earthquake of 1755, followed by a highly destructive tsunami and devastating fires, required the adoption of new urban planning and architecture styles and techniques. The Marquis of Pombal introduced neoclassical principles, earthquake-resistant "Pombaline" buildings and an efficient grid street layout. Today's Lisbon is undergoing urban revitalization, while preserving its historic heritage and embracing modernity: the Parque das Nações was developed for the '98 Expo, simultaneously embracing modern architecture and a waterfront promenade along the Tagus River.

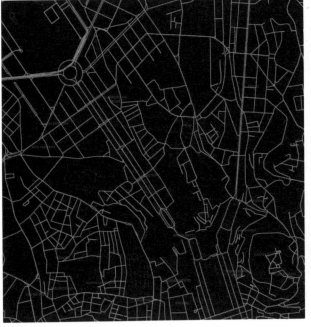

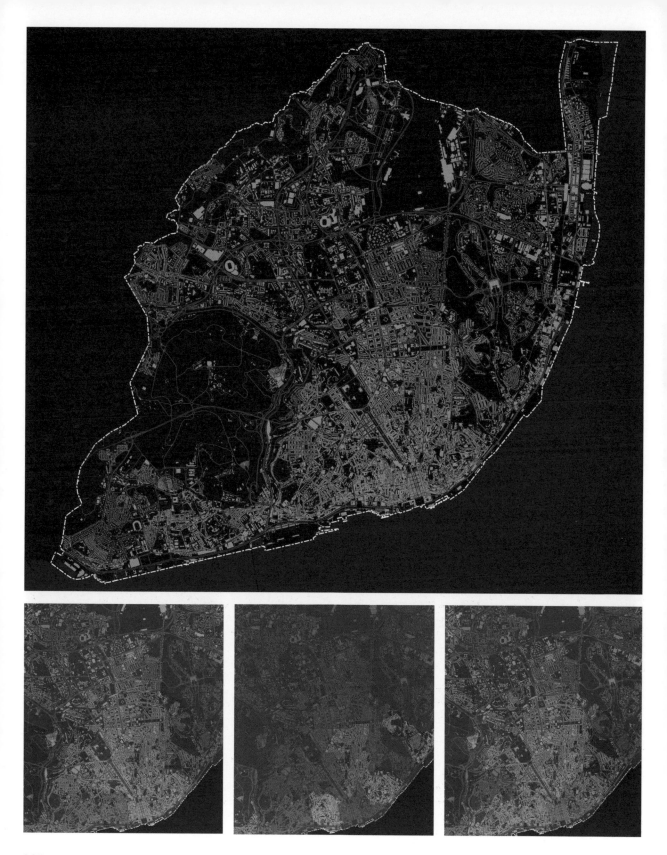

Liverpool

North West England
United Kingdom

City Population
500,500

City Area
112 km²

City Density
4,476.74 /km²

Metropolitan Population
1,551,722

Metropolitan Area
909 km²

Metropolitan Density
1,706.88 /km²

City Form Typologies
Atomized, Random, Garden

Liverpool was once a humble fishing and trading port along the River Mersey. The city's name derived from "Lifer pool" ("muddy pool" in old English), and it was built following an archetypal Small World layout around the Liverpool Cathedral. During the Imperial Era, Liverpool played a central role in the transatlantic slave trade, making it one of Europe's major ports for shipping enslaved Africans to the Americas. Liverpool's docks expanded to accommodate this booming trade and witnessed the construction of merchant houses. During the Industrial Revolution, Liverpool underwent rapid urban expansion, and its port facilities were expanded, making it a vital hub for trade and manufacturing. Beginning in 1830, the Liverpool and Manchester Railway reinforced the centrality of the booming industrial and logistics powerhouses in Northern England. Albert Dock's pioneering dock system was constructed, facilitating the development of new neighborhoods to accommodate population growth. Liverpool experienced some decline following World War II, as it suffered from severe economic challenges affecting the maritime-related industries. Contemporary Liverpool has implemented remarkable urban regeneration projects in neighborhoods like the Baltic Triangle, along with development of waterfront, consolidating the city as a modern and dynamic urban center.

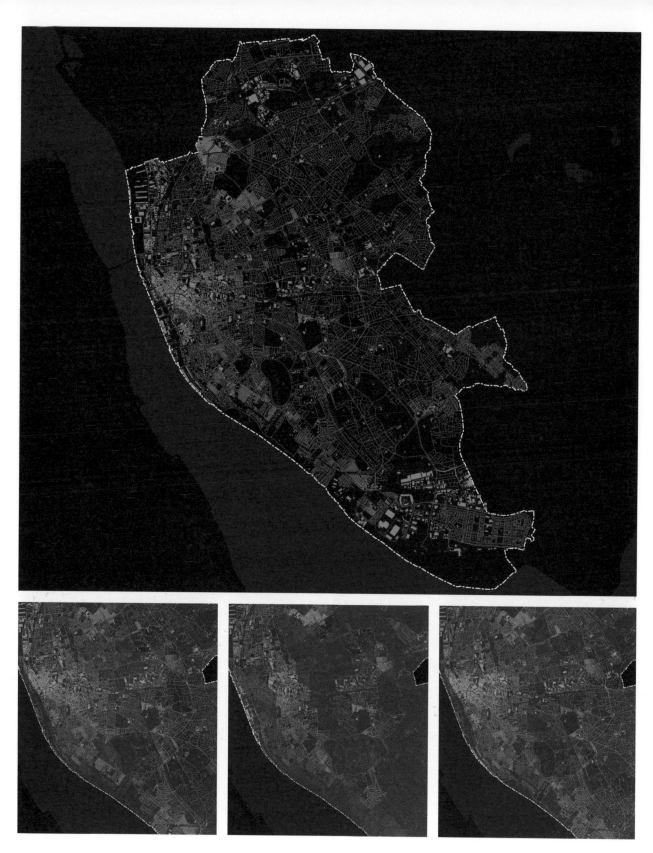

London

London
United Kingdom

City Population
9,002,488

City Area
1,572 km²

City Density
5,726.66 /km²

Metropolitan Population
14,800,000

Metropolitan Area
8,382 km²

Metropolitan Density
1,765.69 /km²

City Form Typologies
Small World, Radial / Organic, Monumental, Atomized, Garden

Originally founded by the Romans as Londinium (1st–5th century AD), the ancient city soon became an important trading and administrative center. The construction of a critical bridge over the Thames River, as well as various buildings and walls, conformed a Small World Network urbs. Medieval London (5th–16th century) subsequently became a trading and commercial hub. The construction of the Tower of London in the 11th century and the London Bridge deeply influenced the city's street layout. The Tudor and Stuart eras made a significant impact on London's urban development. Rapid population growth required an accelerated expansion of the city's boundaries, following a Radial-Organic pattern. The great fire of London destroyed most of medieval London. The city underwent a massive transformation during Victorian times, spurred by the Industrial Revolution: rapid urbanization and outward expansion structured around new means of transportation. New Monumental City landmarks included Westminster Palace and the Victoria & Albert Museum. The development of the London Underground gave rise to the world's first underground railway. The post-WW2 reconstruction efforts embraced contemporary trends such as brutalism, garden city patterns, and linear growth along different railroad edges. The 21st-century metropolis adopted vertical growth patterns that radically modified the old town skyline.

Los Angeles

California
United States of America

City Population
3,769,485

City Area
1,214 km²

City Density
3,105.01 /km²

Metropolitan Population
9,721,138

Metropolitan Area
10,513 km²

Metropolitan Density
924.68 /km²

City Form Typologies
Reticular, Random / Garden, Organic, Linear

The economic and urban development of Los Angeles (LA) is a tale of strategic positioning, natural resources, and historical events that culminated in its rise as a global metropolis. Initially founded in 1781 as a Spanish pueblo, its early economy rested on agriculture, notably viticulture.
The advent of the 20th century marked LA's transformative moment.
With the discovery of oil in 1892 near what is now Dodger Stadium, LA rapidly transformed into a hub for oil production, second only to Texas by the 1920s. Concurrently, the early 1900s witnessed the birth of the American film industry, with many film producers moving to LA to escape Thomas Edison's monopolistic Motion Picture Patents Company. Hollywood thus became synonymous with global cinema. Infrastructure played a pivotal role too. The construction of the Los Angeles Aqueduct in 1913, which diverted water from Owens Valley, allowed for unprecedented urban sprawl. Post-World War II, the defense and aerospace industries flourished in LA, bolstering its economic base. Yet, it was not without challenges. The latter half of the 20th century witnessed racial tensions, notably the 1965 and 1992 riots, hinting at socio-economic disparities amidst growth. Despite such events, LA has continuously evolved, its diverse economy and urban fabric reflecting its multifaceted history.

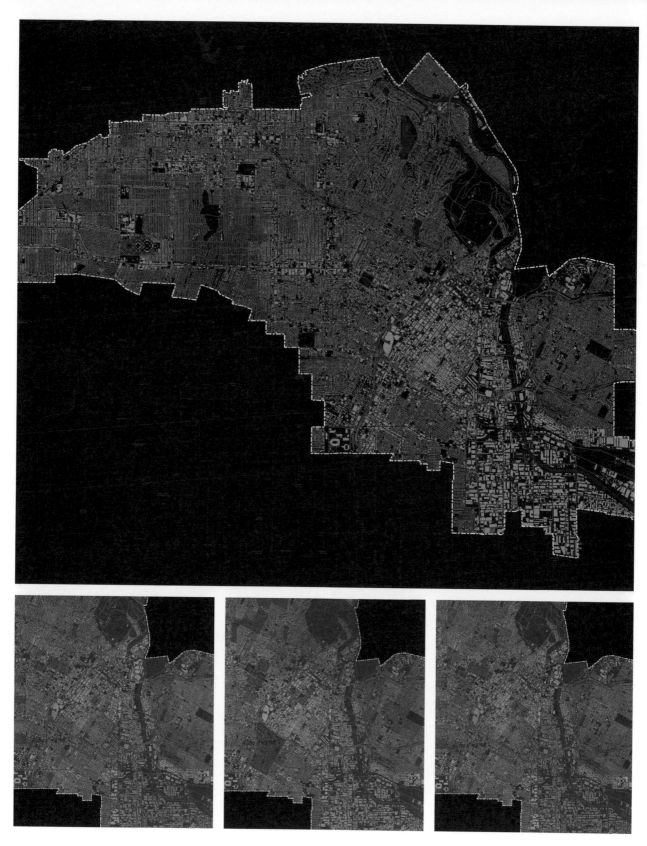

Madrid

Madrid
Spain

City Population
3,305,408

City Area
604 km²

City Density
5,469.72 /km²

Metropolitan Population
6,751,374

Metropolitan Area
5,336 km²

Metropolitan Density
1,265.25 /km²

City Form Typologies
Radial / Organic, Monumental,
Reticular, Linear, Garden

The small fortress town of "Mayrit", characterized by an organic pattern, remained a largely unremarkable settlement and rural cattle crossroads until King Philip II selected the location to host the capital of the Spanish monarchy. It then underwent a major transformation from a provincial town into a major European capital. The Habsburg monarchs propelled a Monumental city pattern, characterized by axial avenues and imposing palaces, political and cultural centers, while building new landmarks such as Palacio Real and Plaza Mayor. The Bourbon regime imposed a radial / concentric growth pattern, and a series of urban planning reforms by King Charles III opened wide avenues, such as Paseo del Prado. The Industrial Revolution introduced new schemes such as the linear city (conceived by Arturo Soria), garden city areas on the outskirts, and modern grid patterns in Barrio de Salamanca and Chamberí. Contemporary Madrid became a modern metropolis, experiencing rapid growth and becoming a global city with new landmarks such as the Nuevos Ministerios complex and the Edificio Telefónica skyscraper.

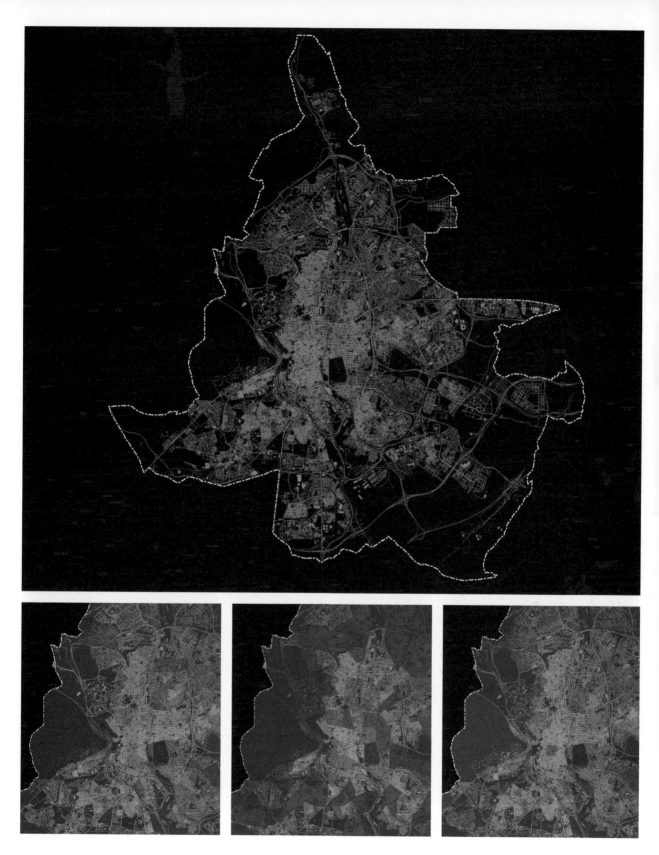

Manchester

North West England
United Kingdom

City Population
551,938

City Area
116 km²

City Density
4,774.55 /km²

Metropolitan Population
2,791,005

Metropolitan Area
1,277 km²

Metropolitan Density
2,185.60 /km²

City Form Typologies
Organic, Garden, Random, Small World, Linear

Initially formed as a small Lancashire market town, Manchester soon became a notable regional enclave for textile manufacturing. The Small World network growth pattern (narrow streets, timber and thatch buildings) that marked the Middle Ages and Renaissance times became obsolete during the Scientific Revolution and the explosion of cotton manufacturing, during which Manchester evolved into a global hub for the British textile industry at the height of the Industrial Revolution. The widespread construction of textile mills and factories shaped an austere yet effervescent urban landscape and permitted rapid population growth, facilitated by a modern canal system (Bridgewater Canal) allowing for the efficient transportation of goods. The prosperity of the Victorian era, however, was dramatically unevenly distributed, giving birth to the term "Manchesterian Capitalism", which became a synonym of income inequality and social injustice. The Manchester Ship Canal opened in 1894, aspiring to connect the city to the major maritime trade routes. Post-industrial decline threatened to deteriorate the city's potential, leading to disinvestment and the closing of mills and factories. However, the city's efforts to diversify its economy by means of the knowledge economy, the finance and culture sectors, and higher education brought substantial regeneration projects (Trafford Centre) and significant urban revitalization (Northern Quarter, Spinningfields).

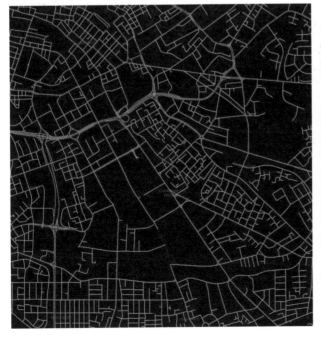

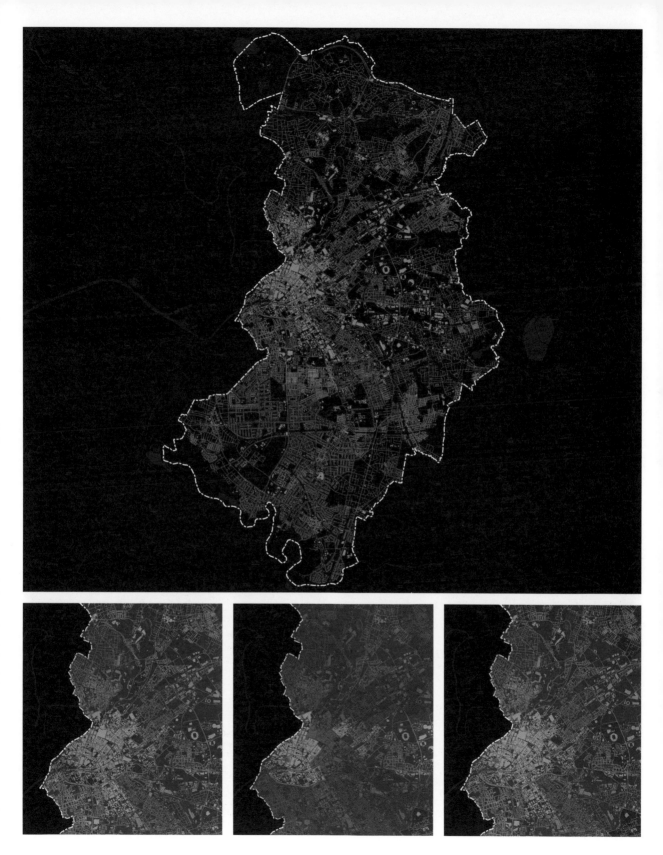

Melbourne

Victoria
Australia

City Population
168,000

City Area
37 km²

City Density
4,540.54 /km²

Metropolitan Population
5,235,000

Metropolitan Area
9,993 km²

Metropolitan Density
523.87 /km²

City Form Typologies
Atomized, Reticular, Organic, Garden

Founded in 1835 as a British colonial settlement at the start of the Australian Gold Rush (1835-1860s), Melbourne was originally a military-style settlement camp. The reticular, grid-based urban street layout was composed of wide streets and laneways, now called the Hoddle Grid. The 1850s were marked by the discovery of gold resources in Victoria, bringing a chaotic growth period known as the Gold Rush. Melbourne's population and economy boomed, preceding the construction of symbolic buildings (Parliament House, Royal Exhibition Building). The city received the informal title of "Marvelous Melbourne" in the late 19th century in reference to the prosperity and social climbing opportunities associated with the economic explosion. Elegant Victorian-era architecture also began cropping up, including ornate public buildings, churches and mansions. New green spaces (Botanic Gardens, Fitzroy Gardens) and the cable tramway system complemented the Garden City patterns. The construction of skyscrapers during the 1980s (Eureka Tower, Rialto Towers) was influenced by contemporary architecture, leading to a new financial and business hub, a thriving arts and culture center, and new sports facilities. Melbourne's Zero Net Emissions plan constitutes an audacious initiative, including the development of green spaces (Federation Square) and the transformation of legacy industrial areas (Docklands) into mixed-use buildings.

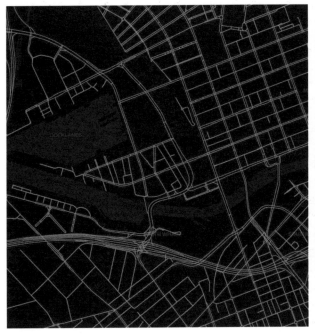

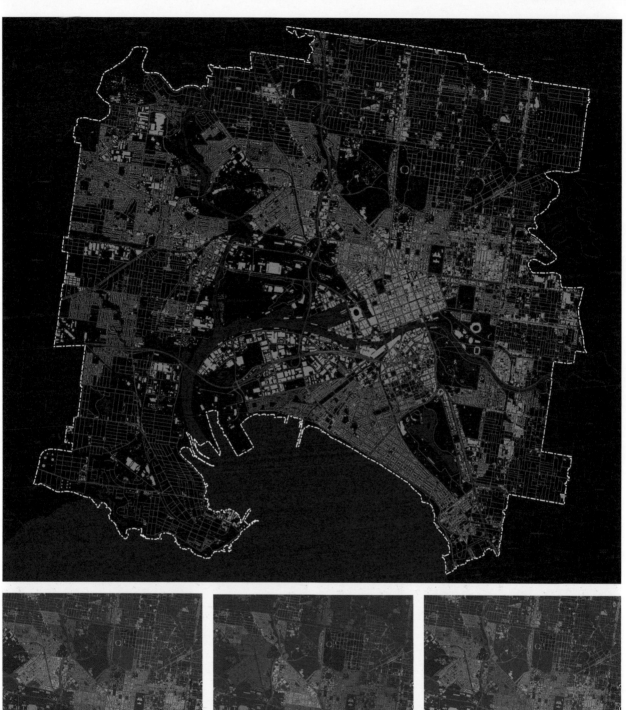

Mexico City
Distrito Federal
Mexico

City Population
9,209,944

City Area
1,485 km²

City Density
6,201.98 /km²

Metropolitan Population
22,281,442

Metropolitan Area
7,866 km²

Metropolitan Density
2,832.59 /km²

City Form Typologies
Organic, Monumental, Random, Garden

The urban and economic trajectory of Mexico City, one of the largest metropolises in the world, is deeply interwoven with the historical fabric of Mexico itself. Founded as Tenochtitlán in 1325 by the Mexica (Aztecs), the city served as the epicenter of a sprawling empire until its conquest by the Spanish in 1521. The Spanish colonial period saw the city transformed into the Viceroyalty of New Spain's administrative and economic hub, and a grid-based urban design was laid down, which is still evident in the Centro Histórico. Following Mexico's independence in the 19th century, Mexico City emerged as the nation's political and economic fulcrum, though it experienced developmental fits and starts due to political upheavals. The 20th century brought accelerated urbanization and industrialization, especially in the 1940s, propelling the city into a period of rapid population growth and spatial expansion. Government-led infrastructural projects and incentives for industries culminated in an influx of migrants, overflowing the city's boundaries. By the 1980s and 1990s, concerns over environmental degradation, informal housing, and economic disparities had become pronounced. Today, while grappling with challenges of pollution, traffic congestion, and housing, Mexico City remains a testament to its resilient economic vitality, diverse cultural tapestry, and intricate urban evolution.

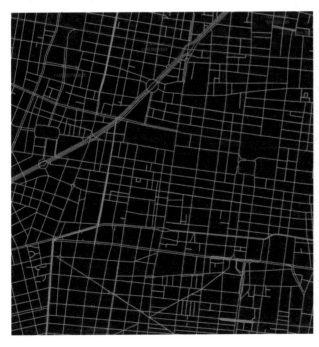

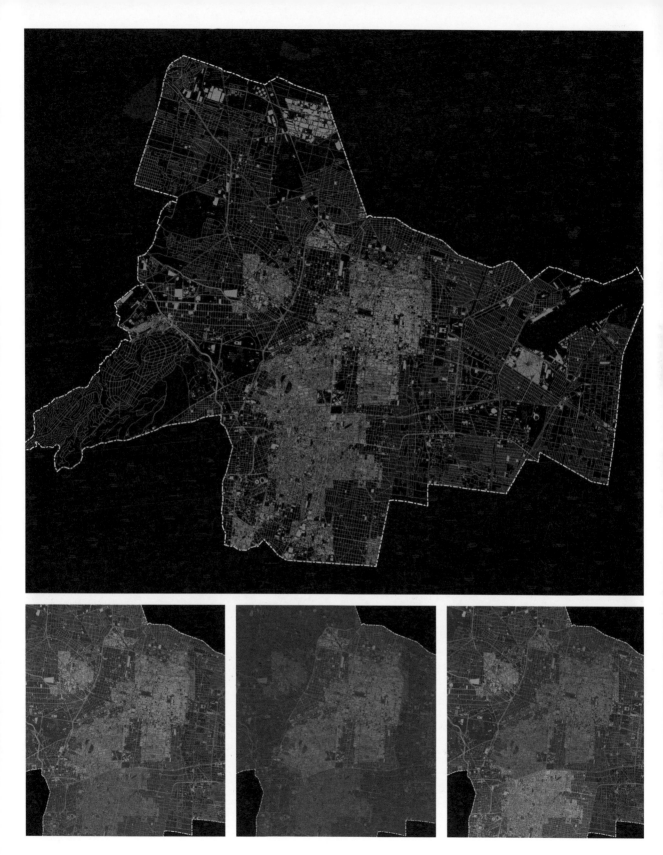

Miami

Florida
United States of America

City Population
435,919

City Area
93 km²

City Density
4,675.74 /km²

Metropolitan Population
6,091,747

Metropolitan Area
15,890 km²

Metropolitan Density
383.37 /km²

City Form Typologies
**Atomized, Random,
Reticular / Organic, Garden**

Miami's evolution as an urban center is intricately linked to its unique geographical position, climate, and historical events. Initially inhabited by Native American tribes, the area's modern development began following the construction of a railway by Henry Flagler in the early 20th century, which turned it into a nexus for tourism and trade. The 1920s saw a land boom fueled by speculative investments, but a devastating hurricane in 1926 and the subsequent Great Depression hindered its growth. Nonetheless, after World War II, Miami re-emerged as a popular tourist destination and saw significant Cuban immigration following Fidel Castro's rise to power in 1959. This influx not only diversified the city's cultural fabric but also became a driving force behind its economic expansion. Miami's location also made it an influential gateway to Latin America, fostering international banking and trade. Furthermore, the development of Miami's Design District and the Art Basel fair strengthened its reputation as a global cultural hub. However, the city also grapples with challenges such as income inequality and the looming threat of sea-level rise due to climate change.

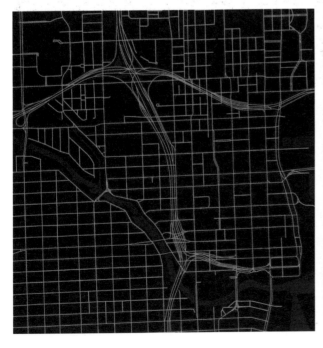

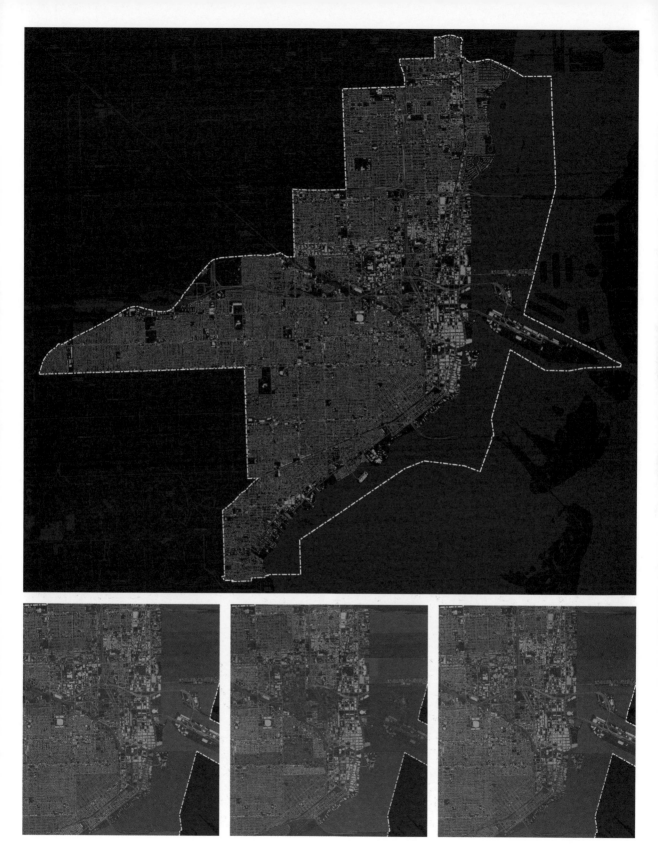

Milan
Lombardy
Italy

City Population
1,371,498

City Area
182 km²

City Density
7,545.65 /km²

Metropolitan Population
3,154,570

Metropolitan Area
1,575 km²

Metropolitan Density
2,002.90 /km²

City Form Typologies
Radial, Small World, Organic, Fractal

The ancient city of Mediolanum was originally a Celtic settlement ("Medhelan"), ultimately conquered by the Romans in the 3rd century BC. Mediolanum inherited a traditional Roman grid, combining orthogonal street patterns with baths, an amphitheater, and a series of religious temples. Milan became the capital of the Western Roman Empire in the 4th century AD, before its boundaries shifted during the turbulent Middle Ages. The city was at some point part of the Byzantine and Holy Roman Empires. During the medieval era, Milan received Small World influences: narrow streets, military fortifications, and numerous churches. The gorgeous Duomo di Milano began its construction in the 14th century. The city experienced cultural and artistic flourishing during the Renaissance, spurred by the patronage of the Sforzas, who promoted projects by virtuoso architects. The Palazzo Reale was built under Spanish rule, before Napoleon's occupation led to profound urban layout alterations. The aftermath of the Congress of Vienna led Milan to become part of the Austrian Empire, but in 1859, the Italian unification marked the beginning of the modernization/industrialization process. Contemporary Milan is a vibrant and cosmopolitan metropolis focused on finance, fashion, and design. The city's skyline presents a mixture of historic and modern architecture (Pirelli Tower, Bosco Verticale).

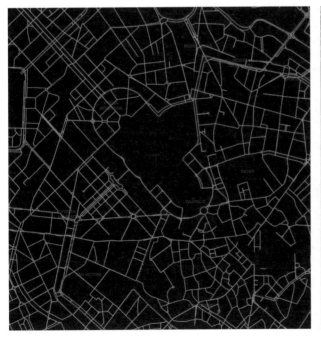

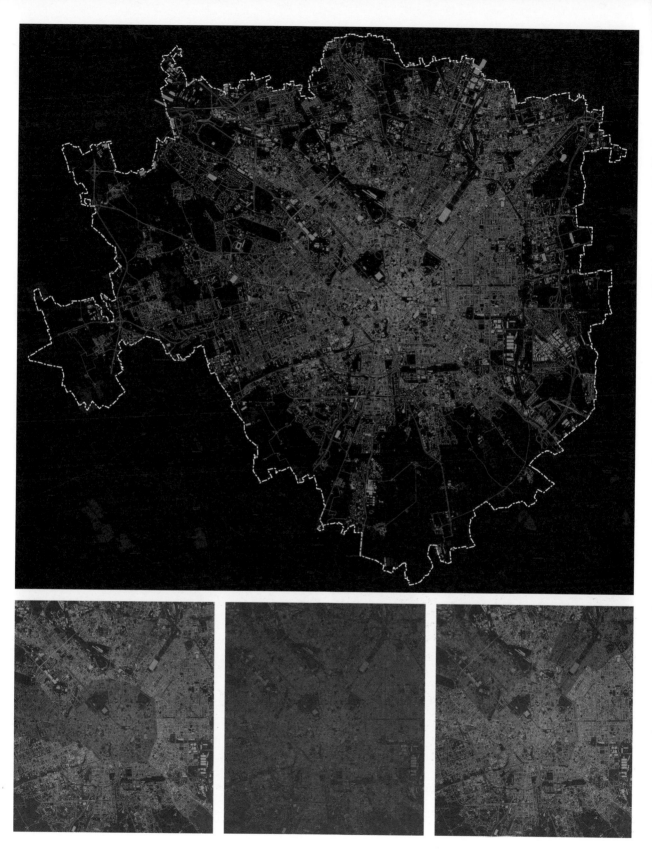

Milwaukee

Wisconsin
United States of America

City Population
555,640

City Area
249 km²

City Density
2,230.41 /km²

Metropolitan Population
1,559,792

Metropolitan Area
3,766 km²

Metropolitan Density
414.16 /km²

City Form Typologies
Reticular, Garden, Organic, Random, Atomized

Milwaukee has a distinctive history rooted in economic and urban development. Founded in the early 19th century, the city grew exponentially during the mid-to-late 1800s, chiefly due to its strategic location at the confluence of three rivers and on the western shore of Lake Michigan. Its waterways facilitated trade and transport, thus supporting the burgeoning industries. By the mid-19th century, the grain-milling industry had flourished in Milwaukee, leveraging the water resources. However, it was the brewing industry, with iconic firms like Schlitz, Pabst, and Miller, that earned the city its reputation as the "beer capital of the world". Concurrently, Milwaukee became a significant manufacturing hub, especially for heavy machinery, owing to the migration of skilled labor from Germany and other parts of Europe. The 20th century saw challenges in the form of deindustrialization, leading to economic restructuring and urban redevelopment. The Menomonee Valley, once a hive of manufacturing, underwent substantial revitalization in the late 20th and early 21st centuries, becoming a model for sustainable urban development. Today, while Milwaukee grapples with issues like segregation and economic disparity, its resilience and diverse economic base have consistently shaped its urban fabric.

Minneapolis

Minnesota
United States of America

City Population
418,075

City Area
140 km²

City Density
2,989.24 /km²

Metropolitan Population
3,693,729

Metropolitan Area
18,259 km²

Metropolitan Density
202.30 /km²

City Form Typologies
Atomized, Random, Organic, Reticular, Garden

The economic and urban development of Minneapolis traces its origins to its strategic position along the Mississippi River. Initially, the city's growth was propelled by its flour milling and timber industries, with the likes of Pillsbury and General Mills establishing their roots there. By the late 19th and early 20th centuries, Minneapolis had evolved into the world's flour milling capital. After World War II, Minneapolis experienced a shift from manufacturing to a more diversified economy. Financial services, commerce, health care, and tech industries began to flourish. Major firms, such as Target and Wells Fargo, established significant operations in the city. Urban planning in the latter half of the 20th century emphasized infrastructure development, including the construction of Interstate 94 and Interstate 35W, which, while enhancing connectivity, also faced criticisms for disrupting established communities, particularly in African American neighborhoods. In recent decades, Minneapolis has been characterized by its efforts towards sustainable urban planning, with initiatives focused on green spaces and public transit, like the METRO Light Rail system. Throughout its history, Minneapolis's urban and economic trajectory has drawn on its natural resources, industrial prowess, and adaptability to a changing global economy.

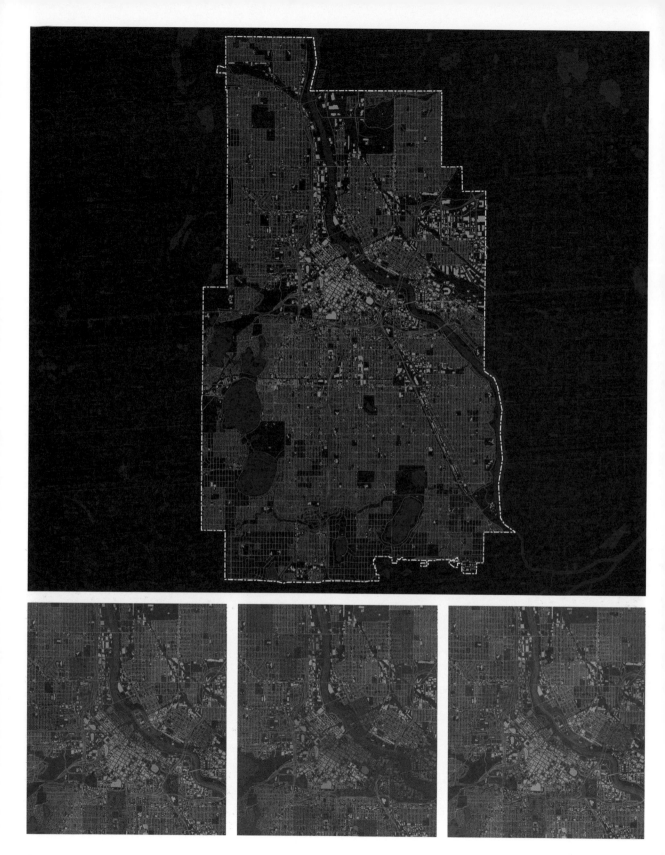

Moscow

Central Federal District
Russia

City Population
12,680,000

City Area
2,562 km²

City Density
4,950.22 /km²

Metropolitan Population
21,700,000

Metropolitan Area
48,360 km²

Metropolitan Density
448.72 /km²

City Form Typologies
Radial, Organic, Garden

The city of Moscow was originally founded as a small fortress on the banks of the Moskva River. The city grew organically as a center of trade and governance, hosting the monumental-style Kremlin fortified complex, standing as a symbol of Moscow's political power and influence in the Slavic world. The medieval city's layout followed Small World patterns, with narrow streets, wooden buildings, and Orthodox churches (Dormition). As the capital of the Tsardom of Russia, Moscow eventually evolved into a major cultural and political center. The Reign of Ivan the Terrible brought the construction of the Great Bell Tower and expansion of the Kremlin, whereas under Peter the Great the city experienced significant westernization, adopting Baroque and Neoclassical architectural styles. The Imperial style propagated an urban pattern composed of a series of concentric rings, establishing Moscow as one of the foremost Radial cities. Moscow underwent rapid urban expansion during the Industrial Revolution (Bolshoi theater, Opera House). The profound influence of the Soviet Era was centered on Socialist Realism, with its grandiose government buildings, wide boulevards and Stalinist architecture. The Seven Sisters skyscraper and the Metro became symbols of the new era. Contemporary Moscow combines the status of a modern metropolis with the conservation of its historical heritage.

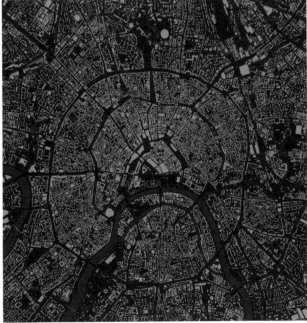

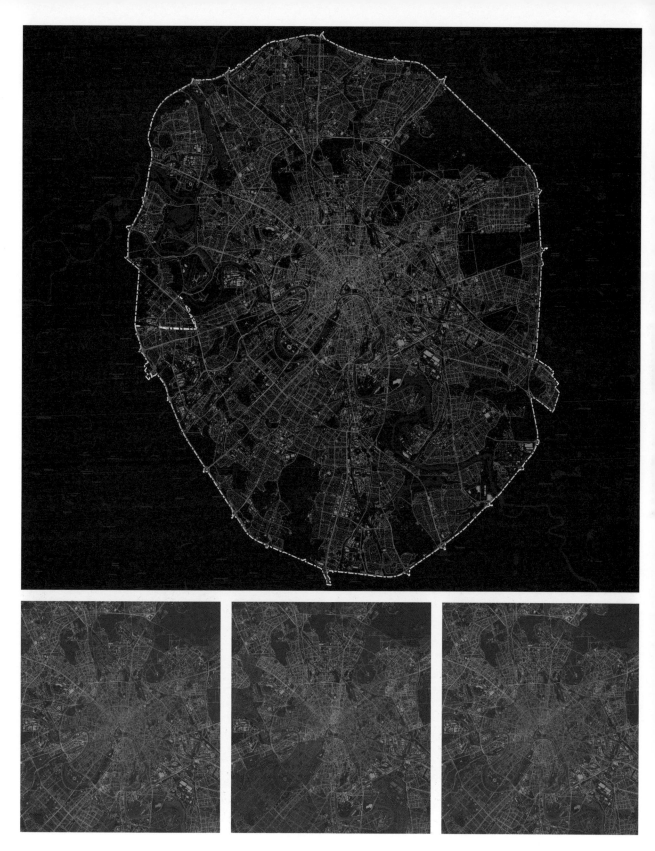

Mumbai

Maharashtra
India

City Population
14,350,000

City Area
603 km²

City Density
23,781.90 /km²

Metropolitan Population
21,296,517

Metropolitan Area
4,355 km²

Metropolitan Density
4,890.13 /km²

City Form Typologies
Random, Organic, Atomized, Garden

Mumbai epitomizes India's urbanization trajectory, evolving from an ancient fishing settlement to a premier global metropolis. Historically, Mumbai's economic centrality emerged from its colonial legacy when the British Crown leased the seven islands of Bombay to the East India Company in 1668. The subsequent construction of the Hornby Vellard in 1784 united these islands, setting the stage for infrastructural development and commercial expansion. During the 19th and early 20th centuries, Mumbai emerged as a prime cotton trading center, further augmented by the American Civil War which disrupted global cotton supplies. The city's economic landscape shifted towards industrialization with the establishment of textile mills. Mumbai's port, one of the finest deep-water ports in the subcontinent, further solidified its role as an economic hub, facilitating trade and movement of goods. Post-independence, the city's economic base diversified into finance, services, and the entertainment industry. The rise of Bollywood positioned Mumbai as a cultural powerhouse. However, rapid urbanization posed challenges, including housing shortages and infrastructural bottlenecks. The juxtaposition of the affluent business districts and sprawling informal settlements underscores Mumbai's economic disparities. Despite these challenges, Mumbai's resilience, demographic dynamism, and economic vigor continue to propel it on the global stage.

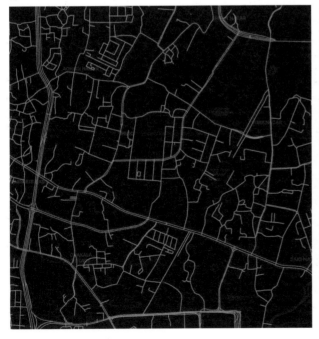

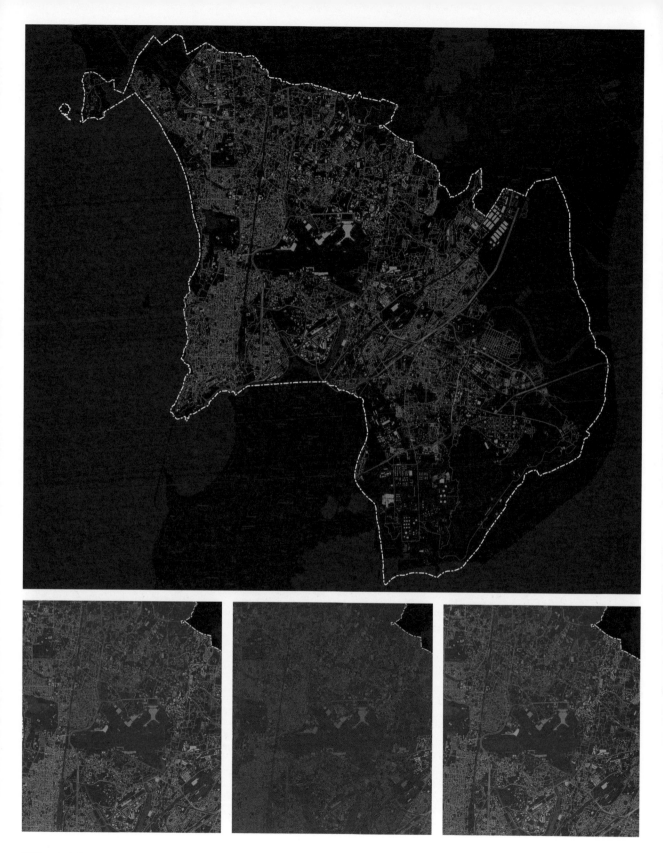

Munich

Bavaria
Germany

City Population
1,578,132

City Area
311 km²

City Density
5,079.28 /km²

Metropolitan Population
5,991,144

Metropolitan Area
27,700 km²

Metropolitan Density
216.29 /km²

City Form Typologies
**Small World, Radial / Organic,
Linear, Garden**

The capital of modern Bavaria emerged in the 12th century as a market town near the banks of the Isar River. Munich eventually grew into a fortified medieval urbs, a quintessential Small World city, the natural capital of the Duchy of Bavaria. Munich expanded beyond its ancient walls by means of a Radial-Organic pattern during the Baroque and Rococo era, undergoing significant architectural and urban development. Embellished by its gorgeous churches, palaces and magnificent squares, and nurturing grand landmarks such as the Nymphenburg Palace and Theatinerkirche, Munich led the Kingdom of Bavaria throughout the early stages of the Industrial Revolution. The economic boom observed during the 19th century demanded a notable urban expansion, mostly characterized by linear-organic morphological features, a development greatly influenced by neoclassical and historicist architectural styles. The rapid industrialization and modernization processes that took place during the late 19th and early 20th centuries brought suburban growth and an expansion of the transportation network, while the city adopted some of the world's largest urban parks: the so-called English Gardens. Contemporary Munich required substantial post-war reconstruction in order to restore historical landmarks and revitalize the now vibrant city center.

Nashville

Tennessee
United States of America

City Population
658,525

City Area
1,305 km²

City Density
504.46 /km²

Metropolitan Population
2,072,283

Metropolitan Area
19,380 km²

Metropolitan Density
106.93 /km²

City Form Typologies
Atomized, Organic, Garden

Nashville often hailed as the "Music City" due to its rich musical heritage, has experienced multifaceted economic and urban developments since its founding in 1779. Originally established as a trading post along the Cumberland River, Nashville rapidly grew into a prominent river port by the early 19th century. However, its strategic location led to its devastation during the Civil War, after which it underwent significant reconstruction, harnessing the railway system to revitalize its economy. The 20th century marked Nashville's diversification away from solely agrarian interests. The emergence of a healthcare sector, with institutions such as the Vanderbilt University Medical Center, began transforming the city's economic landscape. Around the same time, the expansion of the Grand Ole Opry in the 1920s solidified Nashville's reputation as the hub of country music, attracting both tourists and aspiring musicians, thereby fueling both the service and entertainment sectors. Urban development, particularly in the latter half of the 20th century, responded to these economic shifts. The city underwent major infrastructural projects and land-use reconfigurations, leading to the establishment of key urban centers and amenities, reflecting its evolving economic imperatives.

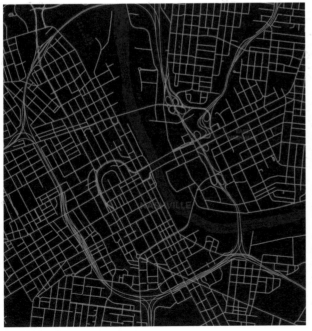

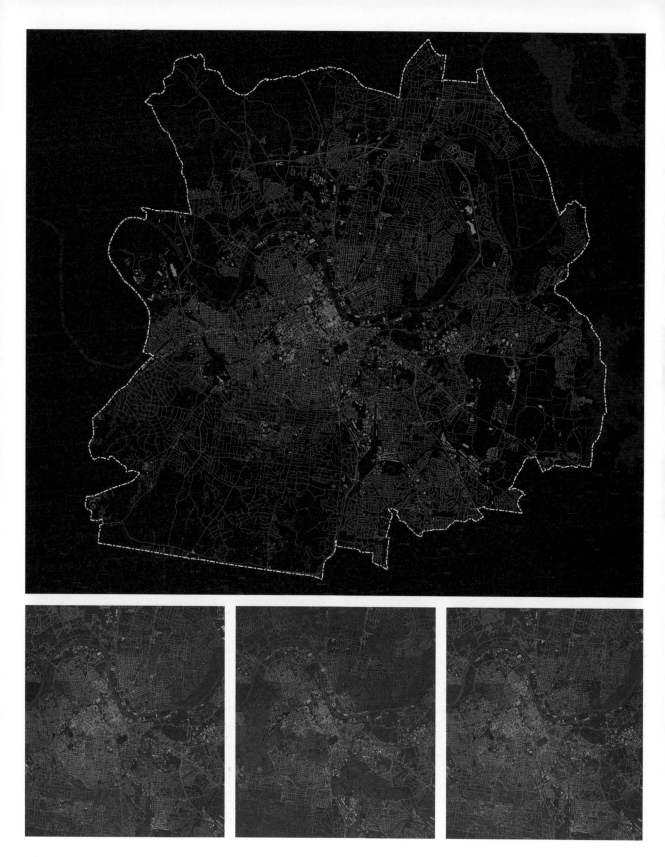

New York City

New York
United States of America

City Population
7,888,121

City Area
778 km²

City Density
10,136.63 /km²

Metropolitan Population
19,617,869

Metropolitan Area
8,936 km²

Metropolitan Density
2,195.37 /km²

City Form Typologies
Reticular, Organic, Atomized, Garden

The colony of New Amsterdam was founded in the early 17th century as a Dutch settlement. Established at the southern tip of the island of Manhattan, it eventually became the capital of New Netherland. The original configuration mimicked those of contemporary cities in the Netherlands, following a Small World urban typology. The subsequent takeover by the British Empire did not dramatically alter the morphological structure during the 18th century, and it was consolidated through the Revolutionary period. The construction of the Erie Canal during the 1820s helped New York achieve commercial primacy. The city embraced a quintessentially Reticular city form pattern as a result of Commissioners' Plan of 1811, which shaped most of the exponential growth that took place during the Industrial Revolution. The eastern strip of Staten Island followed a linear model, whereas Brooklyn adopted a fractured mosaic of small grids displaying multiple orientations. Queens and most of Long Island adopted an organic growth pattern, which was also the main city form configuration in the development of the borough of the Bronx.

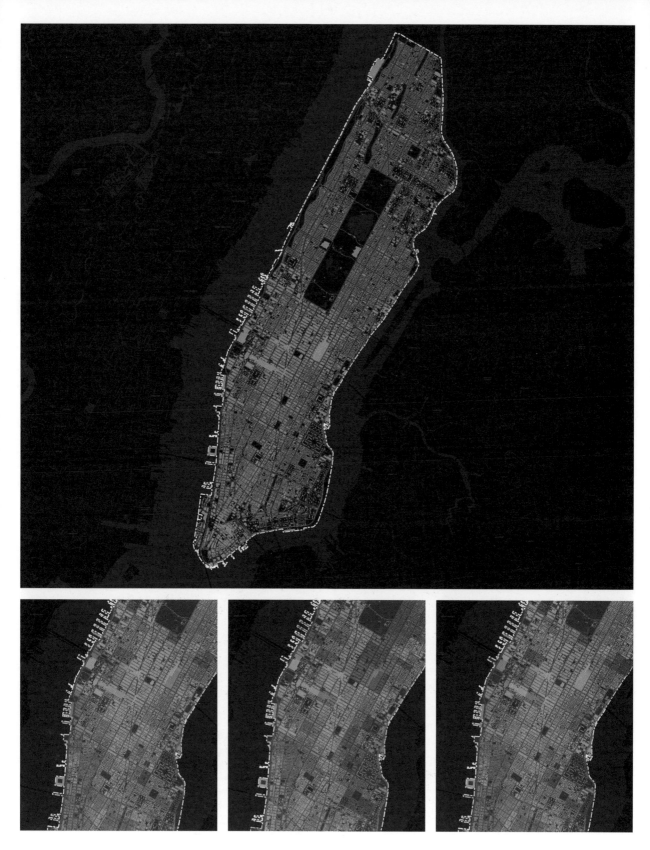

Osaka

Kansai
Japan

City Population
2,753,862

City Area
225 km²

City Density
12,227.97 /km²

Metropolitan Population
19,303,000

Metropolitan Area
13,228 km²

Metropolitan Density
1,459.25 /km²

City Form Typologies
Atomized, Reticular, Organic, Linear

The economic and urban development of Osaka traces its origins to ancient times when it served as the country's political and economic center during the 7th and 8th centuries. During the Edo period (1603-1868), Osaka emerged as a crucial economic hub, often dubbed the "kitchen of Japan", given its role in the rice trade. The unique system of rice brokerage known as the Dojima Rice Exchange, founded in 1697, further bolstered Osaka's economic significance, foreshadowing futures trading practices. The Meiji Restoration (1868) and subsequent industrialization transformed Osaka from a trading nexus into an industrial powerhouse. The city underwent rapid urbanization, bolstered by the establishment of factories, especially in the textile sector. Following World War II, Osaka faced the challenges of rebuilding and emerged as a vanguard in urban planning, with the development of the Osaka Bay Area and the city's bid to host the 1970 World Expo symbolizing its revitalization. Today, Osaka's legacy as an economic dynamo endures, with the city playing an integral role in the Kansai region's development, embracing innovation and continually redefining its urban landscape.

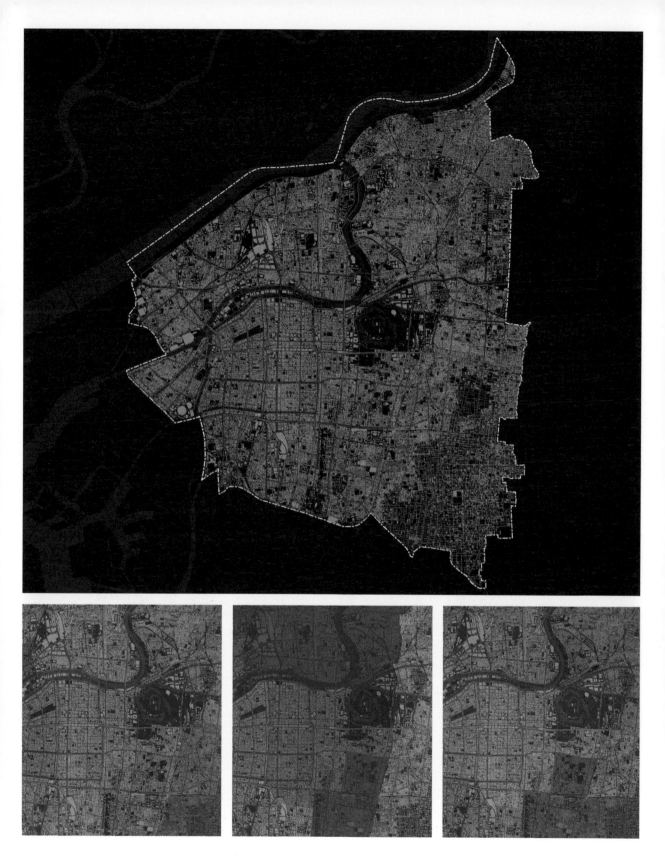

Paris

Île-de-France
France

City Population
2,102,650

City Area
105 km²

City Density
19,949.24 /km²

Metropolitan Population
11,208,000

Metropolitan Area
18,941 km²

Metropolitan Density
591.74 /km²

City Form Typologies
Radial / Organic, Fractal, Garden

Ancient Paris (3rd century BC–5th century AD) was originally called Lutetia, a Gaul settlement that eventually became a Roman metropolis. The development of critical engineering infrastructure, such as roads and bridges, gave rise to a Small World city pattern, consolidated during Medieval times. Île de la Cité became the neuralgic center, built around Notre-Dame Cathedral, constructed in the 12th century. The narrow, sinuous streets and the construction of iconic landmarks like the Louvre Palace and the city walls followed a natural pattern of organic evolution. During the Renaissance and the Enlightenment era the city expanded beyond the boundaries of the medieval wall; grand boulevards and squares (Place des Vosges) followed a Monumental City construct. The expansion of the Palace of Versailles remarkably influenced urban planning and architecture in Paris (three main avenues including one leading to Paris, Avenue de Paris). The urban transformation led by Georges-Eugène Haussmann under Napoleon III constituted a strongly radial system. The plan included widening boulevards, implementing urban parks (Parc des Buttes-Chaumont) and modernizing civil infrastructure, and putting up iconic buildings ("immeubles Haussmaniens"). Post-war urban development involved new/innovative landmarks such as La Défense (business district) and high-tech spaces like the Pompidou Center.

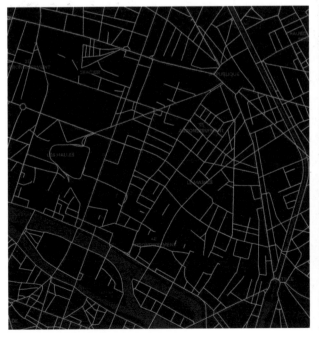

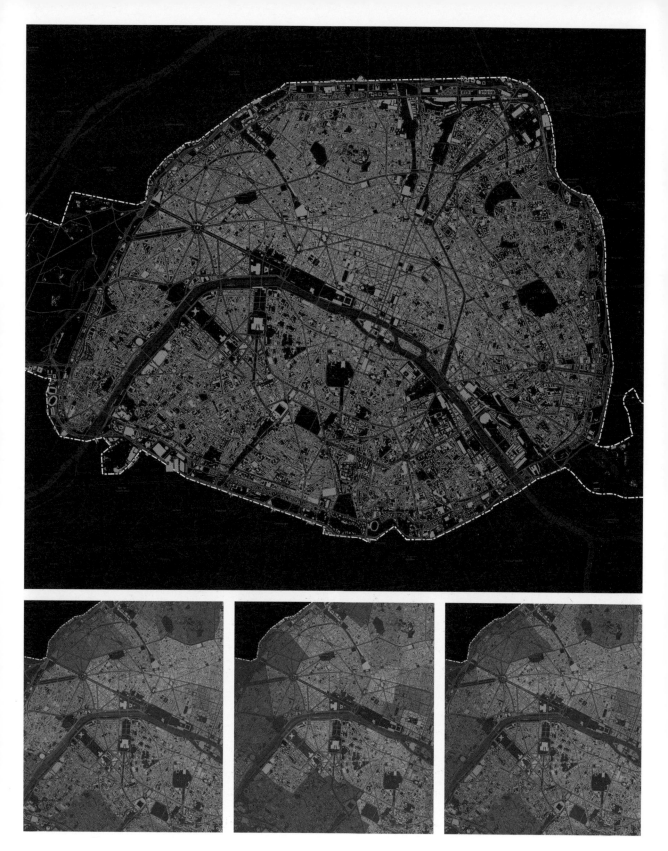

Perth

Western Australia
Australia

City Population
2,043,762

City Area
1,720 km²

City Density
318.44 /km²

Metropolitan Population
2,192,229

Metropolitan Area
6,418 km²

Metropolitan Density
341.58 /km²

City Form Typologies
Atomized, Reticular, Organic, Garden

Founded in 1829 as the Swan River Colony to serve as a British colonial outpost, the city of Perth was originally a modest, grid-like frontier settlement, centered around St. George's Terrace and the Swan River. Historic buildings such as the Government House and St. Mary's Cathedral recreated quintessential European features in a city strongly shaped in an atomized manner due to the orographic conditions of the riverbed. The Australian Gold Rush brought a large influx of wealth and population growth, expanding the city beyond its original boundaries via the construction of grand public buildings such as the Perth Town Hall and the Supreme Court of Western Australia. After World War II, Perth adopted an intense suburbanization pattern, connecting the newly conceived neighborhoods by means of new transportation infrastructure (Narrows Bridge, Mitchell Freeway). In recent decades, Perth benefitted from the impulse derived from mining and natural gas exploration, which led the city to become a hub for natural resource extraction corporations and related industries. Modern commercial and residential complexes (Perth Convention and Exhibition Centre, Elizabeth Quay waterfront redevelopment) placed significant emphasis on the need for sustainable development growth patterns (Perth City Link, Yagan Square).

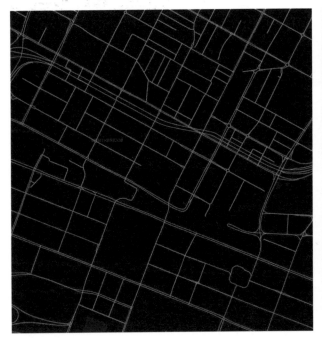

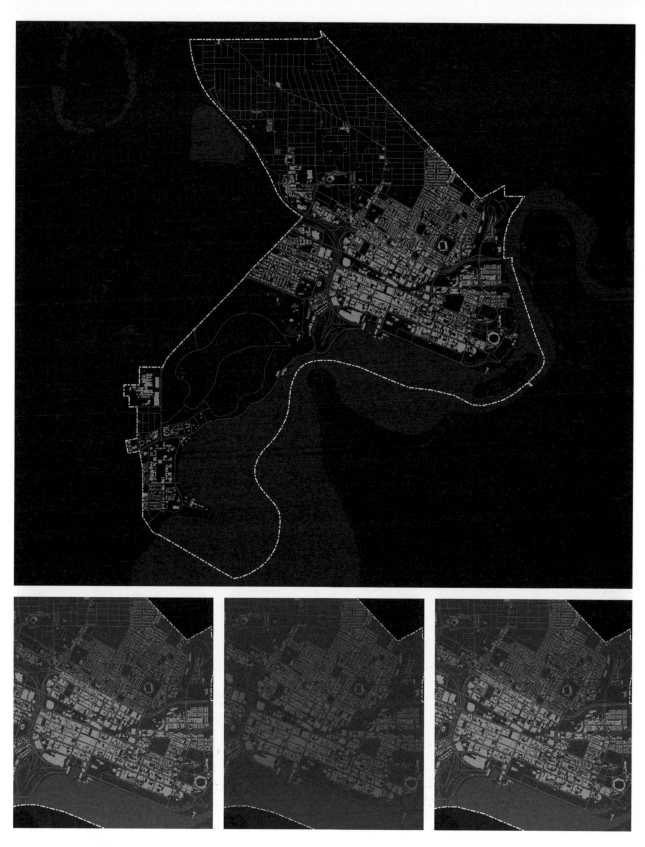

Philadelphia

Pennsylvania
United States of America

City Population
1,527,886

City Area
348 km²

City Density
4,390.73 /km²

Metropolitan Population
6,241,164

Metropolitan Area
11,943 km²

Metropolitan Density
522.60 /km²

City Form Typologies
Reticular, Organic, Small World, Atomized, Garden

The economic and urban development of Philadelphia, Pennsylvania, has been integrally tied to its historical and geographical context. Founded by William Penn in 1682 as a haven for Quakers, the city's early layout emphasized egalitarianism, and Penn's grid system served as a model for many subsequent American cities. By the 18th century, Philadelphia had grown into a major port and was pivotal in the American Revolution and the drafting of the U.S. Constitution. Its economic ascent in the 19th century was spurred by industrialization, particularly in textiles, manufacturing, and shipbuilding, positioning it as a major gateway for immigrants and a transportation nexus with the consolidation of Pennsylvania Railroad. However, the 20th century saw economic stagnation and decline, as deindustrialization led to job losses and population decrease, and the urban renewal programs of the 1960s, intended to rejuvenate the city, often inadvertently displaced marginalized communities. Nonetheless, in recent decades, Philadelphia has been undergoing a resurgence, with revitalized neighborhoods, burgeoning cultural institutions, and a diversified economy driven by education, healthcare, and technology. This cyclical trajectory of Philadelphia's development underscores the dynamic interplay of its historical legacy, economic shifts, and urban planning endeavors.

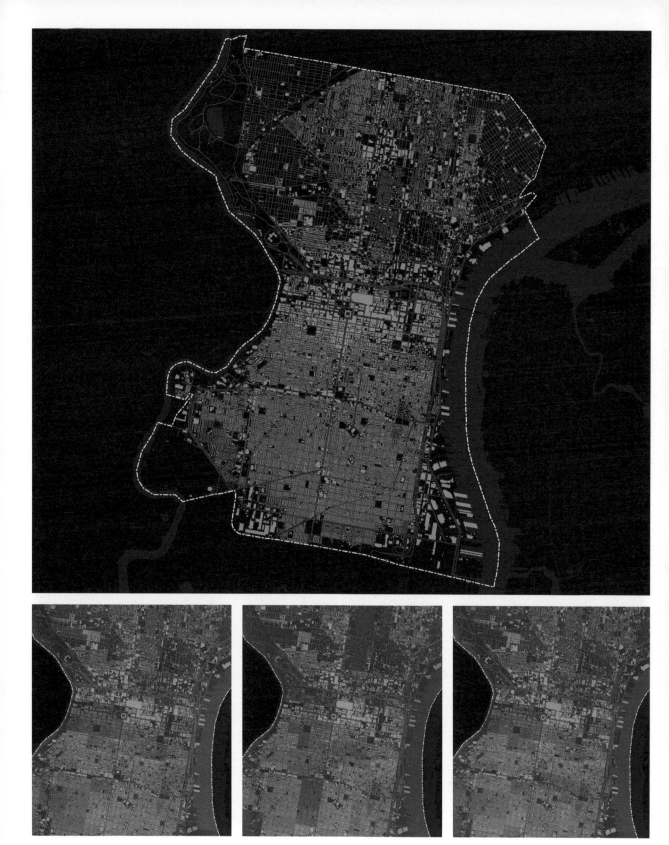

Phoenix

Arizona
United States of America

City Population
1,651,344

City Area
1,342 km²

City Density
1,230.23 /km²

Metropolitan Population
4,845,832

Metropolitan Area
37,810 km²

Metropolitan Density
128.16 /km²

City Form Typologies
Random, Organic, Garden, Reticular

The history of Phoenix's economic and urban development is an emblematic tale of Western urbanization in the United States. Founded in the late 19th century, Phoenix capitalized on the Salt River's irrigation potential to cultivate a robust agricultural economy, becoming a major producer of cotton, citrus, and livestock. With the advent of the federal Reclamation Act of 1902, the construction of the Roosevelt Dam in 1911 significantly expanded Phoenix's agricultural prowess. The mid-20th century brought transformative changes to Phoenix. The burgeoning growth of the aerospace industry, notably with companies like Honeywell and Motorola, paved the way for a more diversified economy. Concurrently, federal investment in highways and the burgeoning allure of Sunbelt cities ignited Phoenix's metamorphosis into a major metropolitan area. As a result, Phoenix experienced rapid suburbanization, a trend further exacerbated by affordable housing and the availability of air conditioning, which mitigated the challenges of the desert environment. However, this growth was not without consequences. The city's rapid expansion precipitated a range of urban challenges, from water scarcity to infrastructural strains. Still, Phoenix stands as a testament to the adaptability and resilience of urban centers in arid landscapes.

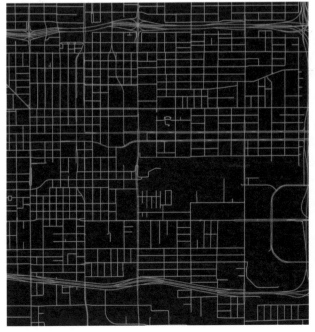

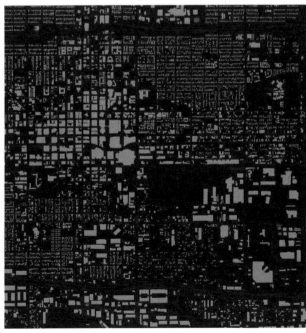

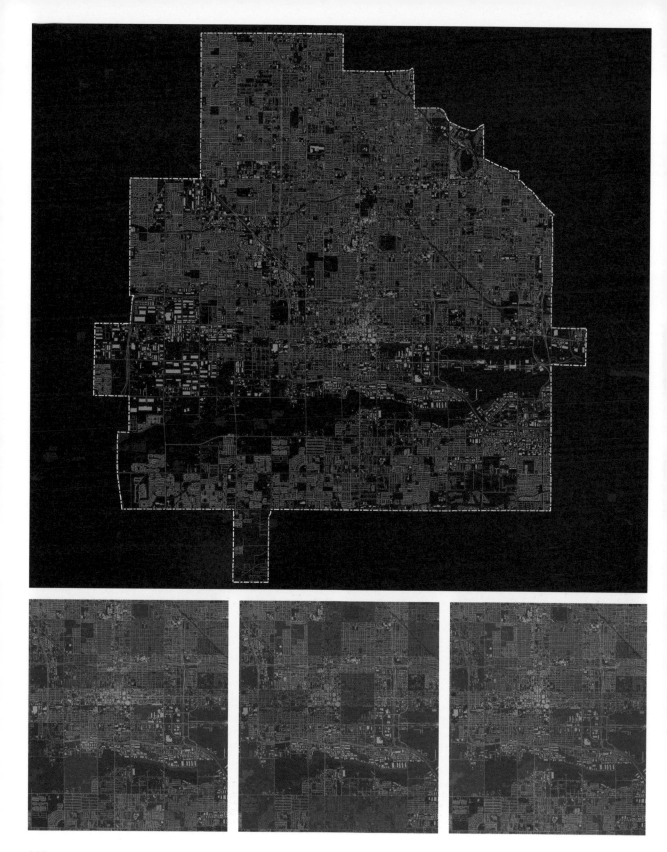

Pittsburgh

Pennsylvania
United States of America

City Population
295,793

City Area
143 km²

City Density
2,062.43 /km²

Metropolitan Population
2,370,930

Metropolitan Area
13,665 km²

Metropolitan Density
173.50 /km²

City Form Typologies
Atomized, Garden, Organic

Pittsburgh, Pennsylvania, historically branded as the "Steel City", embarked on its journey to urban prominence in the late 18th and early 19th centuries due to its strategic location at the confluence of the Allegheny, Monongahela, and Ohio Rivers, proving to be a crucial hub for trade and transportation. In the 19th century, with the advent of the coal and iron industries, Pittsburgh rapidly transformed into a bustling industrial center. The emergence of major steel corporations in the late 19th and early 20th centuries solidified Pittsburgh's status as the heart of America's steel production. However, by the mid-20th century, Pittsburgh was grappling with significant economic and environmental challenges, including severe pollution and an aging industrial base. The decline of the steel industry in the 1970s and 1980s led to massive job losses, pushing the city towards economic turmoil. Yet, the late 20th and early 21st centuries witnessed Pittsburgh's resilient reinvention. Transitioning from a manufacturing-based economy, the city embraced sectors like healthcare, technology, and education. Anchored by institutions like Carnegie Mellon University and the University of Pittsburgh, the city emerged as a hub for robotics, artificial intelligence, and healthcare innovations. Pittsburgh's urban and economic narrative reflects a tale of industrial prowess, subsequent decline, and dynamic rebirth, illustrating the city's resilience and adaptability.

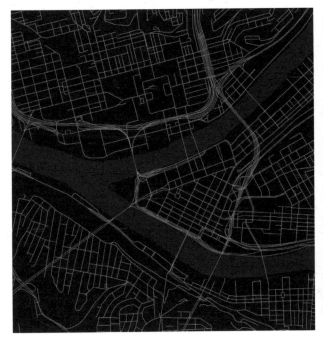

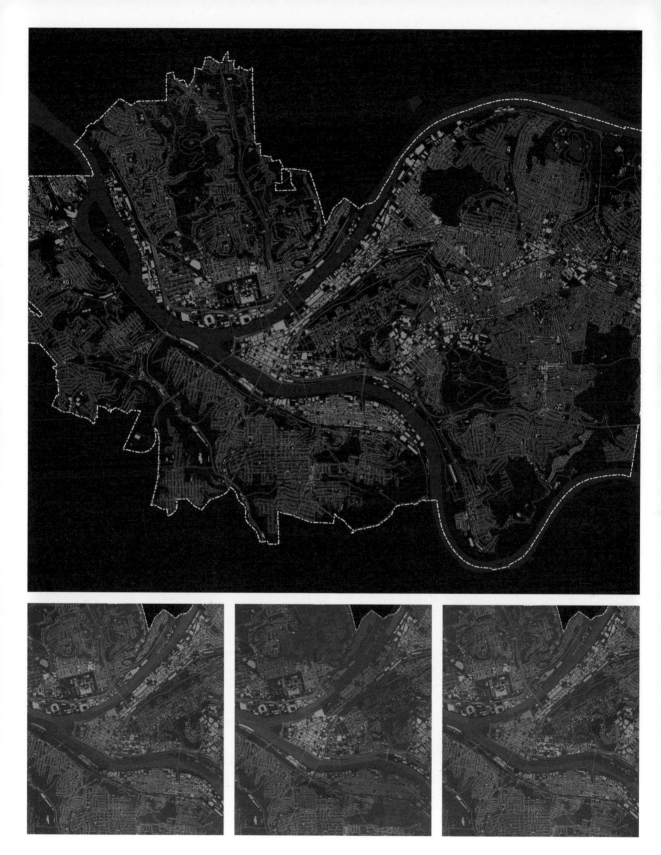

Portland

Oregon
United States of America

City Population
619,286

City Area
346 km²

City Density
1,791.24 /km²

Metropolitan Population
2,509,140

Metropolitan Area
17,359 km²

Metropolitan Density
144.55 /km²

City Form Typologies
Atomized, Linear, Reticular, Organic, Garden

Portland, Oregon, emblematic of the Pacific Northwest's urban and economic trajectory, boasts a rich tapestry of development rooted in its geographical advantage at the confluence of the Willamette and Columbia Rivers. Established in the mid-19th century, Portland initially flourished due to its timber industry, leveraging its extensive forests and serving as a primary hub for the logging sector, which remained a cornerstone of the city's economy into the early 20th century. Thereafter, diversification became its economic hallmark, as maritime trade, manufacturing and, subsequently, technology began to shape Portland's urban fabric. The city strategically capitalized on its riverine assets, creating a robust port system that buttressed international trade. Post World War II, urban planners embraced forward-thinking designs, culminating in the removal of the Harbor Drive freeway in the 1970s and the embrace of public transportation exemplified by the MAX Light Rail in the 1980s. In recent decades, Portland's growth has been underscored by its sustainable urban planning, manifested in policies promoting pedestrian zones, bike-friendly infrastructure, and urban green spaces. Concurrently, the city has emerged as a hub for technology and creative industries, further diversifying its economic portfolio.

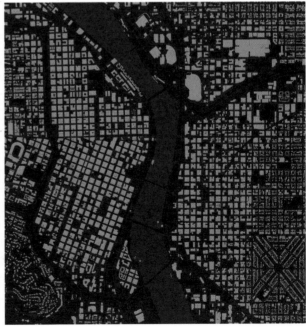

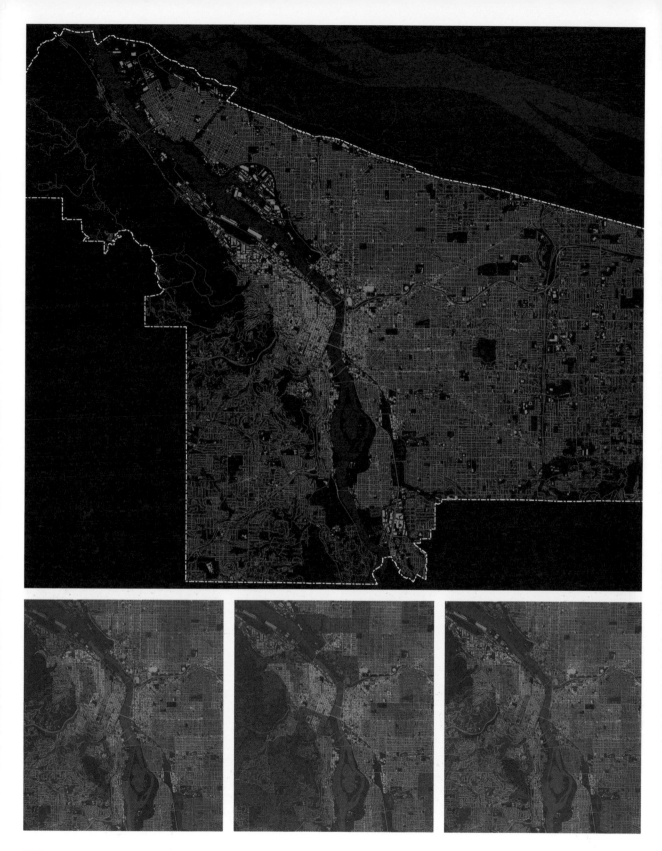

Pretoria

Gaugteng
South Africa

City Population
2,818,100

City Area
688 km²

City Density
4,098.82 /km²

Metropolitan Population
2,921,488

Metropolitan Area
6,298 km²

Metropolitan Density
463.89 /km²

City Form Typologies
Organic, Random, Reticular, Linear

Pretoria, the administrative capital of South Africa, has experienced dynamic economic and urban transformations since its foundation in 1855. Initially founded as a Boer capital in the Transvaal, it has deep roots in the country's colonial and apartheid histories. In the late 19th century, British forces took control of Pretoria, further cementing its significance in the geopolitical landscape of the region. The discovery of gold in nearby Johannesburg in 1886 led to an influx of people, indirectly boosting Pretoria's economy as it served as an administrative and services hub. Post-World War II, Pretoria was transformed into a major industrial center, with a focus on iron, steel, and machinery, diversifying its previously agrarian-based economy. Its urban morphology was, however, deeply shaped by apartheid planning policies, which saw the racial segregation of its population into specific urban areas. Since the end of apartheid in 1994, Pretoria has sought to reposition itself within a democratic South Africa. Recent decades have seen endeavors to undo the spatial legacies of segregation, with major infrastructural projects, such as the Gautrain, bridging previously divided regions.

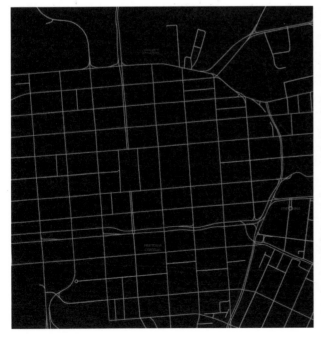

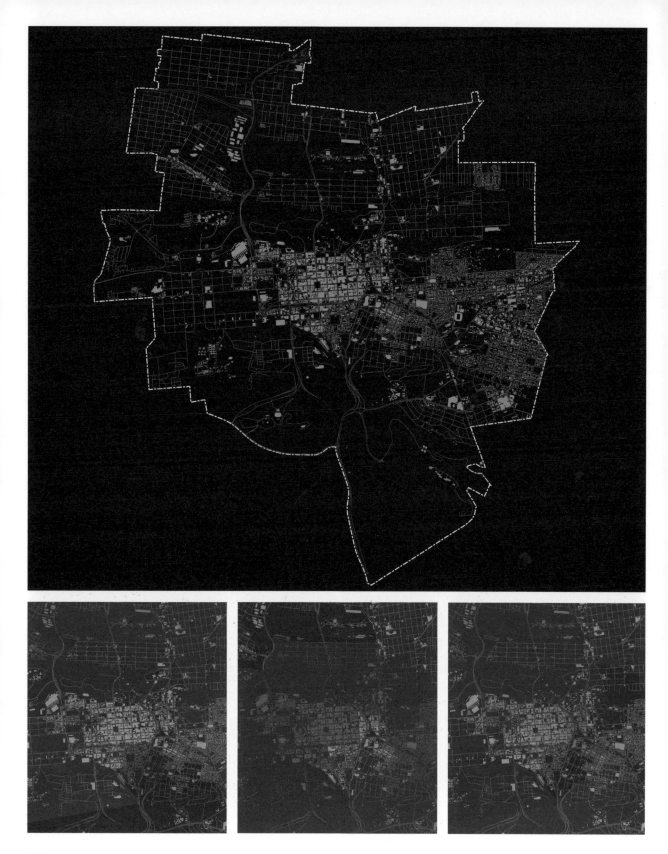

Raleigh

North Carolina
United States of America

City Population
472,540

City Area
381 km²

City Density
1,240.26 /km²

Metropolitan Population
1,484,338

Metropolitan Area
5,486 km²

Metropolitan Density
270.56 /km²

City Form Typologies
Organic, Garden

The economic and urban development of Raleigh, North Carolina, has its roots in its founding in 1792 as a planned city, designated to be the state capital. Strategically located in the state, Raleigh began its growth trajectory associated with governmental functions. In the 19th century, Raleigh's economy was bolstered by the rise of the North Carolina Railroad, which facilitated trade and commerce. This transportation infrastructure helped Raleigh diversify its economy, promoting both agricultural exports and industrial activities. The 20th century witnessed significant growth, particularly with the establishment of the Research Triangle Park (RTP) in 1959, situated between Raleigh, Durham, and Chapel Hill. RTP transformed Raleigh's economy by attracting high-tech firms and research institutions, which leveraged the talent from nearby universities like North Carolina State University. The knowledge-based economy thrived, ensuring steady urban growth. In recent decades, Raleigh has been marked by progressive urban planning initiatives that focus on sustainable development, green spaces, and improved public transportation. As a result, the city has been recognized for its quality of life, attracting both businesses and residents, thus reinforcing its position as a hub for innovation and economic growth in the Southeastern United States.

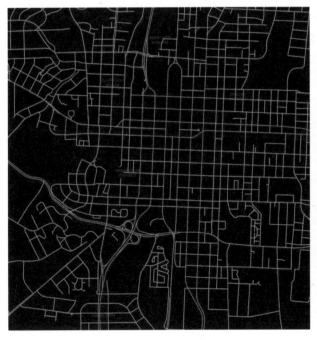

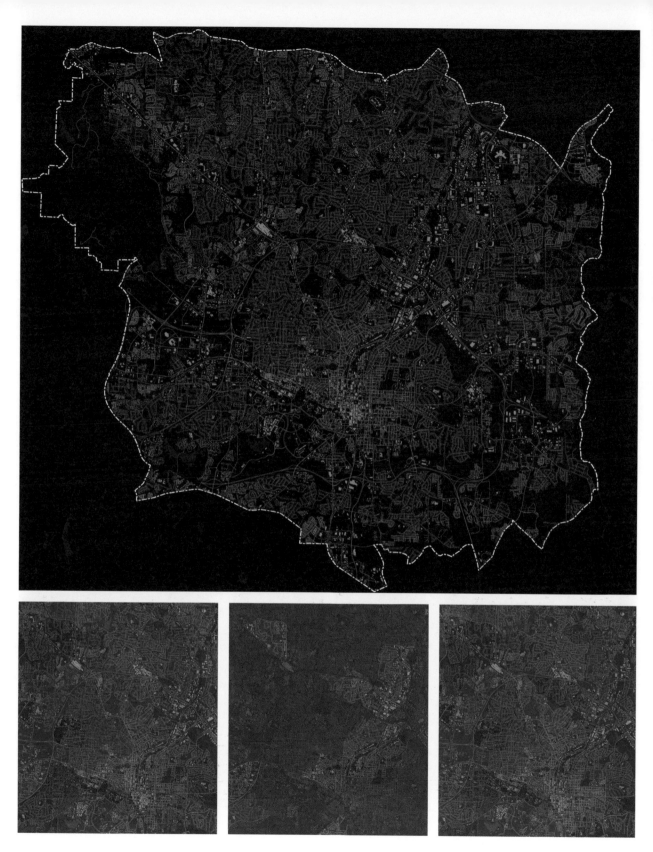

Rio de Janeiro

Rio de Janeiro
Brazil

City Population
6,747,815

City Area
1,221 km²

City Density
5,526.74 /km²

Metropolitan Population
13,727,720

Metropolitan Area
4,540 km²

Metropolitan Density
3,023.86 /km²

City Form Typologies
Random, Monumental,
Atomized, Organic, Garden

Rio de Janeiro, once the capital of Brazil (1763-1960), has a long history of economic and urban development marked by its natural harbor, its colonial past, and its subsequent industrialization. Founded in 1565 by the Portuguese, the city initially thrived due to its port activities and the sugar trade, which was heavily reliant on enslaved Africans. By the 18th century, gold and diamond mining in nearby Minas Gerais bolstered Rio's importance as an export point and led to significant urban expansion. The early 20th century witnessed a series of urban reforms aimed at "modernizing" the city. Influenced by the City Beautiful Movement, Mayor Pereira Passos, with the support of sanitarian Oswaldo Cruz, implemented significant infrastructure projects and demolished overcrowded areas, replacing them with grand boulevards, parks, and monuments. This period also marked the beginning of the expansion of the city's *favelas* (informal settlements), a response to housing shortages and social inequalities. Following World War II, Rio saw rapid industrialization and population growth. The relocation of the capital to Brasília in 1960 did not deter its development; on the contrary, the city transitioned into a major cultural, economic, and tourist hub. However, the economic progress was juxtaposed with increasing spatial segregation, as *favelas* grew alongside elite enclaves, making urban planning a constant challenge.

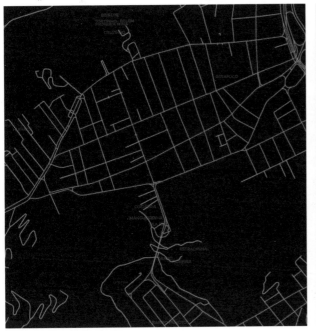

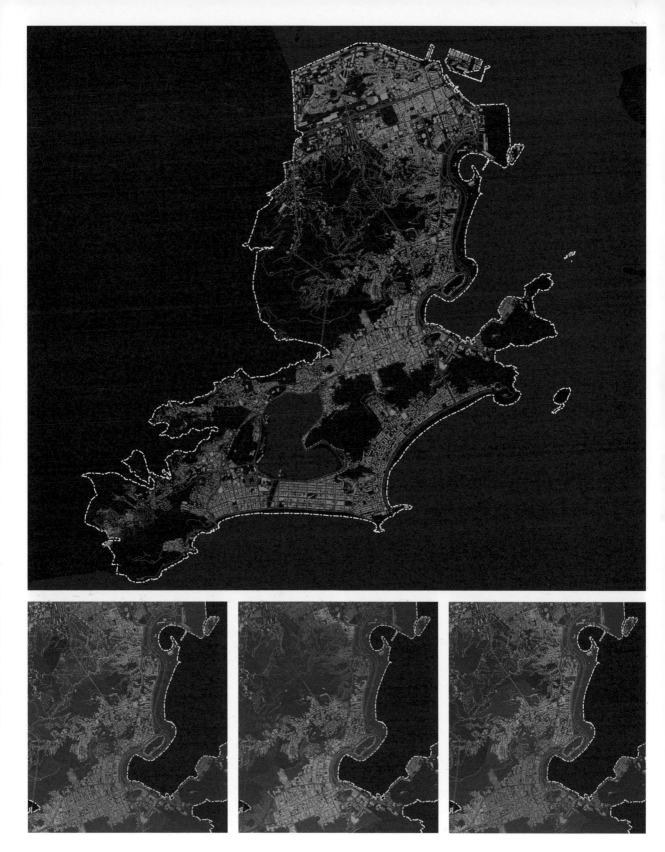

Riyadh

Riyadh
Saudi Arabia

City Population
7,009,100

City Area
1,973 km²

City Density
3,552.51 /km²

Metropolitan Population
8,591,748

Metropolitan Area
404,240 km²

Metropolitan Density
21.25 /km²

City Form Typologies
Organic, Reticular, Random, Monumental

Riyadh, the capital of Saudi Arabia, has a rich history that traces its origins to pre-Islamic times. However, its significant urban and economic transformation began in the 20th century, sparked by the discovery of oil in the Arabian Peninsula in the 1930s. The city, originally a small oasis, witnessed rapid urbanization in the 1960s, largely driven by the immense revenues from oil exports. This influx of wealth funded large-scale infrastructure projects, converting the traditional mud-brick city into a sprawling metropolis. By the 1970s and 1980s, the Saudi state had invested heavily in modernizing Riyadh, constructing wide boulevards, skyscrapers, and state-of-the-art public facilities. The state's emphasis on modernization, however, sometimes came at the expense of preserving historical and cultural landmarks. In recent decades, as part of the Vision 2030 initiative, there has been a push to diversify Riyadh's economy away from oil, with investments in sectors such as tourism, entertainment, and technology. This new direction also considers sustainable urban planning and aims to incorporate green spaces and public transportation networks into the city's design.

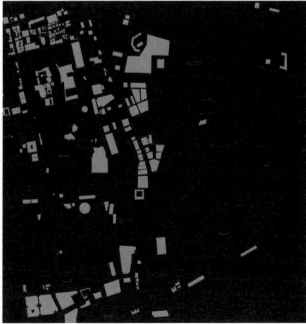

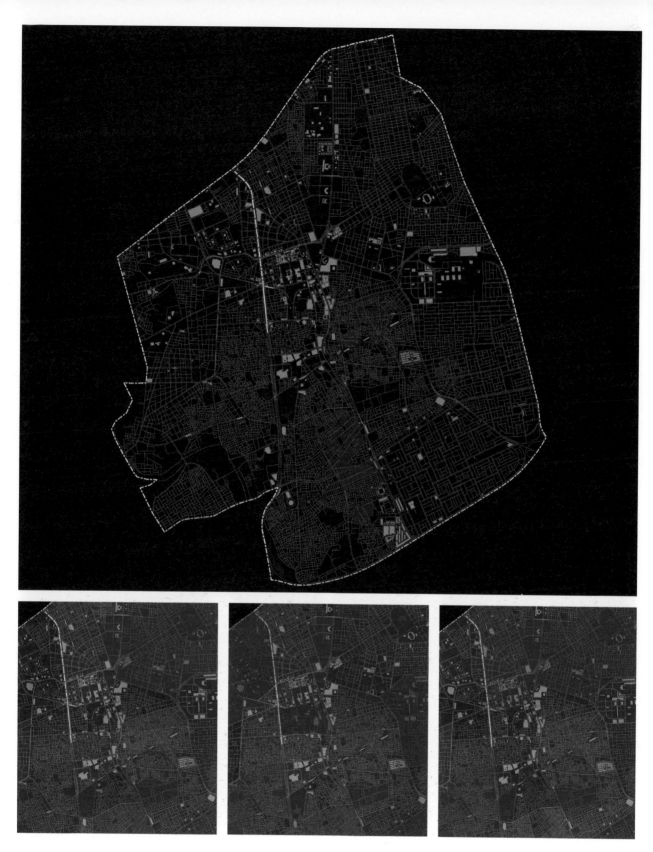

Rome

Lazio
Italy

City Population
2,860,009

City Area
1,285 km²

City Density
2,225.69 /km²

Metropolitan Population
4,315,671

Metropolitan Area
5,352 km²

Metropolitan Density
806.37 /km²

City Form Typologies
Monumental / Fractal, Organic, Atomized, Garden

The mythical foundation of Rome constitutes one of the most memorable legends of European antiquity. Originally ruled by a monarchy since the 8th century BC, Rome became a major continental trade center, propelling the Roman Republic to become a military and political powerhouse, eventually embracing a Monumental growth pattern characterized by iconic structures such as the Roman Forum, the Colosseum, and the Pantheon. Monumental styles were combined with a reticular growth pattern built on a *cardo-decumanus* structure, which influenced a myriad of cities across the vast Empire that grew under the rule of the City of Light. Medieval Rome evolved into a Small World city, adopting a more compact layout, and erecting a peripheral walled structure: a fortified city populated by narrow streets. Rome's personality has been profoundly influenced by its status as the world's capital of Christianity, reinforced by the construction of many churches, including St Peter's Basilica and St. John Lateran. Rome's Renaissance and Baroque expansion brought a renewed sense of grandeur, fueled by widespread piazzas, grand staircases, and boulevards. Contemporary Rome evolved as a modern metropolis, albeit aiming to preserve its rich historical heritage and global influence as the spiritual and administrative center of the Catholic Church.

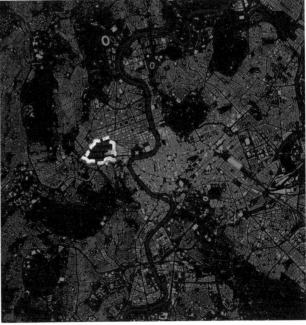

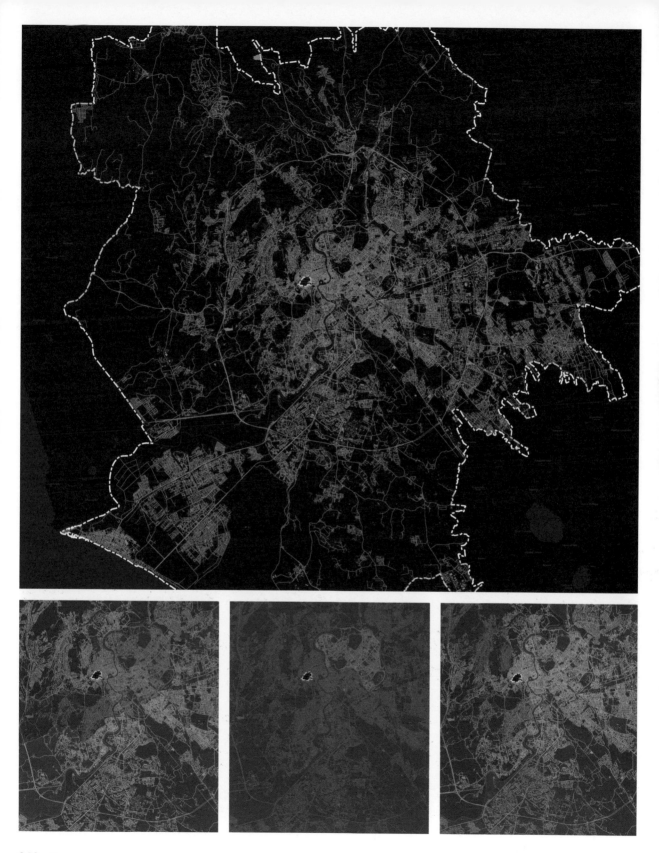

Rotterdam

South Holland
Netherlands

City Population
664,311

City Area
324 km²

City Density
2,049.46 /km²

Metropolitan Population
2,390,101

Metropolitan Area
1,130 km²

Metropolitan Density
2,115.13 /km²

City Form Typologies
Atomized, Linear, Organic, Garden

The majestic and industrious port city of Rotterdam began in the 13th century as a small fishing village near the Rotte River. The city grew in importance because of its strategic location near the North Sea, making it a key trading and maritime center. The golden age and expansion of Rotterdam during the Baroque era brought economic prosperity, as the city's port facilities were expanded to become a global hub for international trade. The development of canal-side archetypal houses reinforced the urban sense of identity, further enhanced by an intense industrialization process, leading to the consolidation of maritime-related industries. The construction of sophisticated infrastructure, complex bridges, and efficient railway systems positioned Rotterdam as a hub for intermodal freight logistics, and the city's port became the largest in all of Europe. During World War II Rotterdam was heavily bombed, and most of its historic center was utterly destroyed. Reconstruction efforts gave rise to a singular and modern cityscape: innovative architecture (Cube Houses, Erasmus Bridge), wide boulevards, and a focus on functionality. Contemporary Rotterdam's port remains the busiest in Europe. The city hosts a series of singular modern buildings and skyscrapers, forming a characteristic urban skyline.

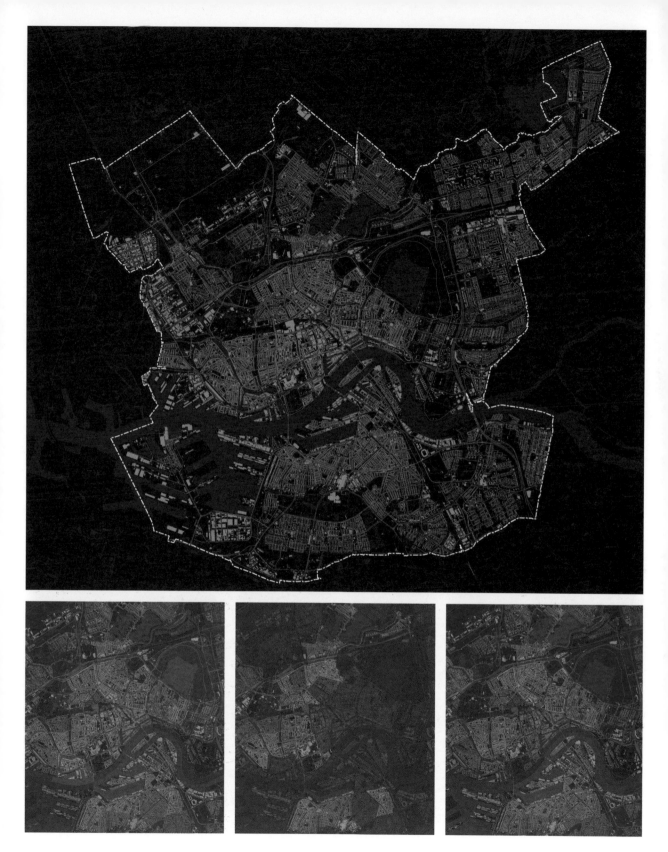

Saint Louis

Missouri
United States of America

City Population
296,262

City Area
160 km²

City Density
1,853.38 /km²

Metropolitan Population
2,809,299

Metropolitan Area
21,910 km²

Metropolitan Density
128.22 /km²

City Form Typologies
Atomized, Reticular, Organic, Garden

The economic and urban development of Saint Louis, Missouri, represents a microcosm of the broader American industrial and post-industrial narrative. Founded in 1764, St. Louis flourished as a river port, becoming a primary hub for the fur trade and later benefiting from its strategic location at the confluence of the Mississippi and Missouri Rivers. The 19th century saw the city further prospering from westward expansion, exemplified by the completion, in 1874, of the Eads Bridge, which became the world's first all-steel bridge, fortifying St. Louis as a critical rail gateway. However, the 20th century posed some challenges. Deindustrialization in the post-World War II era led to an economic downturn, mirrored by urban decay and White flight to the suburbs, which depopulated the city center. This period also witnessed contentious urban renewal projects like the razing of the Mill Creek Valley, displacing thousands of predominantly African American residents, in the 1950s. Recent decades have been characterized by endeavors to revive the city's economic and urban fabric. The establishment of the Gateway Arch as part of the Jefferson National Expansion Memorial in the 1960s is emblematic of these regeneration efforts, symbolizing the city's historical significance and its aspirations for revitalization.

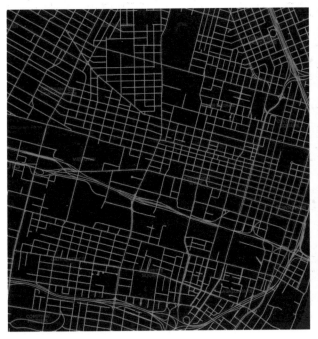

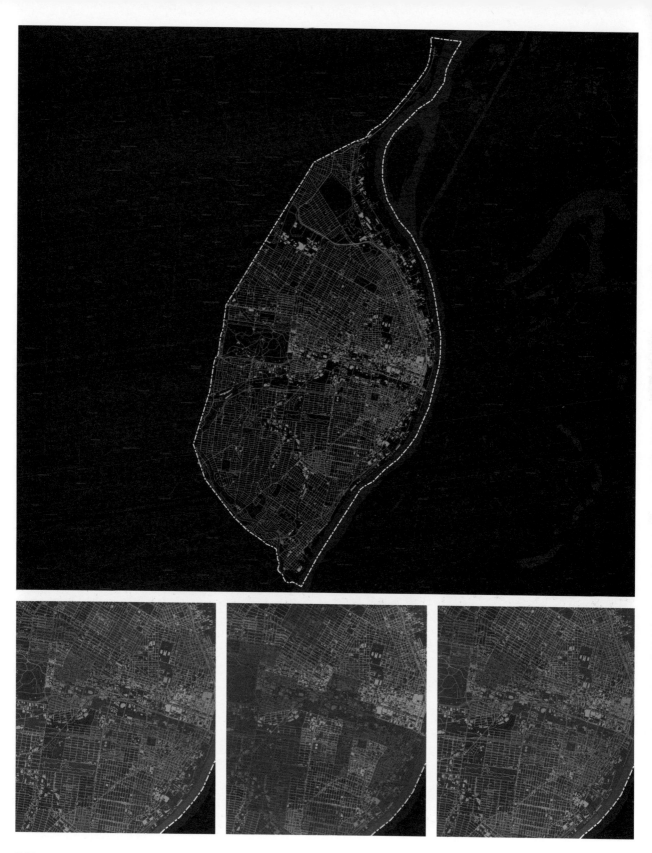

Saint Petersburg

Northwestern
Russia

City Population
5,561,294

City Area
1,439 km²

City Density
3,864.69 /km²

Metropolitan Population
6,200,000

Metropolitan Area
11,600 km²

Metropolitan Density
534.48 /km²

City Form Typologies
Monumental, Small World, Atomized, Reticular, Organic

Founded as a planned, monumental city by Tsar Peter the Great in 1703, Saint Petersburg was destined to become a political power center and strategic port city on the Baltic Sea. The city is one of the foremost global examples of the Monumental city form, alongside Brasilia, Washington DC, Habsburg Madrid, Rome, and central London. Since its inception, Saint Petersburg was intended to adopt a deliberate European style, reflecting the Tsar's desire to modernize Russia. The urban designers involved in the process endowed Saint Petersburg with wide avenues, ample canals, and grand squares, hosting iconic landmarks such as the Winter Palace, St. Isaac's Cathedral, and the Peter and Paul Fortress, adopting Baroque and Neoclassical styles. The city hosted the Imperial capital between 1712 and 1918. Its Baroque Splendor led to a significant cultural renaissance. In 1924, at the beginning of the Soviet Era, the city was renamed Leningrad and became a leading industrial and military center. Post-war reconstruction efforts were necessary to restore significant historic landmarks. After the collapse of the Soviet Union in 1991, the city embraced liberal economic principles, while preserving its historic heritage (Nevsky Prospekt). The construction of Lakhta Center Skyscrapers symbolizes the rebirth of the city.

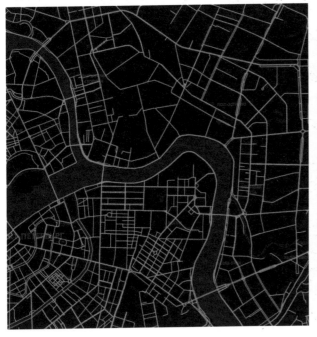

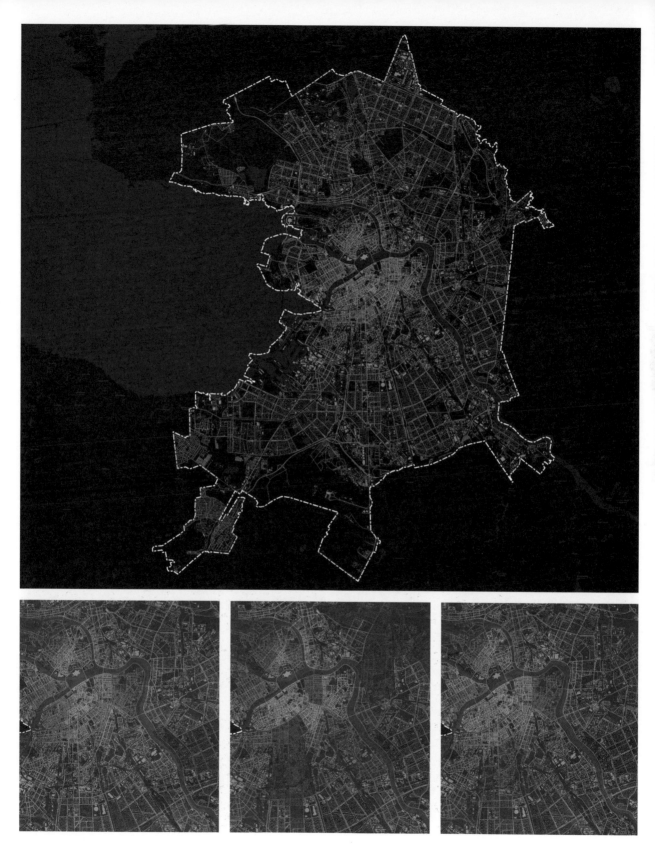

San Diego

California
United States of America

City Population
1,374,076

City Area
844 km²

City Density
1,628.01 /km²

Metropolitan Population
3,276,208

Metropolitan Area
11,036 km²

Metropolitan Density
296.87 /km²

City Form Typologies
Atomized, Garden, Organic, Random Reticular

San Diego, situated in the southwestern corner of California, reveals a rich tapestry of economic and urban development, intertwined with its unique geographical and historical context. Originally inhabited by the Kumeyaay Native Americans, San Diego's urban trajectory took a decisive turn with the establishment of the Spanish presidio and mission in 1769. The city's strategic port positioned it as a pivotal maritime hub during the 19th century, fostering economic trade and military activity, and attracting a myriad of immigrants. With the opening of the Santa Fe Railway in the late 19th century, San Diego witnessed an economic transformation, paving the way for the city's first real estate boom and the introduction of significant infrastructure projects. The 20th century saw the establishment of San Diego as a prominent military and defense center, especially during World War II, leading to significant population growth and urban expansion. The development of the University of California, San Diego in the 1960s catalyzed the city's evolution into a center for biotechnology and healthcare research. Today, San Diego's multifaceted history, combined with its advantageous location near the U.S.-Mexico border, manifests in a diversified economy, encompassing tourism, international trade, research, and technology, among other sectors.

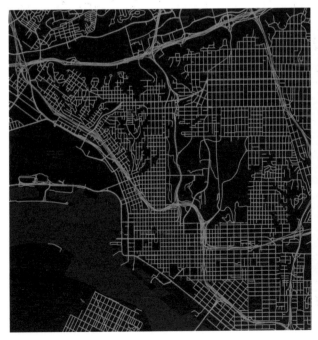

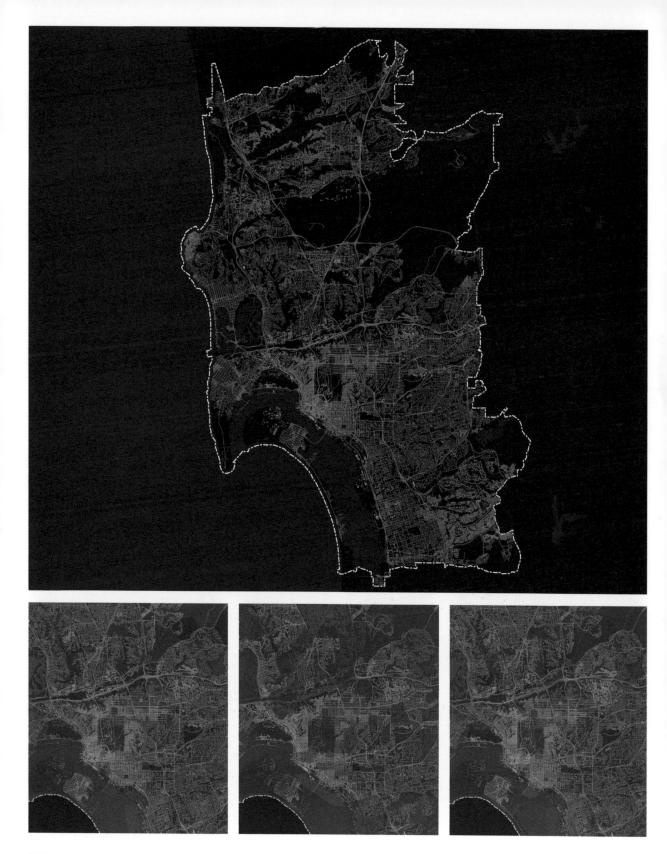

San Francisco

California
United States of America

City Population
715,717

City Area
121 km²

City Density
5,891.64 /km²

Metropolitan Population
4,623,264

Metropolitan Area
9,128 km²

Metropolitan Density
506.49 /km²

City Form Typologies
Reticular, Atomized, Garden, Organic

San Francisco's economic and urban development forms a rich tapestry that interweaves geography, resource booms, and innovation. Its origins as a Spanish mission settlement in 1776 were humble, but the 1849 Gold Rush radically transformed it, ushering in a massive influx of people and capital. The city rapidly evolved from a small settlement to a bustling port catering to miners and businesses eager to exploit the Sierra Nevada's gold reserves. However, San Francisco's geography – a narrow peninsula flanked by the Pacific Ocean and the San Francisco Bay – limited its spatial expansion, necessitating innovative urban solutions. The 1906 earthquake and subsequent fire devastated the city, but it also offered an opportunity for urban renewal and modern infrastructure development. Throughout the 20th century, San Francisco's economy diversified. The rise of the finance and insurance sectors established the city as the West Coast's financial hub. In the late 20th and early 21st centuries, proximity to Silicon Valley positioned San Francisco at the nexus of the technology boom, leading to a surge in housing demand, soaring real estate prices, and an influx of tech firms and workers. By intertwining resource availability, innovation, and its unique geography, San Francisco has perennially redefined urban and economic development paradigms.

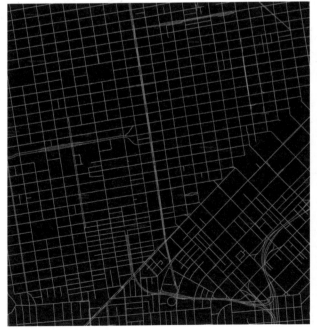

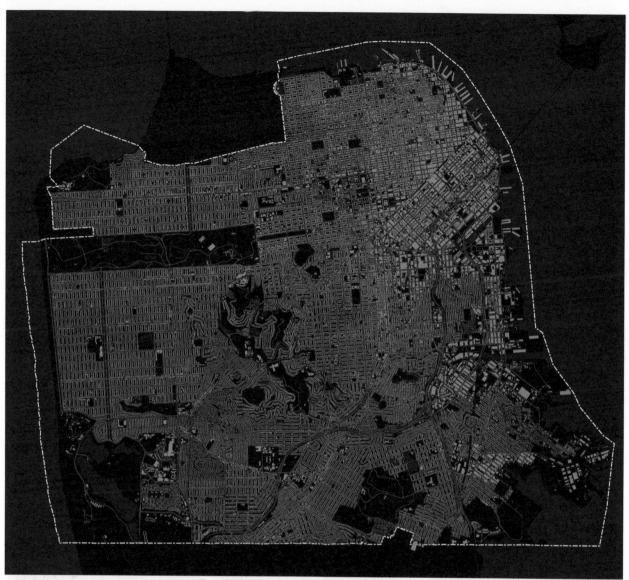

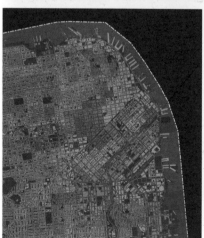
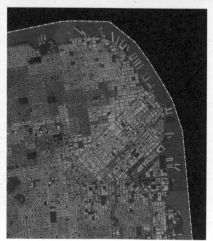
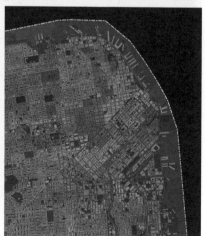

San Jose / San Francisco Bay Area

California
United States of America

City Population
7,760,000

City Area
18,040 km²

City Density
430.16 /km²

Metropolitan Population
9,710,000

Metropolitan Area
26,390 km²

Metropolitan Density
367.94 /km²

City Form Typologies
**Linear, Organic, Reticular,
Garden**

The San Francisco Bay Area's economic and urban development is a dynamic tale shaped by geography, innovation, and sociopolitical factors. Historically, the region's initial growth was spurred by the 1849 Gold Rush, which attracted a diverse range of immigrants and led to the rapid urbanization of San Francisco. Its natural harbor made the city a pivotal maritime hub, while the advent of the transcontinental railroad in the late 1860s further anchored its status as the West Coast's primary port and commercial center. In the post-World War II era, suburbanization trends and the rise of the automobile shaped the spatial growth of the Bay Area, leading to the development of peripheral communities. Stanford University's focus on fostering ties with the tech industry played a key role in the emergence of Silicon Valley in the 1960s and 1970s, and it became a nexus for technological innovation. Companies like Apple, Google, and Facebook eventually headquartered in the region, establishing the Bay Area as the global epicenter of the tech industry. Recent decades, however, have brought challenges. The explosive growth of the tech sector led to soaring housing costs, gentrification, and economic disparities. Addressing these issues remains a pressing concern for urban planners and policymakers.

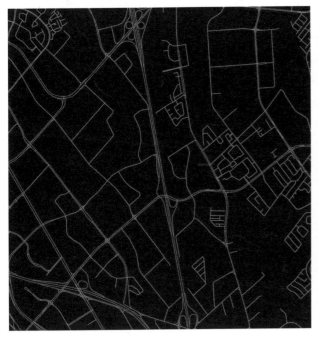

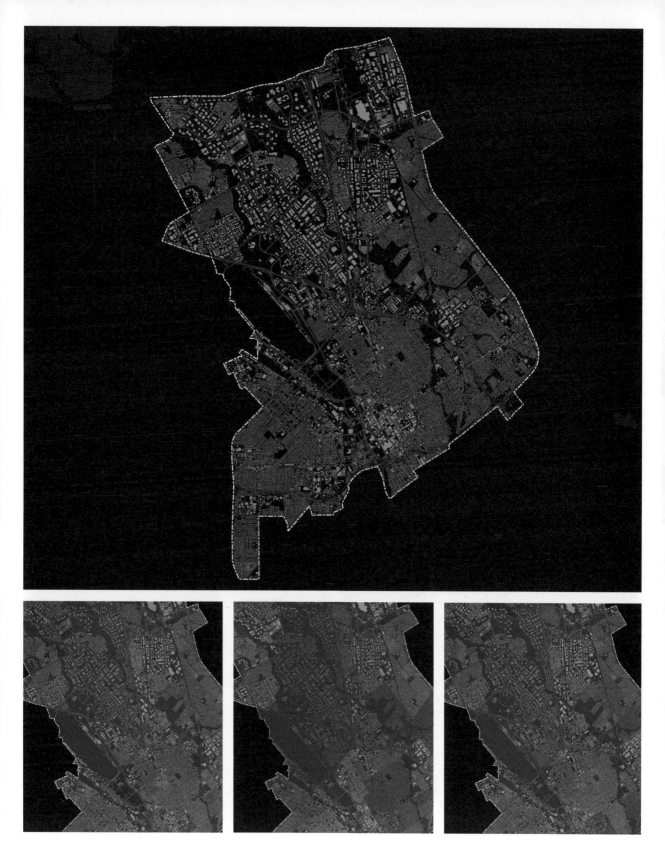

São Paulo

São Paulo
Brazil

City Population
12,400,232

City Area
1,521 km²

City Density
8,152.09 /km²

Metropolitan Population
22,619,736

Metropolitan Area
7,947 km²

Metropolitan Density
2,846.34 /km²

City Form Typologies
Random, Organic, Radial, Garden

The urban and economic history of São Paulo is a remarkable testament to rapid urbanization and economic development in the 20th century. Initially founded in 1554 as a Jesuit mission, São Paulo's early economy relied predominantly on sugar cultivation and export. The late 19th and early 20th centuries saw a shift towards coffee production, propelling the state of São Paulo to the forefront of Brazil's economy, which in turn fostered the arrival of numerous European immigrants. The city's transformation into an industrial hub began in the 1930s, expedited by Brazil's broader industrialization policies. Infrastructure investments, notably in roads and transport, bolstered São Paulo's position. By the latter half of the 20th century, it became Brazil's economic powerhouse, diversifying into the financial services, technology, and manufacturing sectors. The trends in urbanization, however, have not been without their challenges. The rapid influx of migrants searching for better job opportunities has contributed to the sprawling development of informal settlements, known as *favelas*, highlighting issues of housing and infrastructure deficits. Nevertheless, São Paulo's evolution is emblematic of Brazil's broader socioeconomic dynamism, reflecting both the nation's potential and the challenges of uneven development.

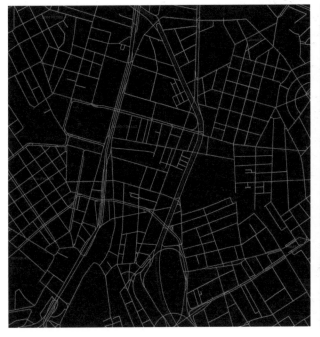

Savannah

Georgia
United States of America

City Population
145,870

City Area
281 km²

City Density
519.09 /km²

Metropolitan Population
418,373

Metropolitan Area
3,494 km²

Metropolitan Density
119.75 /km²

City Form Typologies
Fractal, Reticular, Organic, Garden

Savannah, Georgia stands as a paragon of economic and urban development in the history of the United States. Founded in 1733 by General James Oglethorpe, Savannah was designed with a unique urban plan known as the "Oglethorpe Plan". This plan characterized the city's layout with a system of grids interwoven with open squares, intending to promote community and egalitarian ideals. The layout fostered ease of access and growth, allowing Savannah to flourish as a center of the cotton trade by the 19th century. With the establishment of the Central of Georgia Railway in 1833, Savannah secured its position as a significant hub for transportation and trade in the South, enhancing its economic strength. The railway, complemented by the city's port, supported the export of cotton, lumber, and naval stores, underpinning Savannah's growing economy. The period following World War II brought challenges, with urban flight and economic restructuring shaping Savannah's trajectory. However, efforts in historic preservation during the late 20th century, symbolized by the rehabilitation of the historic district, catalyzed urban renewal and tourism, establishing a new economic pillar. Today, Savannah's economy continues to evolve, balancing its rich history with modern-day economic demands.

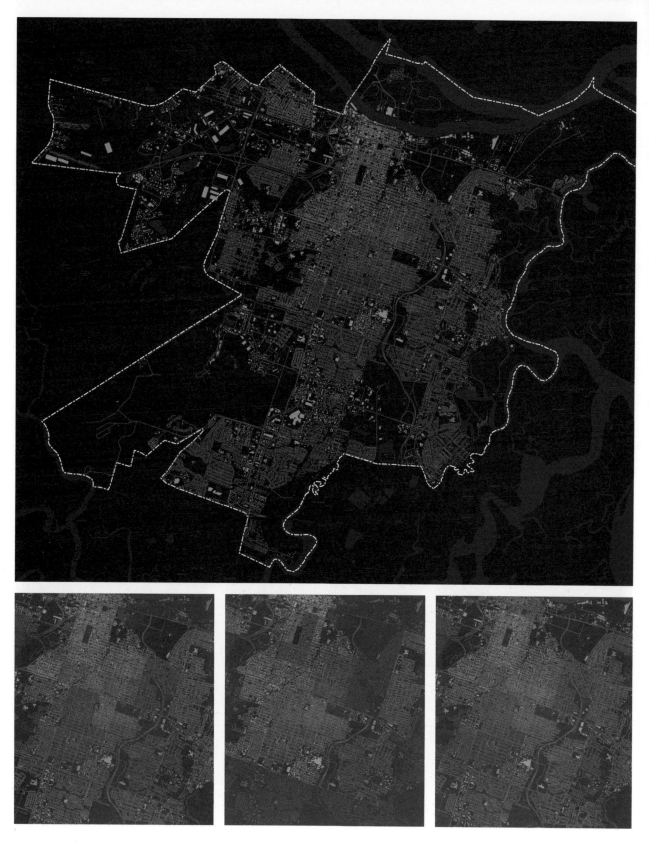

Seattle

Washington
United States of America

City Population
725,487

City Area
218 km²

City Density
3,334.96 /km²

Metropolitan Population
4,018,762

Metropolitan Area
21,202 km²

Metropolitan Density
189.55 /km²

City Form Typologies
Atomized, Reticular, Organic, Garden

Seattle has a dynamic history of economic and urban development that reflects its unique geographical, cultural, and industrial positioning. Founded in the mid-19th century, Seattle initially experienced growth through its timber industry and as a transport hub for miners during the Klondike Gold Rush. By the early 20th century, it had further diversified with shipbuilding and manufacturing, notably aviation with the foundation of the Boeing Company in 1916, which would become a cornerstone for the city's development. After World War II, Seattle witnessed a transformation: as the aviation and technology industries grew, so did urbanization patterns, leading to the emergence of high-density residential areas and suburban sprawl. In the late 20th century and into the 21st, Seattle evolved into a major global tech hub with the presence of companies like Microsoft and Amazon, and numerous startups, which significantly influenced its urban landscape. This tech-driven growth brought with it challenges, such as housing affordability problems and traffic congestion, further shaping its urban development strategies. The city's growth, therefore, reflects a history of industry shifts, from timber and mining to aviation and technology, all of which have left indelible marks on its urban fabric.

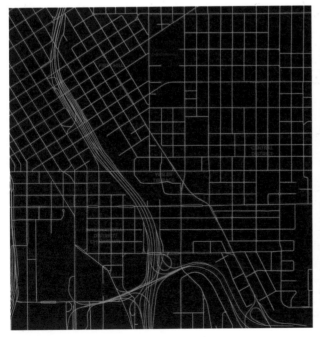
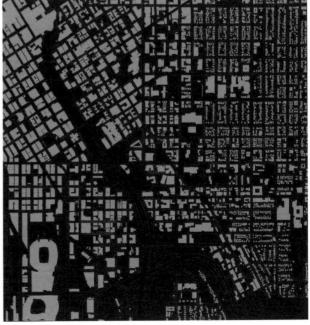

Seoul

Seoul
South Korea

City Population
9,988,049

City Area
605 km²

City Density
16,503.44 /km²

Metropolitan Population
26,037,000

Metropolitan Area
12,685 km²

Metropolitan Density
2,052.58 /km²

City Form Typologies
**Atomized, Linear, Organic,
Random, Garden**

Seoul, the capital and heart of the Republic of Korea, has historically been the center of economic, political, and cultural activities since the establishment of the Joseon Dynasty in the 14th century. The city's transformation from a historical capital to a sprawling metropolis began during the Japanese colonial period (1910-1945) when infrastructure improvements set the groundwork for modern urbanization. Post-World War II, rapid industrialization from the 1960s through the 1980s marked a defining chapter in Seoul's economic evolution. The national government actively promoted export-oriented industrialization, causing significant rural-urban migration, leading Seoul to experience exponential population growth. During the 1988 Seoul Olympics, the city emerged as an international hub, reflecting its growing economic prowess. The 21st century has seen Seoul metamorphose into a global city with the concentration of international businesses, technologies, and cultural exports, such as the Hallyu wave. Its urban planning strategies, like the restoration of the Cheonggyecheon Stream in 2005, emphasize sustainability and livability, indicating a shift from purely growth-driven policies. This intricate blend of historical prominence, post-war industrialization, and modern urban policies makes Seoul's economic and urban trajectory a captivating case of transformative resilience and innovation.

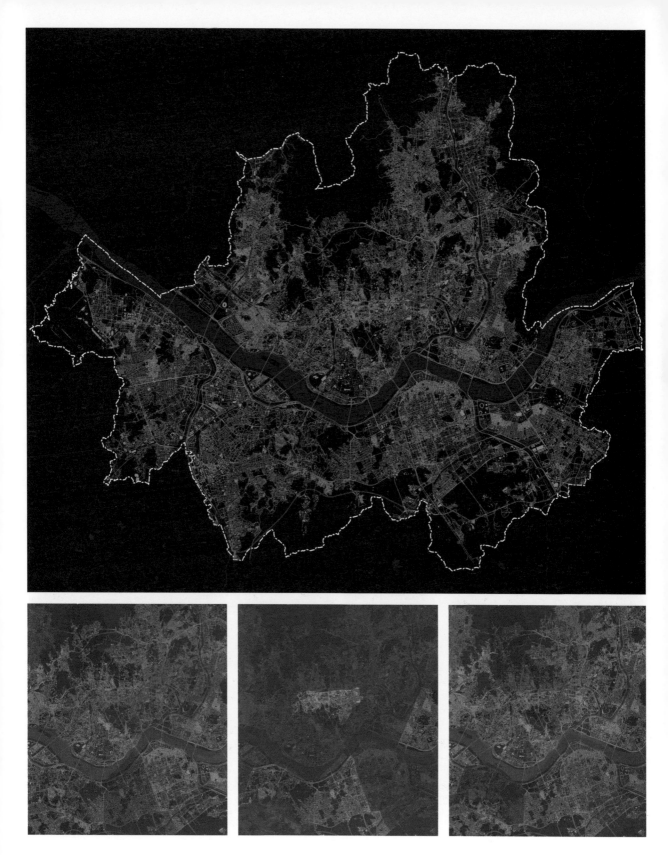

Shanghai

Huangpu
China

City Population
26,875,500

City Area
6,341 km²

City Density
4,238.37 /km²

Metropolitan Population
40,000,000

Metropolitan Area
14,923 km²

Metropolitan Density
2,680.48 /km²

City Form Typologies
Organic, Atomized, Random, Reticular

Historically, Shanghai's Huangpu District has been at the heart of China's urban and economic transformation. As the birthplace of modern Shanghai, Huangpu once served as the primary international port, establishing itself as the nexus of East-West trade and interactions during the late 19th and early 20th centuries. The signing of the Treaty of Nanking in 1842 facilitated the establishment of the Shanghai International Settlement, with the British and American settlements coalescing in Huangpu, adjacent to the bustling Bund area. This international presence catalyzed rapid infrastructural development and urbanization, turning the district into a locus of financial services, trade, and multiculturalism. European-style buildings erected along the Bund stand testament to its colonial past and economic prowess. Following the establishment of the People's Republic of China in 1949, Shanghai underwent substantial political and economic shifts. While initially suffering from post-revolutionary economic stagnation, Huangpu began to experience renewed growth post-1990s, largely driven by China's national economic reforms and open-door policy. Today, Huangpu District remains emblematic of Shanghai's historical legacy and modern aspirations, juxtaposing colonial-era architecture with contemporary urban landmarks.

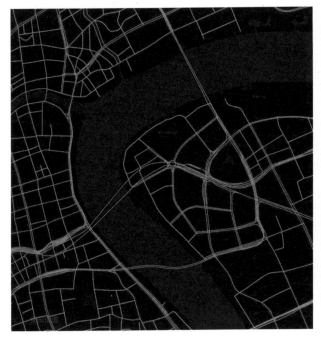

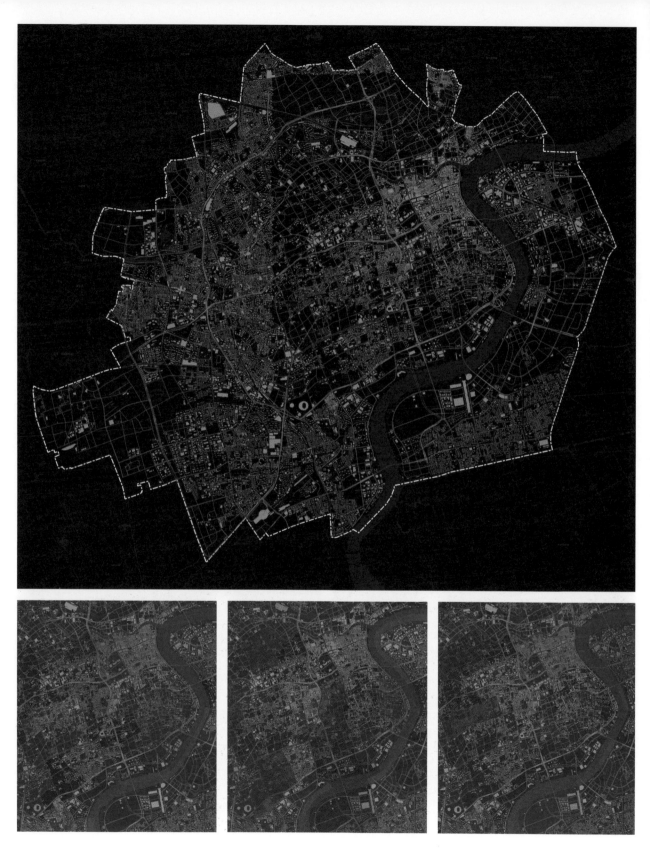

Singapore

Urban Authority of Singapore
Singapore

City Population
6,080,859

City Area
734 km²

City Density
8,281.16 /km²

Metropolitan Population
-

Metropolitan Area
-

Metropolitan Density
-

City Form Typologies
Atomized, Linear, Organic, Garden

The urban and economic trajectory of Singapore is an example of rapid transformation from a colonial port to a global city-state. Founded as a British trading colony in 1819, Singapore's strategic location made it a hub for trade routes between East and West. The early 20th century saw its gradual emergence as a key port in British Malaya, with the rubber and tin industries propelling its growth. However, the post-war years marked economic uncertainty, with Singapore facing challenges after separation from Malaysia in 1965. Under the leadership of Prime Minister Lee Kuan Yew, Singapore embarked on a series of ambitious economic reforms in the 1960s and 1970s, which focused on labor-intensive industrialization, attracting foreign investments, and developing its financial sector. State-led initiatives, such as the Jurong Industrial Estate, bolstered the manufacturing base, while the creation of the Economic Development Board in 1961 played a pivotal role in wooing foreign direct investment. By the 1980s, Singapore had evolved into a knowledge-based economy, emphasizing education, R&D, and technological innovation. The urban landscape was transformed with infrastructural projects like the Mass Rapid Transit system. Presently, Singapore stands as a testament to visionary urban planning and economic foresight, positioning itself as a global hub for finance, trade, and technology.

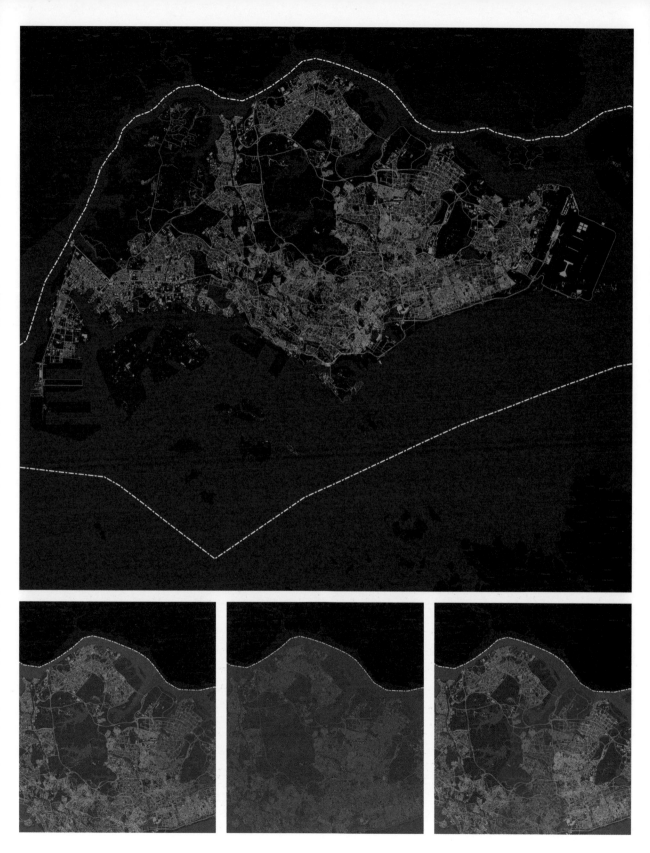

Stockholm

Södermanland
Sweden

City Population
975,551

City Area
188 km²

City Density
5,319.15 /km²

Metropolitan Population
2,415,139

Metropolitan Area
6,519 km²

Metropolitan Density
370.48 /km²

City Form Typologies
**Fractal, Small World,
Monumental, Organic, Garden**

The community surrounding the medieval fortress built on Stadsholmen Island eventually became a relevant Scandinavian trading center. The original city of Stockholm featured typical Small World city properties such as narrow streets and alleys with wooden buildings. Stockholm's strategic intermodal logistics placement across the islands in Lake Mälaren and the Baltic Sea facilitated trade and navigation. Stockholm played a central role in the development of the Swedish Empire, and eventually became its political and cultural heart. The embracement of the Scientific and Industrial Revolutions brought rapid population growth, ambitious urban planning projects and audacious developments in housing, transportation and sanitation. The construction of sophisticated bridges connected the constellation of islands, giving birth to new neighborhoods such as Norrmalm and Södermalm. A series of urban planning initiatives implemented throughout the 20th century aspired to improve the living conditions of working class citizens, and advanced transportation systems (Million Programme, Stockholm Metro) raised the quality of life of its population. Today's Stockholm is one of the foremost examples of the harmonious coexistence of Small World and Fractal layouts and Garden City developments, championing green spaces, while promoting environmentally friendly transportation (cycling) and revitalizing waterfront areas.

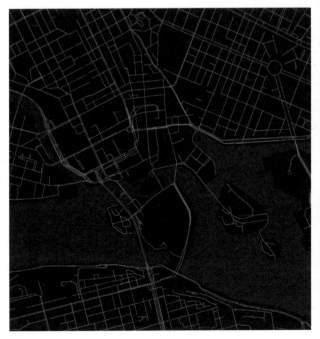

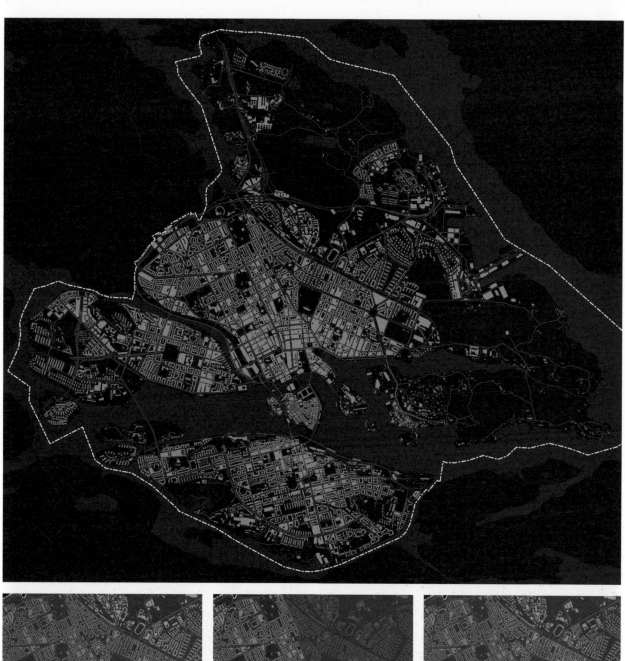

Sydney
New South Wales
Australia

City Population
214,851

City Area
27 km²

City Density
8,052.89 /km²

Metropolitan Population
5,297,089

Metropolitan Area
12,368 km²

Metropolitan Density
428.30 /km²

City Form Typologies
Atomized, Monumental, Organic, Garden

Prior to the arrival of European explorers, the area surrounding Sydney was inhabited by Aboriginal Eora-Gaidal-Darug tribes. The indigenous settlement was composed of traditional shelters, fishing and hunting grounds, and connections to the natural environment. The first British fleet arrived in Sydney Cove in 1788 and founded a penal colony and a permanent settlement around the Circular Quay and Sydney Cove, bringing Georgian and Victorian architecture. The discovery of gold deposits in New South Wales in the 1850s transformed Sydney into a thriving economic center. Grand public buildings (General Post Office, Customs House) epitomized the newly acquired wealth, combined with the affluence of the gentry residing in the suburbs (Paddington, Balmain). Sydney played a major role in the federation of Australia in 1901, becoming its capital. Iconic landmarks such as the Harbour Bridge or the Opera House raised the global profile of the city, in parallel with the Garden City expansion of suburbs (Bondi Beach). Today, Sydney is an attractive multicultural metropolis, presenting a rich tapestry of cultural influences (Little Italy, Chinatown), hosting singular modern architecture and high-rise buildings. Ambitious renewal projects aspire to revitalize the waterfront areas, promote green spaces, expand the light rail system, and regenerate the Darling Harbour area.

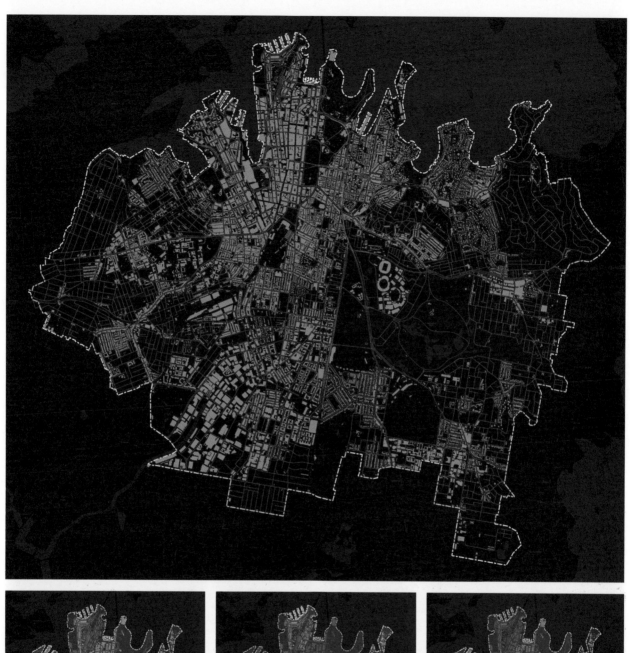

Tehran

Tehran
Iran

City Population
8,300,000

City Area
615 km²

City Density
13,495.93 /km²

Metropolitan Population
9,499,781

Metropolitan Area
2,235 km²

Metropolitan Density
4,250.46 /km²

City Form Typologies
Organic, Random, Monumental, Garden

The urban and economic trajectory of Tehran, the capital of Iran, can be traced back to its establishment in the early 12th century, although its meteoric rise to prominence began in the late 18th century when it was declared the national capital. Initially known for its walled gardens and orchards, by the late 19th and early 20th centuries, Tehran had undergone major infrastructural overhauls with European-inspired avenues and architecture, paving the way for its emergence as a cosmopolitan center. Post World War II, the city experienced rapid urbanization and population growth, driven in part by rural-to-urban migration. This period marked the onset of ambitious modernization projects under the Pahlavi dynasty, which sought to align Tehran with global cities in the West. This expansion, however, was accompanied by a proliferation of informal settlements on the periphery. After the 1979 Revolution, urban development policies shifted, emphasizing Islamic values, though many pre-revolutionary projects continued. The city grappled with issues of congestion, pollution, and housing shortages. Recent decades have seen Tehran making strides in urban transport with the establishment of metro lines and rapid transit bus systems, though challenges in sustainable urban planning persist.

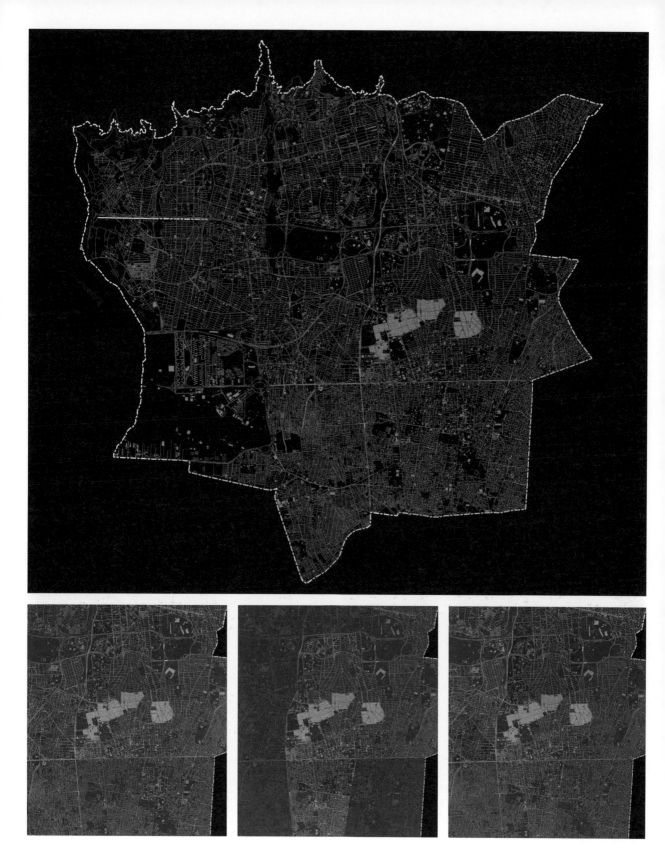

Tel Aviv

Tel Aviv
Israel

City Population
467,875

City Area
52 km²

City Density
8,997.60 /km²

Metropolitan Population
4,156,900

Metropolitan Area
1,516 km²

Metropolitan Density
2,742.02 /km²

City Form Typologies
Organic, Reticular, Random, Linear

Tel Aviv, founded in 1909 on the outskirts of the ancient port city of Jaffa, is emblematic of the dynamic urban and economic evolution of modern Israel. Initially conceptualized as a garden suburb, Tel Aviv swiftly transitioned to become the cultural and financial center of Israel, distinct from its agrarian Zionist settlements. The 1920s and 1930s marked a significant phase in Tel Aviv's urbanization, with the city experiencing rapid population growth, primarily due to Jewish immigration. The Bauhaus architectural movement, introduced by German Jewish architects fleeing the Nazi regime, became prominent during this period, earning the city its characteristic "White City" designation from UNESCO. The economic trajectory of Tel Aviv was driven by the establishment of the State of Israel in 1948. The city, devoid of historical significance, became a fulcrum for diversity and modernity. Consequently, it attracted investments and talent, laying the foundations for its burgeoning tech industry, which earned it the nickname of "Silicon Wadi" in the late 20th century. Today, Tel Aviv's urban fabric reflects a mosaic of historical layers, from Ottoman-era Jaffa, through Bauhaus boulevards, to contemporary skyscrapers, illustrating a narrative of resilience, reinvention, and relentless growth.

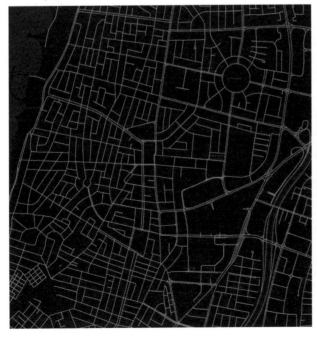

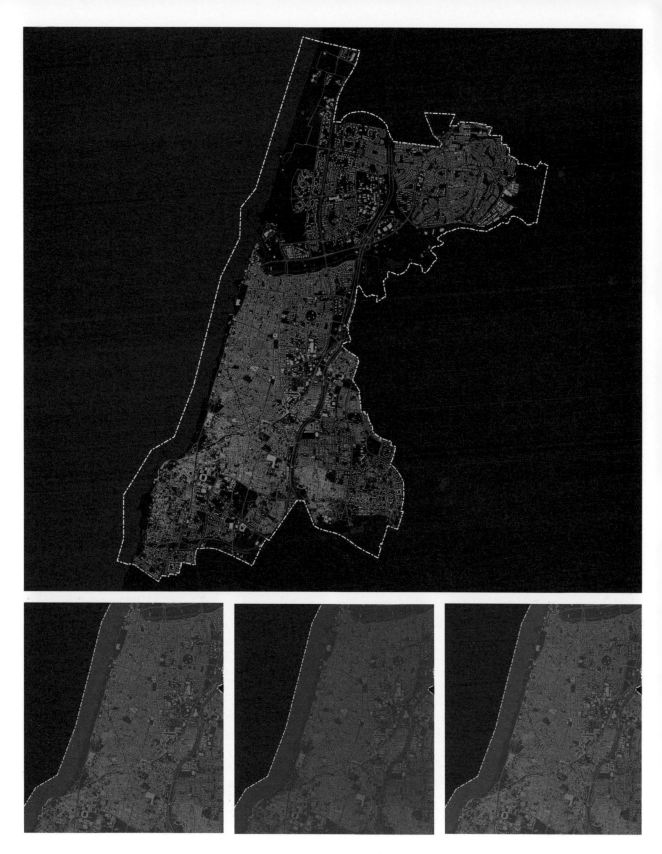

Tokyo

Kantō
Japan

City Population
14,094,034

City Area
2,194 km²

City Density
6,423.69 /km²

Metropolitan Population
40,800,000

Metropolitan Area
13,452 km²

Metropolitan Density
3,033.01 /km²

City Form Typologies
Organic, Monumental, Radial, Atomized, Reticular, Garden

Tokyo's urban and economic evolution offers an insightful chronicle of adaptability, resilience, and strategic growth. Originally known as Edo, by the early 17th century, the city emerged as Japan's political center with the establishment of the Tokugawa shogunate (1603-1868). This feudal era witnessed Edo transforming into one of the world's largest cities, despite Japan's broader policy of sakoku (or national seclusion). Post-1868, with the Meiji Restoration, Edo was renamed Tokyo, symbolizing a new era of modernization and westernization. As Japan's capital, Tokyo underwent infrastructural developments, incorporating railroads and modern architecture. However, the 1923 Great Kantō earthquake significantly devastated the city, necessitating large-scale reconstruction. Post-World War II, Tokyo faced another rebuilding phase, but remarkably by the late 20th century, it stood as a global economic powerhouse. Contributory factors included Japan's post-war economic miracle, state-led urban planning strategies, and Tokyo's role as a central node in global financial networks. Today, Tokyo, as part of the Kantō region, epitomizes a confluence of historical influences and modern dynamism, remaining a linchpin in global economic and urban narratives,

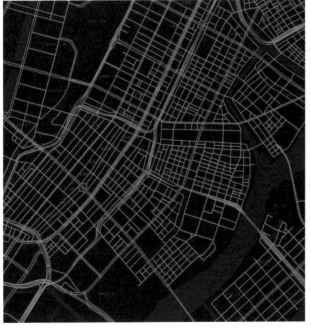

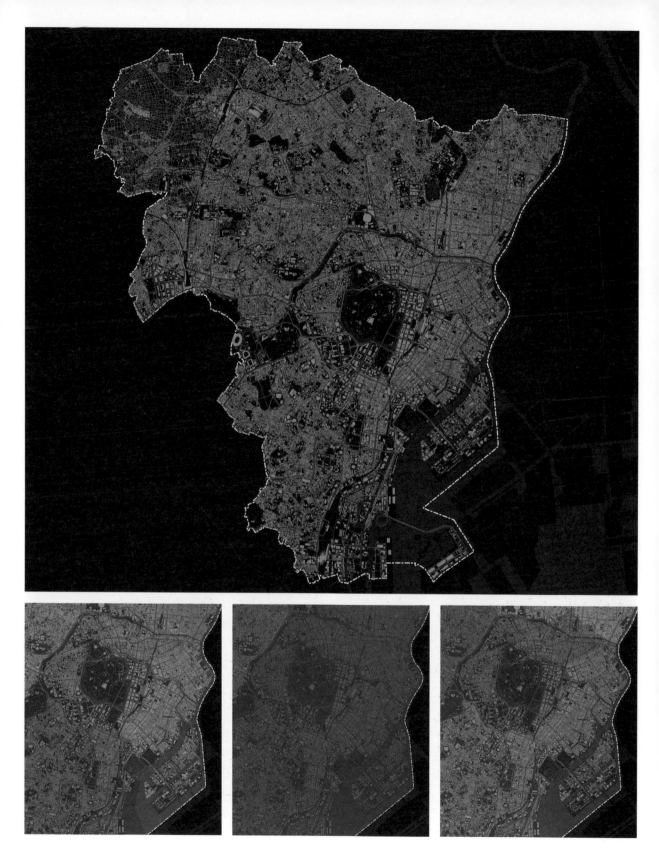

Turin

Piedmont
Italy

City Population
847,287

City Area
130 km²

City Density
6,509.08 /km²

Metropolitan Population
1,801,944

Metropolitan Area
1,127 km²

Metropolitan Density
1,598.89 /km²

City Form Typologies
Linear, Reticular, Organic

Augusta Taurinorum was established by the Romans, strategically located along the Via Augusta, the core transport artery of the Republic. Quintessentially reticular patterns and grand, monumental public buildings (amphitheater) characterized one of the most vital cities of the nascent Empire. Small World network patterns were adopted during the Middle Ages, thus filling the city with narrow, sinuous streets, defensive walls, palaces and churches, like the Saint John the Baptist Cathedral. Turin became the prosperous capital of the Duchy of Savoy and constituted a major focus of Baroque splendor in Northern Italy, hosting luxurious architectural spaces enriched by delicate ornamental decoration. Turin's layout experienced substantial redesign, giving birth to grand squares, wide avenues, elegant gardens and refined landmarks (Palazzo Reale, Madama, Church of San Lorenzo). Turin played a major leading role during the Italian Unification and the Risorgimento. The city underwent a profound industrialization process, propelled by the automotive industries (Fiat). The development of new neighborhoods and the improvement of railroad infrastructure led to a linear growth pattern. Contemporary Turin is a modern and dynamic city, endowed with a rich cultural heritage, currently embracing the revitalization of industrial areas (Lingotto district).

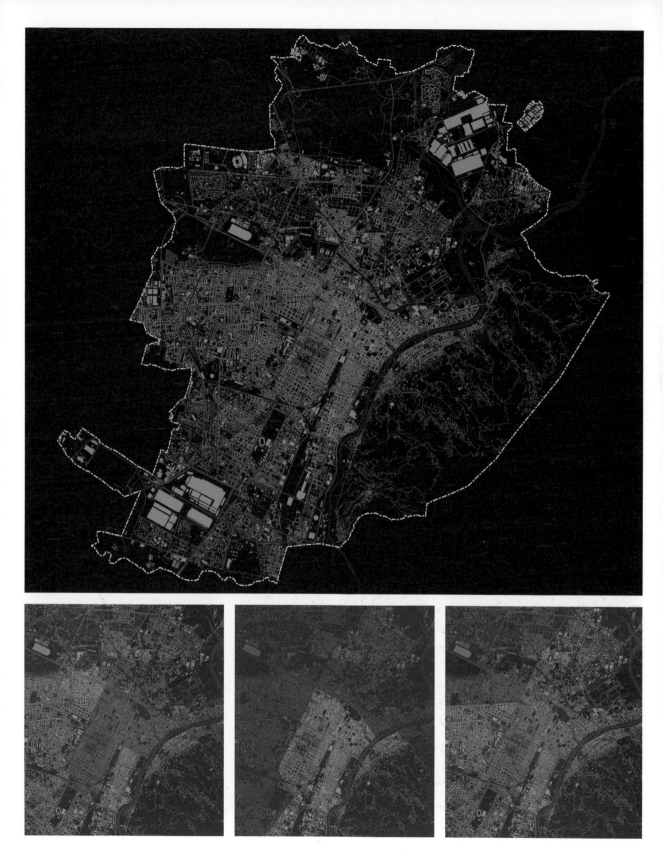

Venice

Veneto
Italy

City Population
258,051

City Area
415 km²

City Density
622.45 /km²

Metropolitan Population
833,703

Metropolitan Area
2,473 km²

Metropolitan Density
337.12 /km²

City Form Typologies
Atomized, Small Wo

The original settlement of contemporary Venice was founded by Veneti refugees fleeing the aggressive invasion of northern Italy by Germanic tribes in the 5th century. A flock of small communities established themselves on the islands of the Venetian Lagoon, ultimately constructing a highly sophisticated network of canals and bridges, and wooden piles upon the marshy ground to create solid foundations for permanent buildings. The construction of the Basilica di San Marco constituted the spiritual center of the highly prosperous trade enclave. The rise of Venice as a Mediterranean maritime power was spurred by its privileged location, advanced financial networks, and its role as a point of contact between Europe, the Byzantine Empire, and the Islamic world. The widespread construction of churches and grand palaces such as the Doge's Palace gave rise to the vibrant political and administrative center of the nascent Republic. A uniquely beautiful and luxurious urban landscape emerged, filled with narrow winding streets and canals. Venice became a major center of Renaissance art (Palladio), but the city struggled to overcome the unexpected decline of its maritime influence. The preservation of the city's precious architectural and urban heritage led to the emergence of a highly profitable tourism industry.

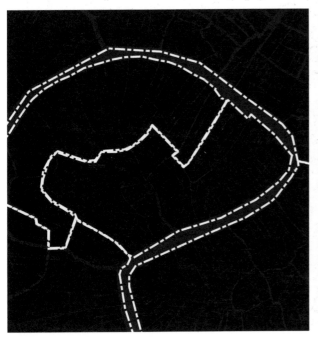

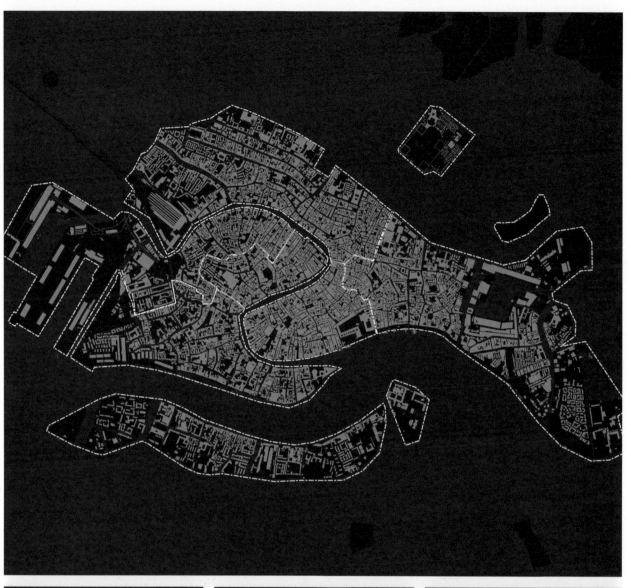

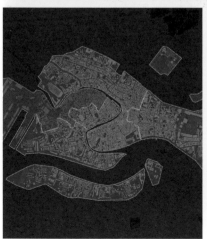
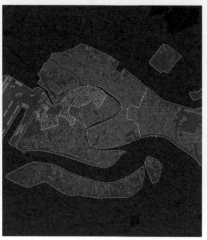

Vienna

Vienna
Austria

City Population
1,975,271

City Area
415 km²

City Density
4,762.21 /km²

Metropolitan Population
2,890,577

Metropolitan Area
3,862 km²

Metropolitan Density
748.47 /km²

City Form Typologies
Monumental, Small World, Atomized, Organic, Garden

The Roman urbs of Vindobona was originally established as a strategic military camp along the Danube River. In its early stages, the city followed a reticular pattern, often adopted by Roman military leaders as the blueprint for city planning. Vienna was a relevant city within the Holy Roman Empire, ultimately becoming the imperial capital of the Habsburg monarchy. Vienna rose to political prominence in central Europe during the Renaissance, contributing to the continent's architectural splendor throughout the Baroque era with the construction of grand palaces (Hofburg, Belvedere), following a Monumental pattern, and with its grand boulevards, parks, and squares articulated around the city core encircled by the Ringstrasse. Following the expansion of the Austro-Hungarian Empire, Vienna grew beyond its traditional boundaries to become a modern, industrial capital (Leopoldstadt, Wieden). Viennese iconic landmarks include the State Opera, St. Stephen's Cathedral, and the Parliament. A celebrated architectural center during the Belle Epoque and Interwar period, Vienna endured severe post-war reconstruction efforts, finally embracing an advanced architectural landscape involving eclectic residential complexes (Karl-Marx-Hof). Contemporary Vienna is a continental center for arts, music and culture, and the city preserves its elegance and charm by means of revitalizing historic districts and supporting sustainable urban planning and transportation.

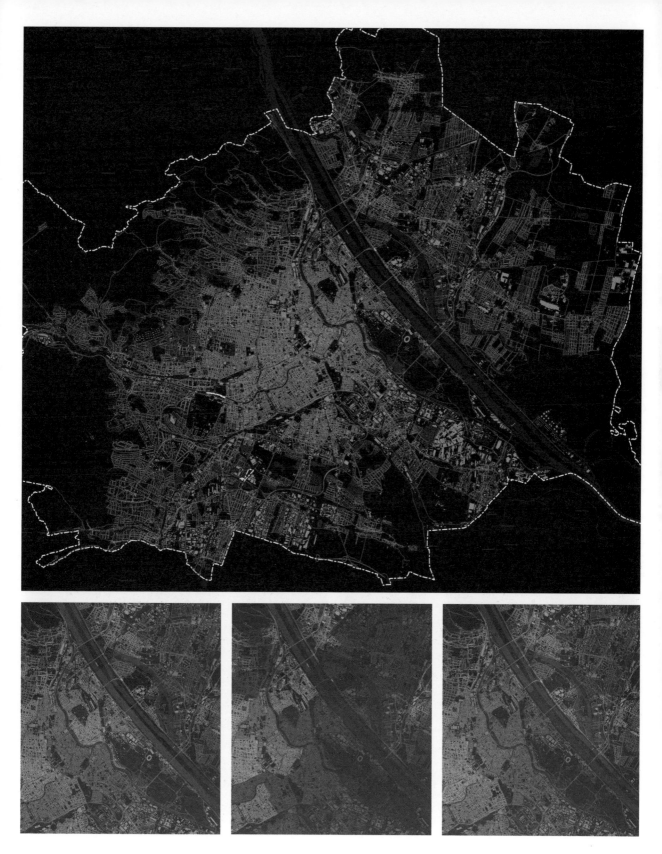

Warsaw

Masovian
Poland

City Population
1,863,056

City Area
517 km²

City Density
3,601.92 /km²

Metropolitan Population
3,100,844

Metropolitan Area
6,100 km²

Metropolitan Density
508.30 /km²

City Form Typologies
**Small World, Monumental,
Radial, Atomized, Garden**

The medieval roots of Warsaw can be traced back to the 13th century, when the city was founded as a small trade settlement. Warsaw's prominence as the capital of Poland occurred in the late 16th century under King Sigismund III Vasa. The Medieval old town followed a typical Small World pattern, crowded with narrow streets, townhouses, and the Royal Castle. The era of Enlightenment witnessed the emergence of Warsaw as a major European cultural and architectural capital. King Stanislaw II Augustus embraced the new intellectual currents and supported the construction of monumental, Neoclassical buildings, majestic boulevards and elegant palaces. The Partitions and Rebirth of Poland during the 19th century caused political turmoil, as a result of a nation being split among neighboring empires. Warsaw's urban layout was redesigned, with new districts and landmarks (Grand Theatre, University). Poland's resurgence as an independent nation in the 20th century conflicted with the Materialist styles imposed by the Soviet regime. The profound scars of the Nazi occupation and the immense destruction suffered during WWII led to an arduous reconstruction of the city's historic core, combined with the appearance of modern architecture (Palace of Culture and Science). Today, Warsaw presents a hybrid skyline composed of multiple architectural styles, from historic buildings to skyscrapers.

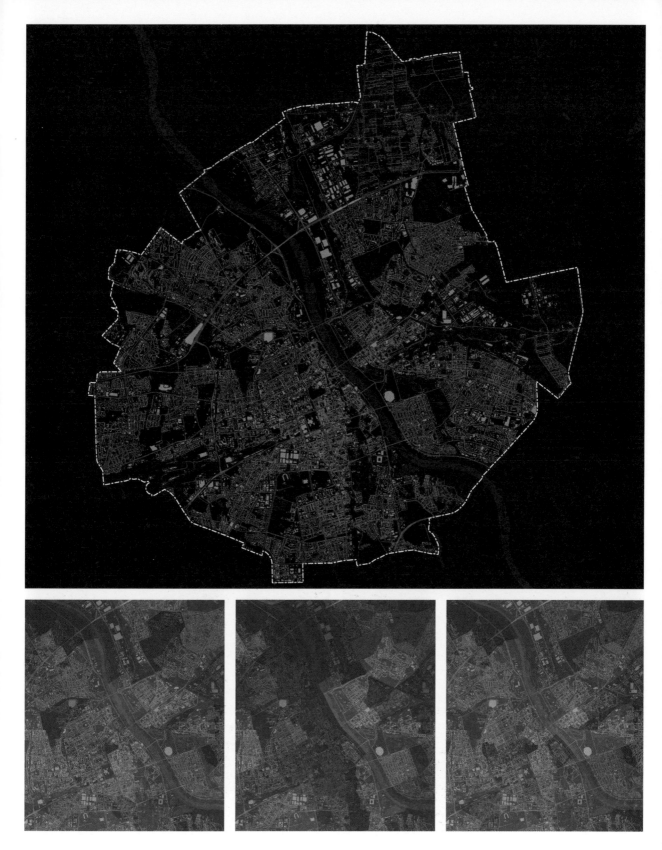

Washington D.C.

Washington
United States of America

City Population
631,693

City Area
158 km²

City Density
3,989.98 /km²

Metropolitan Population
6,373,829

Metropolitan Area
16,984 km²

Metropolitan Density
375.29 /km²

City Form Typologies
**Monumental, Fractal,
Organic / Atomized, Garden**

The economic and urban development of Washington D.C. is deeply rooted in its establishment as the nation's capital in the late 18th century. Founded pursuant to the Residence Act of 1790, its unique location along the Potomac River was a political compromise between the northern and southern states. Pierre Charles L'Enfant, a French engineer, designed the city with a blend of European and American urban ideals, envisioning grand avenues and ceremonial spaces like the National Mall. In the 19th century, the city's economy was dominated by the federal government, and its development pattern was substantially influenced by this. With the advent of the 20th century and large-scale urbanization, Washington witnessed demographic changes and increasing racial tensions, which culminated in the 1968 riots following the assassination of Martin Luther King Jr. These events precipitated an economic decline and disinvestment in certain areas. By the late 20th and early 21st centuries, however, urban revitalization projects, like the development of the Metro rail system in 1976 and the Capitol Riverfront, began transforming D.C.'s economic and urban landscape. The city started attracting businesses beyond the federal sector and saw significant gentrification trends, reshaping its socio-economic dynamics.

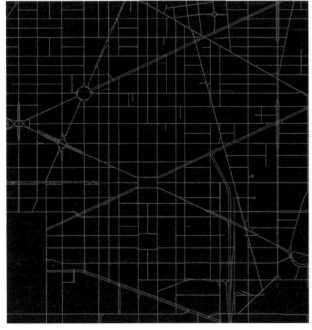

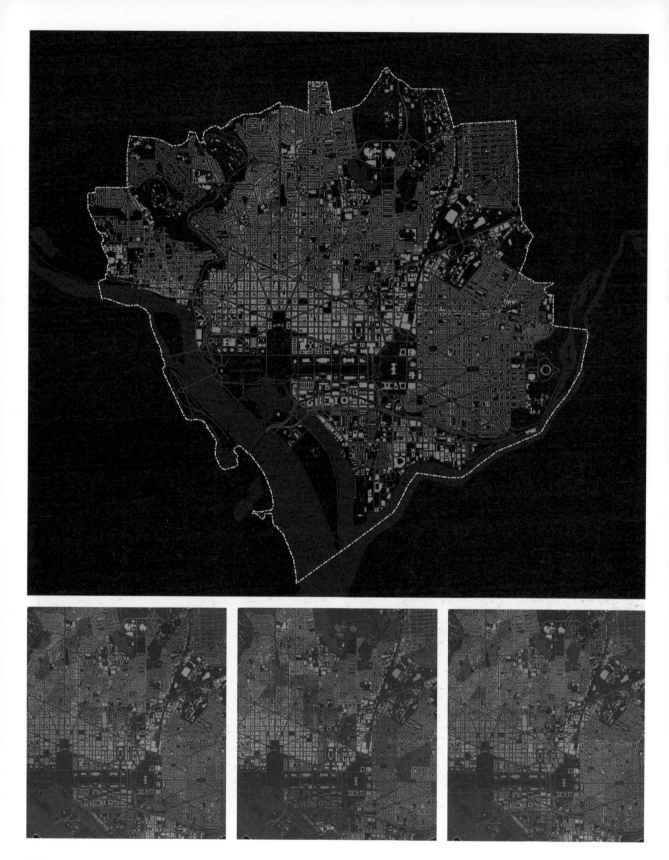

Zurich

Zurich
Switzerland

City Population
443,037

City Area
88 km²

City Density
5,041.39 /km²

Metropolitan Population
1,431,538

Metropolitan Area
2,103 km²

Metropolitan Density
680.71 /km²

City Form Typologies
Small World, Atomized, Linear,
Garden

Turicum was initially established as a Roman customs post and regional trading center. The town was conceived following a reticular grid, but the city adopted Small World network morphological features as it evolved throughout the Middle Ages. Medieval Zurich became known for its crowded, narrow streets, merchant houses, and churches and cathedrals (Grossmünster und Fraumünster), eventually becoming a member of the Swiss Confederation in the 14th century. The growth experienced during the Scientific Revolution required dismantling vast segments of legacy fortifications, leading to urban expansion. Zurich outgrew its confined boundaries, adopting a more structured grid of townhouses and public squares. ETH Zurich was founded in 1855 and soon became one of Europe's leading universities. Zurich emerged as a major economic center (banking and financial services) and welcomed Garden City developments on the outskirts of the city, connected by means of well-designed civil infrastructures (bridges over the Limmat River). Contemporary Zurich is a cosmopolitan city known for its cultural dynamism, its influential finance and pharmaceutical sectors, and its quality of life.

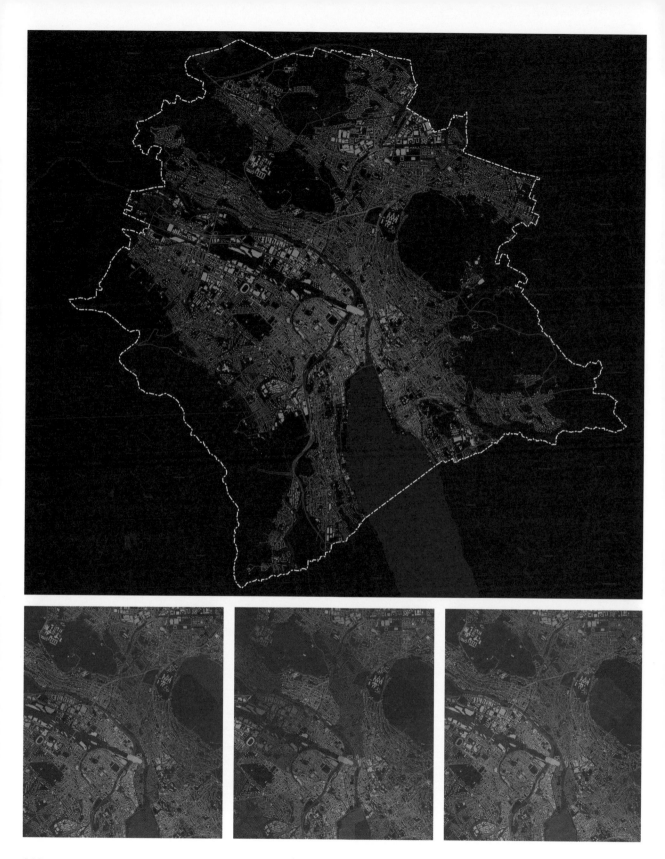

Bibliography

Alonso, L., Doorley, R., Elkhatsa, M., Grignard, A., Noyman, A., Larson, K., Sakai, Y., and Zhang, Y. "CityScope: A Data-Driven Interactive Simulation Tool for Urban Design. Use Case Volpe." In Morales, A. et al. (eds.) *Unifying Themes in Complex Systems IX.* Cham: Springer, 2018.

Arbesman, S., Kleinberg, J. M. and Strogatz, S. H. "Superlinear Scaling for Innovation in Cities." *Physical Review E* 79 (2009): 016115.

Barabási, A. L. "The Elegant Law that Governs Us All." *Science* 357, no. 6347 (2017): 138.

Barabási, A. L. *Network Science: The Scale Free Property.* 2016. https://barabasi.com/f/623.pdf

Barceló, M. *Innocities, urbanismo, economía, tecnología y cambio social.* Barcelona: Innopro Consulting, 2020.

Batty, M. "The Size, Scale, and Shape of Cities." *Science* 319, no. 5864 (2008): 769-771.

Batty, Michael, and Paul A. Longley. *Fractal Cities: A Geometry of Form and Function.* Cambridge, MA: Academic press, 1994.

Bertaud, A. and Malpezzi, S. "The Spatial Distribution of Population in 48 World Cities: Implications for Economies in Transition." 2003. https://alainbertaud.com/wp-content/uploads/2013/06/spatia_-distribution_of_pop_-50_-cities.pdf

Bettencourt, L. M. A., Lobo, Helbing, D., Kühnert, C. and West, G. B. "Growth, Innovation, Scaling and the Pace of Life in Cities." PNAS 104, no. 17 (2007): 7301-7306.

Bettencourt, L. M. A., Lobo, J. and Strumsky, D. "Invention in the City: Increasing Returns to Scale in Metropolitan Patenting." *Research Policy 36,* no. 1 (2007): 107-120.

Bettencourt, L. M. A., Lobo, J., Strumsky, D. and West, G. B. "Urban Scaling and the Production Function for Cities." *PLoS ONE 8,* no. 3 (2013): e58407.

Bettencourt, L. M. A., Lobo, J. and West, G. B. "Why Are Large Cities Faster? Universal Scaling and Self-similarity in Urban Organization and Dynamics." *The European Physical Journal B* 63 (2008): 285-293.

Bettencourt, L. M. A., Lobo, J. and West, G. B. "The Self Similarity of Human Social Organization and Dynamics in Cities. In Lane, D. Pumain, S. E. van der Leeuw, S. E. and G. West (Eds.), *Complexity Perspectives in Innovation and Social Change.* Dordrecht: Springer, 2009.

Bettencourt, L. M. A., Lobo, J., Strumsky, D. and West, G. B. (2010). "Urban Scaling and Its Deviations: Revealing the Structure of Wealth, Innovation and Crime Across Cities." *PLoS ONE 5,* no. 11 (2010): e13541.

Bitácora Urbano Territorial: La planificación teritorial y urbana en América Latina, vol. I, no. 11 (2007), 96–115.

Boeing, G. (2019), "Urban Spatial Order: Street Network Orientation, Configuration, and Entropy." *Applied Network Science* 4, no. 67 (2019).

Burke, J. and Gras Alomà, R. (2019). *Atlas of Innovation Districts.* Aretian and Opinno. Cambridge (MA)

Burke, J. and Gras Alomà, R. (2020) "El reto de las ciudades, los distritos de innovación y las cadenas de valor en la era de la economía global y la automatización." *Panorama Social* 32 (2020): 33-48.

Burke, J. and Gras Alomà, R. "Cinco claves para impulsar el éxito de los distritos de innovación." *MIT Technology Review* (July 29, 2019). https://www.technologyreview.es/s/11331/cinco-claves-para-impulsar-el-exito-de-los-distritos-de-innovacion

Burke, J. and Gras Alomà, R. "Hacia una nueva ciencia para entender y diseñar mejor las ciudades." *MIT Technology Review* (August 8, 2019). https://www.technologyreview.es/s/11355/hacia-una-nueva-ciencia-para-entender-y-disenar-mejor-las-ciudades

Burke, J. and Gras Alomà, R. "Urban AI: The Science behind the 15-Minute City." *Urban AI* (June 8, 2021).

Burke, J., Gras Alomà, R., Yu, F., and Kruguer, J. "Multiplying Effects of Urban Innovation Districts: Geospatial Analysis Framework for Evaluating Innovation Performance within Urban Environments." In Piselli C., Altan, H., Balaban, O. and Kremer, P. (eds.) *Innovating Strategies and Solutions for Urban Performance and Regeneration.* Cham: Springer, 2022.

Burke, J., Gras Alomà, R., Yu, F., Kruguer, J. "Geospatial Analysis Framework for Evaluating Urban Design Typologies in Relation with the 15-minute City Standards." *Journal of Business Research* 151 (2022): 651-667.

Cerdà, I. *General Theory of Urbanization 1867.* Barcelona: Actar, 2018.

Cervero, R. *The Transit Metropolis: A Global Inquiry.* Washington, D.C.: Island Press, 1998.

Christensen, C. M. "What Is Disruptive Innovation?" *Harvard Business Review,* (December 2015). hbr.org/2015/12/what-is-disruptive-innovation

Chui, M., Manyika, J., and Miremadi, M. "Where Machines Could Replace Humans–and Where They Can't (Yet). *McKinsey Quarterly* (July 8, 2016). https://www.mckinsey.com/capabilities/mckinsey-digital/our-insights/where-machines-could-replace-humans-and-where-they-cant-yet

Durand, J. N. L. (1809). *Recueil et parallèle des édifices en tout genre, anciens et modernes.* Paris: Gillé, 1801.

Durand, J. N. L. (1825). *Précis des leçons d'architecture données à l'École polytechnique* Vol. 2, Paris: Hachette, 2013.

Ekmekci, O., Kalvo, R., and Sevtsuk, A. "Pedestrian Accessibility in Grid Layouts: The Role of Block, Plot and Street Dimensions. *Urban Morphology* 20, no. 2 (2016): 89-106.

Ellison, G. and Glaeser, E. "The Geographic Concentration of Industry: Does Natural Advantage Explain Agglomeration?" *American Economic Review* 89, no. 2 (1999): 311-316.

Florida, R. *The Rise of the Creative Class: And How It's Transforming Work, Leisure, Community and Everyday Life.* New York: Basic Books, 2002.

Gehl, Jan. *Cities for People.* Washington, DC: Island Press, 2010.

Granovetter, Mark S. "The Strength of Weak Ties." *American Journal of Sociology* 78, no. 6 (1973): 1360–1380.

Gras Alomà, R. "Discoveries from the Atlas of Innovation Districts." UD:ID (2019). https://www.ud-id.com/equity-1/grasaloma

Gras Alomà, R. "Metropolis fractales: un nuevo enfoque para mejorar la gestión urbana." Anuario internacional CIDOB. Barcelona: CIDOB, 2022. https://www.cidob.org/es/articulos/anuario_internacional_cidob/2022/metropolis_fractales_un_nuevo_enfoque_para_mejorar_la_gestion_urbana

Gras Alomà, R. "Ildefons Cerdà, the Art and Science of City Design: The Founder of Modern Urbanism as a Source of Inspiration for a New Generation of City Designers." *UD:ID*. 2018. https://www.ud-id.com/reaction/2018/4/11/cerda

Gras Alomà, R. "Ciudades – Diseño Urbano." In *La Década Decisiva: Transformaciones para la Agenda 2030.* Barcelona: Acciona, 2023, 36-43.

Harris, K., Kimson, A. y Schwedel, A. (2018). "Labor 2030: The Collision of Demographics, Automation and Inequality." *Bain and Company* (February 7, 2018). https://www.bain.com/insights/labor-2030-the-collision-of-demographics-automation-and-inequality/

Hartmann, D., Guevara, M. R., Jara Figueroa, C., Aristarán, M. and Hidalgo, C. A. "Linking Economic Complexity, Institutions, and Income Inequality." *World Development 93,* (2017): 75-93.

Hausmann, R., Hidalgo, C. A., Bustos, S., Coscia, M., Simoes, A. and Yildirim, M. A. *The Atlas of Economic Complexity. Mapping Paths to Prosperity.* Cambridge, MA: MIT Press, 2013.

Hausmann, R., and Klinger, B. "Structural Transformation and Patterns of Comparative Advantage in the Product Space." CID Faculty Working Paper No. 128, August 2006.

Hidalgo, C. A. and Hausmann, R. "The Building Blocks of Economic Complexity. *PNAS* 106, no. 26 (2009): 10570-10575.

Ho, M.-W. "Large cities in USA Less Green than Small Ones." *Permaculture News*, September 24, 2014. https://www.permaculturenews.org/2014/09/24/large-cities-usa-less-green-small-ones/

Jacobs, J. *The Death and Life of Great American Cities.* New York: Vintage Books, 1993.

Kant, I. Observations on the Feeling of the Beautiful and Sublime and Other Writings. (Frierson, P. and Guyer, P., eds.). New York: Cambridge University Press, 2011.

Katz, B. and Wagner, J. "The Rise of Urban Innovation Districts." *Harvard Business Review* (November 12, 2014). https://hbr.org/2014/11/the-rise-of-urban-innovation-districts

Kharas, H. "The Unprecedented Expansion of the Global Middle Class: An Update." *Brookings.* (February 28, 2017). https://www.brookings.edu/articles/the-unprecedented-expansion-of-the-global-middle-class-2/

Kühnert, C., Helbing, D. and West G. B. "Scaling Laws in Urban Supply Networks." *Physica A: Statistical Mechanics and its Applications* 363, no. 1 (2006): 96-103.

Lane, D., Pumain, S., van der Leeuw, S. E. and West, G. B. "Power Laws in Urban Supply Networks, Social Systems, and Dense Pedestrian Crowds." In *Complexity Perspectives in Innovation and Social Change.* Dordrecht: Springer, 2009.

Matheson, R. "New Report Outlines MIT's Global Entrepreneurial Impact." *MIT News* (December 9, 2015). https://news.mit.edu/2015/report-entrepreneurial-impact-1209.

McKinsey Global Institute. "How Will Automation Affect Jobs, Skills, and Wages?" *McKinsey & Company* (March 23, 2018). https://www.mckinsey.com/featured-insights/future-of-work/how-willautomation-affect-jobs-skills-and-wages

Moreno, C., Allam, Z., Chabaud, D., Gall, C., Pratlong, F. "Introducing the 15-Minute City: Sustainability, Resilience and Place Identity in Future Post-Pandemic Cities." *Smart Cities* 4, no. 1 (2021): 93-111.

Moretti, E. *The New Geography of Jobs.* Boston: Houghton Mifflin Harcourt, 2012.

Mumford, E., (2011), *The CIAM Discourse on Urbanism 1928–60.* Cambridge, MA: MIT Press, 2002.

Pan, W., Ghoshal, G., Krumme, C., Cebrian, M. and Pentland, A. "Urban Characteristics Attributable to Density-Driven Tie Formation." *Nature Communications* 4 (June 4, 2013). https://doi.org/10.1038/ncomms2961.

Roberts, E. B., Murray, F. and Kim, J. D. *Entrepreneurship and Innovation at MIT: Continuing Global Growth and Impact.* MIT Innovation Initiative, 2015. https://innovation.mit.edu/assets/EntrepreneurshipInnovationMIT-8Dec2015-final.pdf

Salingaros, N. *A Theory of Architecture.* Solingen: Umbau-Verlag, 2006.

Saña, H. *Breve tratado de Ética: Una introducción a la teoría de la moral.* Córdoba: Almuzara, 2009.

Saña, H. *Tratado del hombre: de sus orígenes a hoy.* Córdoba: Almuzara, 2010.

Sassen, S. *The Global City: New York, London, Tokyo.* Princeton: Princeton University Press, 2002.

Schläpfer, M., Bettencourt, L. M., Grauwin, S., Raschke, M., Claxton, R., Smoreda, Z., West, J., and Ratti, C. "The Scaling of Human Interactions with City Size." *Journal of the Royal Society Interface* 11, no. 98 (2014).

Schopenhauer, A. *Arthur Schopenhauer: The World as Will and Representation.* Volume I. (Kolak, D., ed.) Abingdon: Routledge, 2008.

Sevtsuk, A and Mekonnen, M. "Urban Network Analysis: A New Toolbox for Measuring City Form in ArcGIS." Proceedings of the 45th Annual Simulation Symposium, 2012.

Smith, A. (1776). *The Wealth of Nations.* New York: Random House, 2000.

Speck, Jeff. *Walkable City: How Downtown Can Save America, One Step at a Time.* New York: Farrar, Straus and Giroux, 2012.

Stibe, A. and Larson, K. "Persuasive Cities for Sustainable Wellbeing: Quantified Communities." *Mobile Web and Intelligent Information Systems* (August 2016): 271–282.

Torres, C. "La planificación teritorial y urbana en América Latina." *Bitácora* 11 (2007): 96–115.

Youn, H., Bettencourt, L. M. A., Lobo, J., Strumsky, D., Samaniego, H. and West G. "The Systematic Structure and Predictability of Urban Business Diversity." *Journal of the Royal Society Interface* 13. https://arxiv.org/pdf/1405.3202.pdf

Zhang, Y., Grignard, A., Lyons, K., Aubuchon, A. and Larson, K. 2018. *Real-time Machine Learning Prediction of an Agent-Based Model for Urban Decision-making (Extended Abstract).* Proceedings of the 17th International Conference on Autonomous Agents and MultiAgent Systems (AAMAS '18). International Foundation for Autonomous Agents and Multiagent Systems. Richland, SC: 2171-2173.

Contributors

Fernando Yu
Co-author of the
Atlas of Global Cities

Fernando Yu is the Lead Economist at Aretian, and a former Harvard University researcher interested in productive diversification strategies of countries, regions and cities. Fernando's research combines economic modeling and Big Data analysis to study the tradeoffs between diversification opportunities and growth strategies, utilizing state of the art statistical tools, network analysis and economic modeling, both from the perspective of job creation but also economic, fiscal and financial risk mitigation. As a Research Fellow at Harvard Kennedy School of Government, Fernando developed a framework to evaluate the financial risk of alternative growth strategies. This tool was implemented by the Ministry of Economics of Buenos Aires for the Economic Development Plan 2019. Previously, he has worked at the Fiscal Affairs Department of the International Monetary Fund where he developed a strategy to evaluate and measure the cost of trade wars on the world economy and as a consultant for the Inter American Development Bank where he studied the impact of the financial crisis on international trade flows.

**Gauthier de
La Ville de Baugé**

Gauthier de La Ville de Baugé is in charge of Project Management, Business Development, Communication and Marketing at Aretian. He graduated from IE University in July 2019 where he studied a Bachelor in International Relations with minors in Business Development, Management and Artificial Intelligence. Raised in Paris, he got to discover the full international experience by living in different cities such as San Francisco, London, Rabat, Madrid, and now Boston. Before Aretian, Gauthier worked in the creation of ecological real estate where he developed projects to build wooden infrastructures in France. He was also part of a research team working for the European Commission on the topic of Cybersecurity, addressing the issue of security of the European Union's citizens, companies, and states online.

Céleste Richard

Céleste Richard is an Urban Design Senior Consultant at Aretian, working on innovative urban environments, bridging urban design planning and digital engineering with a human-centric approach. Céleste is interested in fostering sustainable, smart and innovative future cities by tackling complex urban challenges. She holds a Bachelor's degree in Architecture from the National Architecture School of Versailles, and an MSc in Urbanism from TU Delft with Honours. Previously, Céleste was part of the Sustainable Cities & Transport team at ARUP, developing strategies and urban visions, using parametric design and pedestrian modeling. Céleste gained experience on human-centric design from ETH Zurich when she joined the Cognition, Perception and Behaviour team at the Future Cities Laboratory in Singapore.

Authors

Ramon Gras
Co-founder at Aretian

Ramon Gras is an Urban Designer, City Science Researcher, and Civil Engineer from Barcelona, working on the urban innovation space. At Harvard, Ramon graduated from the inaugural cohort of the Harvard MDE program, where he developed research on urban design criteria for innovation districts and agritechnology campuses. Prior to developing his joint thesis at Harvard, Ramon worked at Ferrovial's Innovation office in London, where he led design and technology projects at the London Heathrow Airport and the London Underground. Ramon developed urban design projects at MIT for the Kendall Square expansion and Somerville Innovation Districts in the Boston Area. Ramon's thesis at MIT addressed the consolidation problem in air freight transportation by designing an advanced Business Intelligence platform. He expanded his training at MIT after working as a designer in major infrastructure projects involving urban design, bridge design, maritime infrastructure, high speed rail, and singular architecture projects. Ramon's early research at BarcelonaTech focused on urbanism, bridge design, high performance materials, and nanotechnology applications for structural engineering. Ramon is interested in enhancing innovation around Cities, Technology and Infrastructure, by designing creative and rigorous interdisciplinary solutions to address large, complex challenges facing the cities of our time.

Jeremy Burke
Co-founder at Aretian

Jeremy Burke is a City and Architectural Designer and Researcher interested in how new modeling techniques can describe complex social systems. At Harvard, Jeremy graduated from the inaugural cohort of the Harvard MDE program, where he developed research around design criteria for innovation districts operating in synergy with logistics hubs and developed industrial infrastructure to support local agriculture. Jeremy explores how traditional design methodologies can be informed through computational thinking. The resulting systems-level understanding of a space can be used to inform the design and development of sustainable architectural and infrastructure projects and to foster healthy communities. In addition, Jeremy has worked with a variety of start-ups to plan, market, and create new strategies for continued growth. Prior to his joint thesis with Ramon Gras at Harvard, Jeremy worked with Kennedy Violich Architecture, BRU Architects, and Alon Development, and has experience completing a wide range of projects from smart sustainable houses, to modern renovations within historical contexts, and the master plan and design of a four million square foot resort and entertainment facility. Jeremy is originally from Santa Fe, NM.

City Science: Performance Follows Form

Published by
Actar Publishers, New York, Barcelona
www.actar.com

Authors
Ramon Gras Alomà, Jeremy Burke | Aretian Urban Analytics and Design

Editor
Ramon Gras Alomà

Editorial Development and Supervision
Marta Bugés

Graphic Design
Sofia Sandoval, Ramon Prat | Actar Publishers

Drawings, Visualizations and Concept Illustrations
Ramon Gras Alomà, Jeremy Burke | Aretian Urban Analytics and Design

Co-author of the Atlas of Global Cities
Fernando Yu

Illustrations
Van Saiyan

Copy Editing
Angela Kay Bunning

Printing and binding
Arlequin & Pierrot, Barcelona

All rights reserved
© edition: Actar Publishers
© texts: Aretian Urban Analytics and Design
© drawings, visualizations and illustrations: Aretian Urban Analytics and Design
© photographs: Their authors

This work is subject to copyright. All rights are reserved, on all or part of the
material, specifically translation rights, reprinting, re-use of illustrations, recitation,
broadcasting, reproduction on microfilm or other media, and storage in databases.
For use of any kind, permission of the copyright owner must be obtained.

Distribution
Actar D, Inc. New York, Barcelona.

New York
440 Park Avenue South, 17th Floor
New York, NY 10016, USA
T+1 2129662207
salesnewyork@actar-d.com

Barcelona
Roca i Batlle 2
08023 Barcelona, Spain
T+34 933 282 183
eurosales@actar-d.com